World Englishes:
A Critical Analysis

World Englishes: A Critical Analysis

MARIO SARACENI

Bloomsbury Academic
An imprint of Bloomsbury Publishing Inc

BLOOMSBURY
LONDON • NEW DELHI • NEW YORK • SYDNEY

Bloomsbury Academic

An imprint of Bloomsbury Publishing Plc

50 Bedford Square	1385 Broadway
London	New York
WC1B 3DP	NY 10018
UK	USA

www.bloomsbury.com

BLOOMSBURY and the Diana logo are trademarks of Bloomsbury Publishing Plc

First published 2015

British Library Cataloguing-in-Publication Data
A catalogue record for this book is available from the British Library.

ISBN: HB: 978-1-6235-6380-6
PB: 978-1-6235-6263-2
ePDF: 978-1-6235-6972-3
ePub: 978-1-6235-6452-0

Library of Congress Cataloging-in-Publication Data
Saraceni, Mario, 1969–
World Englishes : a critical analysis / Mario Saraceni.
pages cm
Includes bibliographical references and index.
ISBN 978-1-62356-380-6 (hardback) – ISBN 978-1-62356-263-2 (pb) –
ISBN 978-1-62356-452-0 (epub)   1. Language and languages–Varitation.
2. English language–Globalization.   3. Critical discourse analysis
4. English language–Globalization.   I. Title.
P120.V37S273   2015
420–dc23
2014027578

Typeset by Newgen Knowledge Works (P) Ltd., Chennai, India
Printed and bound in Great Britain

To Charlotte

Contents

Preface

I first began studying 'World Englishes' about 20 years ago, under the guide of John McRae at the University of Nottingham. I will always owe it to him for inspiring enthusiasm and passion that have never left me. With multilingual ease, he showed us that boundaries – between languages, sexes, nationalities, races, rules – only exist in the mind and are there to be trespassed. English*es* broke rules, and this was what made them intrinsically interesting. Before and above anything else.

In the last 20 years, I've learned a great deal about the subversive nature of Englishes. My ideas have evolved, become more complex, less naïvely certain. In a cliché sort of way, it is also fair to say that the world has changed a great deal, too. Globalization has brought about an unprecedented level of diversity – linguistic, cultural, ethnic, religious and so on – within communities. To use a mathematical metaphor, while *addition* (one language plus another language plus another language and so on) used to be sufficient to understand plurality in the twentieth century, now *multiplication* is a better representation of the kind of intersecting and multi-layered diversity that characterizes especially urban areas. Languages don't just exist alongside each other, but merge, blend, mesh, coalesce into a symbiosis where traditional labels struggle to find a place.

Meanwhile, the nature of World Englishes has begun to feel less subversive and more comfortably, and therefore *un*comfortably, settled into what seems to be a paradigm of permanently two-dimensional, harmless, plurality. Fundamentally, a trajectory can be traced from a point in which revolutionary ideas were put forward against the old notion of one monolithic English, and all the ideological baggage that came with it, to a point where those very ideas now need updating, revamping, modernized, perhaps changing, in order to continue to be relevant and equally revolutionary in the twenty-first century. In order to rekindle its anti-conventional, rule-breaking, paradigm-shifting ethos, World Englishes needs to catch up with developments that are taking place all around. There are signs that this might be happening.

In many ways, this book reflects that trajectory. The paradigm through which we understand English(es) has changed over the years, and this book traces the steps with which that paradigm has shifted, and continues to shift, more or less swiftly. It also reflects the ways in which my own ideas have evolved over the years, through reading and reflection, as well as through teaching, experience, research and practice. Of course, through dialogues that I've had with many scholars whom I've been lucky to meet and who have inspired me, sometimes even with a couple of words. It would be futile for me to attempt to list everybody's names without inexcusable omissions, but I wish to mention at least the following individuals for the ways in which they have contributed to the development of my own understanding of World English: Ahmar Mahboob, Alan Maley, Alastair Pennycook, Andy Kirkpatrick, Henny Zacharias, John Joseph, Kingsley Bolton, Lubna Alsagoff, Rani Rubdy, SueWright, Suresh Canagarajah, Suzanne Hilgendorf. In addition, my students are a constant source of inspiration, challenge and healthy self-doubt and it is very much also thanks to them that my thinking continues to evolve.

Just as importantly, this book would not have been possible without the support of the Centre for European and International Studies Research and the School of Languages and Area Studies at the University of Portsmouth.

Finally, my thanks go to Gurdeep Mattu, for having believed in this project from the beginning.

Mario Saraceni, May 2014

1

Introduction

1.1   What this book is (and isn't) about

The term *World Englishes* refers to a well-established academic field in sociolinguistics, whose main concern is the study of world (with a small 'w') Englishes, namely the varieties that emerged around the world largely as a result of British from the eighteenth century to the middle of the twentieth century. In turn, 'academic field' can be understood in a narrow sense or in a broad one. In the first case, the 'field' is institutionalized, typically via a professional organization, a journal and an annual (or biennial) conference. 'World Englishes' has all three and fits this description. This book is not directly concerned with this meaning. Nor is it concerned with providing an overview of world Englishes. It does, instead, examine 'World Englishes' in a broader sense, where 'field' is intended as the synthesis of scholarly activity that is conventionally named after an identifiable common theme and is driven by a common investigative and/or methodological impetus.

The analysis is not a neutral, detached one. The general premise to this entire book is that the field of World Englishes currently finds itself in a situation of 'crisis', as it faces some new, and old, challenges. A crisis, of course, can be a very productive process, favourable for a paradigm shift to take place and new ways of thinking to be put forward. So the core aim of this book is twofold: on the one hand, it presents what can be defined as 'traditional' concepts within the World Englishes framework; on the other hand, it highlights possible limitations that have been identified by various scholars and possible avenues for new directions and new conceptualizations of world Englishes. It is in this sense that the analysis is a 'critical' one, as the subtitle of this book promises.

1.2   Why another 'World Englishes' book?

The field of World Englishes experienced something very similar to a 'boom' in the first decade of the millennium. Books with *World Englishes* in the title went forth and multiplied at an astonishing pace, and some of them were even re-published in second editions. Textbooks, more theoretical treatises and edited collections chased one another, made their way into libraries and populated reading lists for university courses. Some of the better known publications with very similar titles are Brutt-Griffler (2002), Jenkins (2003, 2009b), Y. Kachru and Nelson (2006), Melchers and Shaw (2003, 2011), Kirkpatrick (2007), Mesthrie and Bhatt (2008), Wolf (2009), Nelson (2011), Schneider (2011), Seargeant (2012b) among the textbooks and monographs, and B. B. Kachru et al. (2006), Bolton and Kachru (2006), Rubdy and Saraceni (2006), Y. Kachru and Smith (2008), Saxena and Omoniyi (2010), Kirkpatrick (2010b), Seargeant and Swan (2012) among the edited volumes. We're now at a point where, clearly, the same pace couldn't be kept. Given the great quantity and quality of publications, one might be tempted to get to the conclusion that, perhaps, we may have now reached a point of 'saturation', where there isn't much left to say that hasn't already been said.

1.2.1   *Expanding the scope of World Englishes*

One fairly obvious response to anyone feeling this kind of lingering suspicion is given by the fact that there are still areas of the world whose Englishes are under-researched or not researched at all. The so-called Expanding Circle (see Section 3.2.3), namely world regions that were not part of the British empire but where the importance of English as an international (and, to an extent, intranational) language is obviously rising, is attracting a considerable amount of scholarly attention in this field. The main research aim, for scholars investigating English in these areas, is twofold: (i) to establish the extent to which English has acquired local forms and functions that are sufficiently stable as to constitute a distinct variety of the language and, if this is the case, (ii) to describe phonological, lexical, grammatical and discourse patterns that characterize such a variety.

China is probably the part of the world that has attracted the greatest amount of attention in this sense, undoubtedly because of its sheer size, but primarily because of the rapid and profound changes and developments that, in the space of only two decades, have made the country one of the largest economies and a key player in world affairs, fully involved in globalization not only from an economic point of view but also from a cultural one (despite certain restrictions imposed by the government). The presence and the importance of English have therefore risen dramatically in the country. Statistics regarding the numbers of speakers of English are notoriously difficult to produce, the main obstacle being the difficulty in establishing who 'counts' as a 'speaker of English'. Yet, the suggestion that there are more learners of English in China than speakers of the language in the United States and the United Kingdom combined, which has been circulating virally in (para-)academic contexts for a number of years, reflects the undeniable growth of English in this 'new' territory. Hence, the attraction for scholarly research in World Englishes. Bolton's *Chinese Englishes* (2003a) was a milestone along this particular path.

This is a path that has continued to be trodden. Hadikin's (2014) study on Korean English is, at the time of writing, the latest effort to document a 'new' variety of English in the Expanding Circle. His work makes use of methodological opportunities offered by corpus linguistics, something which, in itself, constitutes a relatively new avenue of investigation. The ability to store large amounts of authentic language, spoken and written, in digital datasets allows researchers to study varieties of English more systematically and with more precision. The International Corpus of English (http://ice-corpora.net/ice/) is a project that has been active for a numbers of years and has precisely these aims.

1.2.2   *A slight impasse*

However, despite their importance and value, these developments are relatively marginal, and there is a sense that, on the whole, the field of World Englishes may have reached something like an impasse. Indeed, although each one of the books listed earlier – and many more – makes a very useful contribution to the field, sometimes one feels that things may not have progressed as much as the volume of publications suggests, especially considering the way the main World Englishes tenets are re-iterated over the years.

World Englishes began very much as an anti-establishment, revolutionary philosophy, which opposed old, traditional, anachronistic, stale and unrealistically monolithic ideas about English, and proposed new, fresh, modern ideas that would take into consideration the diverse sociolinguistic realities in which English had relocated. Now, the novelty is somewhat wearing off. One of the latest textbooks, for example, states that the time has come to look at English in a different way:

> . . . in the modern world, the language needs to be viewed not as a single, monolithic entity, but as something that has multiple varieties and forms. The use of this term [*Englishes*] is motivated by an attitude which argues that it is no longer accurate to say that there is just one 'English' in existence around the world – but that instead we need to begin our investigation that

diversity is the norm, and that the multiple forms the language takes are, each and every one, both linguistically and sociolinguistically interesting. (Seargeant, 2012b, pp. 1–2)

The need to view English not as a single entity is undeniable, but this has been *the* core principle which has formed the foundations of the entire World Englishes ethos for decades now. Braj Kachru and Larry Smith explained the meaning of 'Englishes' and the significance of the plural *-es* in 1985 in the editorial of the first issue of the newly named *World Englishes* journal:

> The term 'Englishes' is significant in many ways. 'Englishes' symbolizes the functional and formal variation in the language, and its international acculturation, for example, in West Africa, in Southern Africa, in East Africa, in South Asia, in Southeast Asia, in the West Indies, in the Philippines, and in the traditional English-using countries: the USA, the UK, Australia, Canada, and New Zealand. The language now belongs to those who use it as their first language, and to those who use it as an additional language, whether in its standard form or in its localized forms. (B. B. Kachru & Smith, 1985, p. 210)

If, nearly 30 years later, we're still advocating the need to *begin* to favour plurality against singularity, one could be excused for feeling that, perhaps, there *may* have been a certain amount of 'congestion' in the field. Where do we go from here?

There's a sense that the field might be to an extent lagging behind advancements that have taken place in sociolinguistics since the beginning of the millennium. In particular, the World Englishes framework has been feeling 'pressure', as it were, from two separate fronts of scholars: on the one hand, those who have been engaged with research aimed at providing insights into the forms and functions of English as a lingua franca (ELF) (see Section 4.5); on the other hand, those who have concentrated their attention on phenomena related to globalization, such as 'super-diversity', language 'hybridity', 'translanguaging', 'metrolingualism' (see Chapter 5). In some ways, it could be said that both ELF and the sociolinguistics of globalization have 'eroded' some of the scope of World Englishes.

1.2.3   New challenges

1.2.3.1   English as a lingua franca

ELF research is primarily interested in the ways English is used internationally as a shared language by people in the Expanding Circle. This field of investigation began to be established towards the turn of the new century and has since gained considerable ground. Research findings are disseminated in a dedicated annual international conference, in monographs and in articles which, more recently, have begun to appear in a journal entirely dedicated to this particular research area: the *Journal of English as a Lingua Franca*. As I mentioned earlier, this is also a direction in which World Englishes is expanding its scope, but ELF seems to have 'claimed' this space more resolutely.

There has also been a certain degree of slight academic attrition between some World Englishes and ELF scholars, the main source of it being cases of purported 'misconceptions' and 'misinterpretations' of ELF research and its aims (see, e.g. Seidlhofer, 2006; Jenkins, 2006a, 2007; Cogo, 2008). However, despite this, it is also quite clear that the two areas of research shared a general common de-centralized and pluralistic view of English but were more complementary than in competition with one another (Seidlhofer, 2009b). As Cogo and Dewey (2012, p. 8) state:

> WE is concerned with the empirical study of *nativized* (also often referred to as *indigenized* or *institutionalized*) varieties of English in Kachru's *Outer Circle*. By contrast, *ELF* is a term used to describe the use of English in settings where it is spoken as a contact language by speakers of varying linguacultural backgrounds for whom there is not usually another shared language available.

1.2.3.2   The sociolinguistics of globalization

As regards the sociolinguistics of globalization, the position of World Englishes is slightly more complicated. It is in this area that the framework is beginning to show its 'age', so to speak. It's no longer simply a matter of investigating English in certain parts of the world rather than in others. More profoundly, the challenge relates to a re-conceptualization of language and communication that new trends in sociolinguistics are bringing to the fore:

> Over a period of several decades . . . there has been ongoing revision of fundamental ideas (a) about languages, (b) about language groups and speakers, and (c) about communication. Rather than working with homogeneity, stability and boundedness as the starting assumptions, mobility, mixing, political dynamics and historical embedding are now central concerns in the study of languages, language groups and communication. (Blommaert & Rampton, 2011, p. 3)

This is more of a 'problem' for World Englishes. As the field has always been driven by an innovative impetus to promote plurality over singularity, and has therefore seen itself as proposing a paradigm shift in the way we understand English, it may now be struggling to come to terms with the fact that another paradigm shift has been under way for some time which destabilizes the very concept of plurality. The realization that what was new for decades may now be getting 'old' can be uncomfortable. Particularly so given that the World Englishes paradigm has been explicitly critiqued for being somewhat 'stuck' in positions that are beginning to show signs of ageing.

The main critique has been that it is 'too tied to the linguistics and politics of the twentieth century and ill-equipped to deal with current modes of globalization' (Pennycook, 2007a, p. 12) and 'doesn't go far enough in pluralizing English or reflecting the dynamic changes in communicative practices' (Canagarajah, 2013, p. 58). The limitation that some scholars have identified lies in the fact that plurality is, in itself, unable to capture the kind of diversity brought about by globalization, and ends up producing 'pluralization of singularity' (Makoni, 2011, p. 683). Positing the existence of different, discrete varieties of English presupposes that these varieties are relatively homogeneous, stable and bounded systems but struggles to take account mobility and mixing as fundamental traits of language as social practice. As Otsuji and Pennycook (2010, p. 251) point out:

> . . . a world Englishes focus reacted against the homogenising tendencies of scholars, textbooks, industries and language policies that sought to belittle the diversity of English, and produced a model based on pluralisation: where there had been one (or a few) Englishes, now there would be many . . . . Yet clearly, as with emerging critiques of multilingualism, there need to be alternative ways of understanding diversity other than pluralisation (making English into Englishes and monolingualism into multilingualism).

This is an era where global cultural flows, unprecedented mobility and new modes of communication made available by technology are revealing forms of language practice, especially in urban settings and in online social networks, where linguistic amalgams are so pervasive as to force us to reconsider and challenge traditional precepts about language as divided up into separate systems. The kind of diversity that we are now dealing with in the twenty-first century has been called 'super-diversity' (Vertovec, 2007), in order to signify the fact that societies aren't simply characterized by the addition of many cultures (multi-cultural), many ethnicities (multi-ethnic), many languages (multi-lingual) and so on, but by an interplay of different and layered variables that can be configured in very complex ways (see Section 5.4).

As far as the use of language is concerned, this produces situations where the boundaries between different languages have become increasingly fuzzier or even irrelevant. Accordingly, the concept of 'varieties of English' has similarly come under close scrutiny and been seen as 'less appropriate for sociolinguistic analyses in an increasingly globalised world' (Leimgruber, 2013, p. 126). Even more importantly, though, while it may have been triggered by the analysis of language practices in such new communicative situations, this new perspective needs to apply to language in general, including, that is, rural settings and, historically, precolonial conditions (Canagarajah, 2013).

So, sociolinguistics seems to be advancing while 'it would be unfortunate if the world Englishes paradigm remained static, at a time when new patterns of language contact and linguistic flow are emerging and gaining recognition' (Bolton, 2013, p. 249). In a sense, however, it could afford to continue to do so. To many specialists in the field, the citation from Seargeant (2012b) earlier may sound as if it was produced in the 1970s, but to the vast majority of laypeople the idea that 'it is no longer accurate to say that there is just one "English"' is still controversial and doesn't really apply to more than the awareness that there are differences between British and American English. This is certainly the case in TESOL (Teaching English to Speakers of Other Languages), for example, where preference for British/American English and for 'native speakers' as models continues to be rather solid (see Part Four) and other varieties of English are either discarded as unsuitable or simply ignored. So, depending on the interlocutors it chooses, World Englishes still has considerable scope for portraying itself as innovative and cutting-edge.

However, legitimate as it may be, that position doesn't encourage academic enquiry and development. A more productive orientation is to seek ways in which World Englishes research 'may involve new frameworks accommodating code alternation, hybridisation and fresh perspectives on linguistic contact' (Bolton, 2013, p. 233). It is by taking this route, I believe, that World Englishes can renew its original innovative nature and, especially, remain relevant in the twenty-first century. All of this is discussed in Part Two of this book, which looks at the core of the World Englishes paradigm, where notions of plurality and variety reside, and discusses both its original egalitarian and revolutionary ethos and the ways in which it has been somewhat destabilized by recent developments in sociolinguistics, as briefly sketched earlier.

1.2.4 *Old challenges*

1.2.4.1 Linguistic imperialism

Apart from recent developments in sociolinguistics that it needs to keep apace with, World Englishes continues to face 'older' challenges too. One comes from the proponents of a very negative and cynical interpretation of the spread of English in the world, which is seen as the principal vehicle of all-conquering Anglo-American imperialism which, octopus-like, engulfs the entire planet.

This particular frame of analysis goes by the name *linguistic imperialism*, which is also the title of the book in which its best-known proponent, Robert Phillipson, expounded it in detail (1992). From this particular perspective, the World Englishes paradigm doesn't take into sufficient, or any, account the detrimental effects of the omnipresence of English in the world, which goes hand in hand with the unstoppable diffusion of neoliberalist models of economy, the homogenization of cultures and *linguicide*, that is, the extinction of minor languages overpowered by the expansion of English. So, according to this view, the concept of the pluralization of English is at best a rather naïve reading which fails to recognize darker intents that lie just beneath the surface of global English(es), at worst somewhat complicit in enthusiastically glorifying economic and cultural trends that work in favour of a system where the world is increasingly dominated and controlled by a handful of powers. This theme is discussed in Part Three of this book.

1.2.4.2   English language teaching

Part Four deals with the pedagogical implications that the World Englishes paradigm has for the teaching of English as a foreign/second language. This has always been a very central – and, possibly, *the* central – preoccupation in the field. The initial debates that sparked in the 1960s (see Section 4.2) were ostensibly about language pedagogy and revolved around the issue of the (un-)suitability of models of English that weren't British or American. Also, the vast majority of scholars in this field are or have been English language educators, and one of the main aims in World Englishes has always been that of promoting the idea that pluralizing the language means being able to adopt models of English flexibly according to the learners' cultural context. Essentially, the principle is that learners should be taught varieties of English that are culturally relevant to them, rather than those imposed by old, but very established, convictions about the superiority of one or two varieties.

I call this a 'challenge' because it is an ongoing 'battle' against deep-rooted beliefs about English and its pedagogy. Significantly, not very long ago B. B. Kachru (2009, p. 180) commented that 'our current paradigms of constructs and teaching of English continue to be based on monolingual and monocultural – and essentially Western – traditions of creativity and canon formation'.

There are, however, signs that things *are* changing. The pluralization of English, for example, is finding its way into previously uncharted territories, such as secondary education curricula in Britain. At the same time, World Englishes principles are being embraced by language educators in various world regions, with Southeast Asia probably being at the forefront. Over the last two decades, three concurrent factors have contributed to making

'World Englishes' a very visible presence, especially in higher education, and to inspiring a certain degree of attitudinal change regarding the adoption of models based on different varieties of English. These are: (i) the large volume of publications in the field, including papers in journals such as *World Englishes* and *English Today*, (ii) the annual conference run by the International Association for World Englishes (IAWE), which has been held in a number of countries across the world for two decades and (iii) the inclusion of World Englishes as a subject primarily in master's courses in applied linguistics and TESOL. All these three factors have produced 'impact' (to use a word currently fashionable in research) in the sense that the message has slowly begun to reach outside the confines of academia. Of course, as alluded to earlier, the process is a slow one. Resistance towards, or simple lack of awareness of, the diverse roles and functions of English in the world and the possibility of adopting local varieties as models for teaching is still predominant. The Malaysian government, just to cite and example, continues to spend large amounts of money to send young Malaysians to study in teacher training courses in Britain and, at the same time, invites 'native speakers' to come and teach English in Malaysia, in what seems to be an odd contradiction of intents, which can however be explained by an absolute certainty in the superiority of 'British English' for teaching purposes, as explicitly stipulated in the national curriculum. The challenge for World Englishes is still on.

The conviction that 'British English' must be the 'best' English is generally based on the belief that Britain is the 'birthplace' of the language. Britain, therefore, is the country where the 'original' English is. With typical wit and irony, Henry Widdowson remarked in a now classic article: 'If you want real or proper English, this [England] is where it is to be found, preserved, and listed like a property of the National Trust' (1994, p. 377). Indeed, it appears almost commonsensical that *Engl*ish should come from *Engl*and and that, consequently, the British variety of English should be the purest.

The myth of the 'origin' of English (or of any language) is discussed in Part One, which takes a historical perspective, both with regard to the 'birth' of English and within the context of the 'spread' of English in the world. Mainstream views are problematized and alternative ones proposed. Traditional ideas are often presented in the forms of questions: can we really talk of the 'birth' of the English language? Who were the 'Anglo-Saxons'? How pure are the Germanic roots of English? Why have they been represented as such? Can the history of English be traced in a linear fashion? In answering all these questions, it becomes evident that discourses about English aren't just concerned with language in terms of vocabulary, grammar and so on but, quite pervasively, with ideology and politics. The ideological dimension gets even more prominent in the next chapter, as it examines the early discourses on varieties of English, much before World Englishes, completely entrenched in issues of national independence and identity.

So, the subtitle *a critical analysis* is what really defines this book. It invites the reader to engage critically with many of the core issues within the World Englishes framework, but it seeks to do so in a constructive way. As I said earlier, the 'crisis' that the field of World Englishes finds itself in can be very productive, if it stimulates reflection and helps us find ways in which World English can remain relevant in the twenty-first century.

One fundamental theme running through this book is the proposition that in order for this development to truly take place, a re-conceptualization is necessary whereby the idea that language is divided up into a number of separate, self-sufficient and bounded systems, each one tied to a specific group of people who use it to communicate with one another, gives way to a different understanding of language; one where language is recognized and analysed as integral of social practice in which people *do* things and communication is only a part, sometimes rather small, of it.

1.3   Understanding language

Language is one of those words that we use all the time but whose meaning is far less straightforward than its frequent use suggests. Attempting to define, in an exhaustive way, the nature of language is in fact extremely complex. While a comprehensive account of the conceptualizations of language is well beyond the scope and the purposes of this book, it will be nonetheless useful to briefly synthesize and outline two of the main approaches to the study of language that have characterized modern Western linguistics. It is very important to stress that the reciprocal opposition in which these two views will be presented here is only a simplification at the service of clarity and is instrumentally useful as groundwork underpinning the critical analysis of W/ world Englishes.

One, very influential, developed towards the beginning of the twentieth century, sees language as a *system*, which can be described and studied in its own right. The other considers language a form of *social practice*, that is, inseparable from any human activity that it is used as an integral part of.

1.3.1   *Language as system*

A sensible way to try and get a satisfactory explanation of what 'language' means is to consult relevant reference material. The Oxford English Dictionary (OED), which always radiates with a sense of confident reliability, looks like a good place to start. The *OED* defines 'language' as 'the system of spoken or written communication used by a particular country, people, community, etc., typically consisting of words used within a regular grammatical and syntactic structure'. This definition, which sounds intuitively well-founded, adheres very faithfully to the structuralist tradition initiated by Ferdinand de Saussure, whose *Cours de linguistique générale* (1916/1983) has had enormous and enduring influence on modern linguistics. Saussure's main object of investigation was *langue*, that is, a self-contained system of verbal signs, with its own internal structures, shared by a particular community of speakers.

One key notion, for Saussure, was the nature of the verbal sign, comprising two facets: the *signifier* and the *signified*. The former is the physical aspect of the sign, for example, a sound or a mark on a piece of paper, while the latter is the abstract idea that the signifier refers to. So, for example, the sequence of letters 'c', 'a' and 't' constitute a signifier which refers to the idea of 'cat' as understood by speakers of English. The clause 'as understood by speakers of English' is a central point. This is because for Saussure the links between signifiers and signifieds are arbitrary, in the sense that they are based on no special inter-connection but depend, instead, on the conventions that exist in each individual language and that are shared by its speakers. For speakers of languages other than English the signifier 'cat' (the sequence c+a+t) refers to no signified or to a signified other than the idea of 'cat', demonstrating that there is nothing in this word that would naturally conjure up the idea of a cat. The same applies to any other word in any other language, if we exclude the special class of words whose sounds resemble, to some extent, their signified, such as the sounds *bang* or *gulp* in English.

The arbitrariness of linguistic signs implies that meanings are based on conventions constructed and shared by all the speakers of a given language. However, the connection between *langue* and speakers was not Saussure's primary concern. The actual manifestations of language in use, which he called *parole*, is inevitably tied to each individual speaker and, therefore, is subject to potentially idiosyncratic patterns of use. As such, it escapes systematic study and is only interesting to the linguist insofar as it provides evidence for the rules governing *langue*.

Half a century later, Noam Chomsky developed his own theory of language drawing partly from the same Saussurean structuralist tradition. According to Chomsky (1957, p. 13), a language is 'a set (finite or infinite) of sentences, each finite in length and constructed out of a finite set of elements' and 'the fundamental aim in the linguistic analysis of a language L is to separate the *grammatical* sequences which are the sentences of L from the *ungrammatical* sequences which are not sentences of L and to study the structure of the grammatical sequences'. He also suggests that 'One way to test the adequacy of a grammar proposed for L is to determine whether or not the sequences that it generates are actually grammatical, i.e., acceptable to a native speaker'. In other words, language L is constituted by the set of all sentences considered grammatical by the community of natives speakers of L.

What is particularly interesting in this view is how each language is uniquely tied to a well-defined group of speakers, that is, its native speakers, who are, by definition, the only ones able to make judgements on the acceptability of language forms. So, if each language is defined by a set of rules which determine what is and isn't possible in that language, and if those rules derive from judgements made by native speakers, then this sets very clear demarcation lines not only between one language and another, but also between one speech community and another. The strong connection between languages and their respective speech communities is, as will be discussed more in detail later, a concept that has been a very influential.

Indeed, this idea is sometimes taken to rather extreme interpretations. Returning to the *OED* definition, it is very interesting and significant to pay attention to the grammatical role assigned to 'country': not that of adjunct of place (a language is spoken *in* a country), but that of agent: a language is spoken *by* a country. Here *country* is used as a virtual synonym of *speech community*, and this equivalence in meaning adds a third element to the language-community bond: that of territory. So, there is a tripartite relationship which ties a language to a community that speaks that language to a country in which that community lives. This concept will be discussed more in depth in various points of this book.

In the meantime, another good place where one is likely to find a reliable definition of 'language' is an introductory book to linguistics, the science of language. One of David Nunan's books has the perfect title for this purpose: *What is this Thing Called Language?* (2012). As his entire book is dedicated to explaining what language is, Nunan provides his readers with more than one dictionary-style definition. First of all, he calls language 'a defining characteristic of humanity', that is, 'the phenomenon that defines us as humans' (p. 4). There is already an obvious difference between this definition and the *OED*'s, in that Nunan considers language from a more universal entity, available to all human beings, and not defined according to its being bound to any particular setting or group of people. In this sense, language is an uncountable noun – not language x or y, but just language.

Nunan also defines language as 'a tool for communication' (p. 5) 'for achieving ends that go beyond the language itself' (p. 9). That is, the meanings created and exchanged via language are normally not *about* language (except, of course, in cases where the subject matter *is* language, as it is right now) but reach beyond its boundaries. In other words, language is a tool for communication, and communication takes place in order to get (non-linguistic) things done. To illustrate this, Nunan uses simple examples, such as ordering food at a restaurant, where language isn't used in order to demonstrate the capacity to formulate requests but to actually have the chosen dishes served.

1.3.2 *Language as social practice*

The bridge between language and the world around it that Nunan alludes to gains centre stage in the more recent tradition of Social Semiotics (Halliday, 1978; Hodge & Kress, 1988). For Halliday (1978, p. 2), seeing language as a social semiotic 'means interpreting language within a socio-cultural context, in which the culture itself is interpreted in semiotic terms'. 'Language', Halliday continues, 'does not consist of sentences; it consists of text, or discourse – the exchange of meanings in interpersonal contexts of one kind or another'. By being engaged in discourse, 'people act out the social structure, affirming their own statuses and roles, and establishing and transmitting the shared systems of value and of knowledge'.

As in the previous view of language, for Halliday, too, language is a semiotic *system*, but one fundamental difference: *meaning* and *function* are emphasized much more. In each social activity involving the use of language, people make choices at the level of lexico-grammar principally on the basis of three main variables: (i) the nature of the particular activity they are engaged in, (ii) the relationship they have with the other participants and (iii) the role that language plays in it. Only very secondarily, or not at all, are such choices based solely on their intuitions of grammatical acceptability. These three variables form the core of Halliday's concept of *register* and are called *field*, *tenor* and *mode*, respectively. Language use is therefore 'shaped' by the force that these contextual variables concurrently exercise upon it. The ways in which *field* determines language choices is straightforward. If the social activity is, for example, assembling a piece of furniture, the language produced is likely to contain lexical items related to the task, imperatives and relatively short utterances. Clearly, however, the word 'activity' doesn't have to be interpreted as referring to one, goal-oriented task that people undertake single-mindedly. As they help each other put together a bookshelf, two friends might of course do other things, such as tell stories, joke, discuss politics, make plans and so on. The point is that the nature of all of these activities will influence the language choices that the participants will make. *Tenor* is equally important. The relationship that exists between the participants in an activity can vary according to different or equal levels of power, how close they feel to one another and how frequently they see each other. Again, all these factors will contribute to determining how they use language. Two partners who have been a couple for many years will have a different linguistic behaviour while talking about the next day during dinner compared to an employer and a prospective employee during a meal that is part of a job interview. *Mode* has two main aspects. One has to do with how central language is to the activity of which it is part. In writing a novel, for example, the use of language plays a very key role, while in a chess game it may be minimal and fairly peripheral. The other aspect relates to the physical distance between the participants. Using the same examples, the distance between a novelist and her readers is far greater than that between two chess players, and the types of interaction profoundly different. Once again, these variables will affect the ways in which people draw from the linguistic (and other semiotic) resources at their disposal. As a *social* semiotic system, therefore, language interacts with the context within which its resources are utilized. *Discourse*, in turn, is the deployment of semiotic systems in close and inextricable relationship with their surrounding context.

This conception of discourse is inspired by the work of anthropologist Bronisław Malinowski at the beginning of the twentieth century. In his pioneering ethnographic fieldwork, Malinowski also devoted much attention to language and, in particular, to its connection to 'human action':

> . . . the main function of language is not to express thought, not to duplicate mental processes, but rather to play an active pragmatic part in human behaviour. Thus in its primary function it is one of the chief cultural forces and an adjunct to bodily activities. Indeed, it is an indispensable ingredient of all concerted human action. (Malinowski, 1935, p. 7)

Stemming directly from the insights offered by social semiotics, Critical Discourse Analysis (CDA) emphasizes even more the social nature of language and inextricable two-way relationship to the context of situation. As Fairclough et al. (2011, pp. 357–358) explain:

> CDA sees discourse (or semiosis) as a form of social practice. This implies a dialectical relationship between a particular discursive event and all the diverse elements of the situation(s), institutions(s), and social structure(s) which frame it. A dialectical relationship is a two-way relationship: the discursive event is shaped by situations, institutions and social structures, but it also shapes them. To put it a different way, discourse is socially constitutive as well as socially shaped: it constitutes situations, objects of knowledge, and the social identities of and relationships between people and groups of people.

The two conceptualizations of language briefly outlined here can be summarized in the Table 1.1.

TABLE 1.1 Two conceptualizations of language

System	Social practice
A relatively stable, uniform self-contained system	A process in perpetual flux
Independent from action	Dependent on action
Regulated by internal rules	Regulated by contextual factors
Tied to a particular community	Tied to individual situations

On the one hand, the 'system' view induces one to represent language as an object, perhaps even characterized by physical qualities. In the 'practice' view, on the other hand, it's much more difficult to delineate the exact boundaries of language, since it is so inextricably integrated within action and constantly subject to change. The opposition suggested here underpins much of the discussion which unfolds in the rest of this book. In particular, the next chapter examines how the main narrative recounting the 'history of English' (the use of the inverted commas will become apparent later) has derived from the notion that language is a self-contained bounded system.

PART ONE

History

2

Old Englishes

Credence in a mythical past crafted for some present cause suppresses history's impartial complexity.
DAVID LOWENTHAL

Keywords

Anglo-Saxons • history and ideology • myth • Old English

2.1 Introduction

Most historical accounts on the early development of the English language follow a common narrative line and are based on certain fundamental assumptions, taken more or less for granted:

- the 'birth' of the English language can be traced back to the time when, in the middle of the fifth-century AD, Germanic tribes, commonly referred to as 'Anglo-Saxons', arrived from the north-western shores of Europe and settled in various regions of Britain, having exterminated and/or chased away the indigenous Britons;

- those Germanic invaders spoke closely related (or even mutually intelligible) dialects which, in a short period of time, amalgamated into one, distinctively English, language, while preserving certain features which marked the four main varieties of English of the time: Northumbrian, Mercian, West Saxon and Kentish;

- it is therefore possible to trace the historical evolution of English linearly from that early period onwards, as is reflected in the names 'Old English', 'Middle English' and 'Modern English', each phase being characterized by development primarily on the lexical level, leaving the Germanic backbone of the language intact.

Despite the fact that some of the details (e.g. dates and names) may be disputed, and that the extent to which those assumptions are adhered to may vary, the degree of consistency in the majority of historical reconstructions is high and so, apparently, is the level of confidence in the most important aspects of the facts recounted. Significant departures are very rare and, in a sense, it can be said that the 'history of English' has been *institutionalized*.

However, the factuality of the events recounted in these histories contrasts with the scarcity of contemporary sources. While the arrival of Germanic invaders/settlers in Britain in the fourth and fifth centuries is undisputed, much of the information that we have available about those invasions is based on Gildas's *Excidio et Conquestu Britanniae* (sixth century) and, above all, *Historia Ecclesiastica Gentis Anglorum*, which the monk Bede wrote in the eighth century, in part relying on Gildas's work. More importantly from a linguistic point of view, actual language data from the time generally considered the 'birth' of the English language is completely unavailable. The earliest, very sparse, samples date back to Bede's times, nearly 300 years after the arrival of the so-called Anglo-Saxons.

This chapter first examines the discrepancy between the confidence with which the development of the English language is generally narrated and the lack of actual evidence to support it. It then discusses the reasons why the mainstream narrative has nevertheless been enshrined as canon and suggests possible alternatives to it.

2.2   Mainstream narrative

One of the firm points in the history of English and other European languages is the idea that they share a common ancestry. The striking similarities observable among virtually all European languages and several Asian ones have led linguists to hypothesize a common *Indo-European* origin for these languages, dating back to migrations that took place during a long period, possibly from as early as 10,000 years ago. Since there is no written record from that time, much of the scholarly work that has been conducted has been based on hypotheses.

One such hypothesis is about the actual place of origin of the people who presumably spoke languages that are now referred to as *proto-Indo-European*. Not surprisingly, there is no universal agreement, but one possibility that has been proposed in recent years is that the original 'centre' of Indo-European migration might have been in Anatolia, in central Turkey.

While a discussion on hypotheses about a common genesis of European languages is entirely outside the scope of this book, it is interesting to examine aspects of how this has been represented in what might be called a 'popular-science' approach to linguistics. In particular, I wish to pay attention to the metaphorical representations of language that are evident in such popular descriptions.

2.2.1 *Metaphorical representations of language*

With reference to studies suggesting that Indo-European languages may have originated from Anatolia, a headline in a popular-science magazine read 'Language tree rooted in Turkey' (*Nature*, 27 November 2003). A few years later, a newspaper headline, somewhat more dramatically, informed readers that 'English language comes from Turkey, say experts' (*The Scotsman*, 24 August 2012). These headlines are clearly underpinned by metaphors: one sees language as a plant, the other as an object that is capable of moving from one place to another. These are in no way exceptional representations.

Nor is the use of metaphor to describe language particularly remarkable, as the simplification of complex and abstract concepts through metaphor is entirely normal. As Lakoff and Johnson (1980) explained, metaphors are not special figures of speech that one expects to find in literary texts, but are cognitive devices that we use all the time to make sense of the world. By using metaphors we treat complex and/or abstract concepts as if they were more concrete and simpler entities.

In particular, ontological metaphors allow us 'to refer to, to quantify, or to identify aspects of the experience that has been made more delineated' (Kövecses, 2010, p. 39). Through this kind of metaphor, complex aspects of human experience are typically conceived as if they were physical objects, substances, containers, or even people. Accordingly, metaphors are generally represented in the form of 'X is Y', where X is the complex/abstract concept and Y the simple/concrete one.

Language is very often construed through ontological metaphors, and treated as if it possessed physical qualities: LANGUAGE IS A PHYSICAL OBJECT. It is also often seen as a living organism. Genealogical terms such as *family*, *birth*, *death* and so on are frequently used with reference to language and are evidence of the pervasiveness of this metaphor. Indeed, one of the most common ways to categorize languages is by placing them in kinship relationships through the 'family tree' model. *Life*, in turn, is routinely understood as *a journey*, in which a living being travels from an origin (birth) to a destination (death). In this way, language becomes *a traveller*.

The use of metaphor pervades academic discourse, too. Just opening one of the more popular textbooks on the history of English (Freeborn, 2006), one notices 'The English language is brought to Britain' and 'How the English language came to Britain' as the titles of a chapter and a section of it. These, and countless similar titles commonly found in other publications in the field, entail an understanding of the English language as a well-identifiable physical object, capable of moving or being moved, from one place to another. This is exactly the same LANGUAGE IS A MOVABLE PHYSICAL OBJECT metaphor underpinning the headline about English coming from Turkey.

Such metaphors can indeed be extremely useful. However, the fact that, by their very nature, they entail simplification means that sometimes the cognitive reformulations that they afford can be exploited for reasons that go beyond making a complex notion easier to understand. In particular, metaphors can be instrumental in *ideological* representations of reality. When this is the case, it is useful to unpack a metaphor and deal with the complexity of the concept at hand, in order to try and tease out ideological forces that exploit particular metaphorical representation and that may also contribute to the establishment of the metaphor.

In the next section, I will take a closer look at conventional academic discourse about the history of English and examine how the cognitive shortcuts afforded by metaphors are realized.

2.2.2   *The arrival of English in 449 AD*

As mentioned earlier, most modern accounts of the events that are generally seen as having caused the 'birth' of the English language are based directly on Bede's *Historia* and, to some extent, Gildas's *Excidio*. Given that neither Gildas nor Bede were contemporary to the facts recounted in their narratives, dates, names and facts reported in those early medieval texts are subject to varying degrees of dispute, ranging from faithful reproductions to more sceptical approaches.

An example of the former type is evident in the statement holding that 'English officially starts when the Germanic tribes and their languages reach the British Isles, in 449' (van Gelderen, 2006, p. 2). Here, the use of the phrase 'officially starts' and the exact date 449 may sound fairly extreme in its over-simplistic definiteness, but some versions go even further. The titles in Freeborn's book cited at the beginning of this section, for example, imply that the English language existed even *before* the so-called Anglo-Saxons arrived to Britain, giving it a sort of timeless character. Indeed, by drawing from the LANGUAGE IS A MOVABLE PHYSICAL OBJECT or the LANGUAGE IS A TRAVELLER metaphor, these descriptions portray the English language as an entity that has always existed and that the 'Anglo-Saxon' invasions finally brought to Britain.

Interestingly, this is true even in some interpretations which seem to want to dispel some of the myths about the 'beginning' of the English language. In what is probably the best-known book on the history of English, Baugh and

Cable (2002, p. 43) explain that one should not be induced to believing that the English language has always been bound the English people:

> We are so accustomed to thinking of English as an inseparable adjunct to the English people that we are likely to forget that it has been the language of England for a comparatively short period in the world's history. Since its introduction into the island about the middle of the fifth century it has had a career extending through only 1,500 years.

Here, while arguing against the inseparability of the English language and people, the idea that the language was 'introduced' into the island clearly implies the fact that it existed prior to the fifth century.

Others adopt a more nuanced and cautious approach, highlighting the complexities both of languages in general and of accounts that attempt to trace their histories. Mugglestone (2012), for example, makes it very clear that any endeavour to document the early history of English is bound to face significant challenges due primarily to the scarcity of linguistic data, which is directly proportional to how far back in time one goes, and the inevitable selectivity that the language historian is therefore forced to adopt. For this reason, she concedes that her volume aims to construct '"a history" rather than "the history", recognizing that many other pathways could be navigated through the past – and present – of the English language' (2012, p. 2).

The problem is that alternative pathways are rarely trodden. Indeed, in the historiography of English there seems to be one 'highway' and a number of smaller pathways that run more or less parallel to it, without really moving very far from that main route.

In another popular textbook, I. Singh (2005, pp. 67–68) questions the historical validity of both the date 449 and the name 'Anglo-Saxons' but, while doing so, doesn't really move away from the conventional narrative:

> This date [449] is [. . .] often cited in relation to the initial emergence of the English language. However, it is important to note that these initial migrants, known collectively but somewhat erroneously as the Anglo-Saxons, were not English speakers. They spoke instead the closely related Germanic dialects that would become the roots of English within a few generations of settlement and interaction in England. We will therefore [. . .] take 500 AD as a more sensible birth-date for English.

The postponement from 449 to 500 doesn't alter the basic idea that it is indeed possible to name a particular year as the 'birth-date' of the English language. The arrival of the Germanic tribes in England is seen as a very special event which unified their dialects into one distinctive language.

2.2.3   *From closely related to one language*

So, even when they don't explicitly suggest that the language pre-existed the arrival of Germanic settlers in Britain, many histories of English do insist on the fact that the newcomers 'spoke neighbouring Germanic dialects and were no doubt able to communicate with each other' (Svartvik & Leech, 2006, pp. 17–18) and that such dialects soon became unified into one recognizably English language.

The common ancestry of those proto-English acquires even more substance and scientific factuality if it can be given a name. Following the theory put forward by German philologist Friedrich Maurer (1953), Gramley (2012, p. 25) claims that

> it is unlikely that there were any major linguistic differences [among the four tribal groups of Angles, Saxons, Jutes, and Frisians]; all of the newcomers were speakers of *'North Sea Germanic'*, sometimes also known as Ingvaeonic.

The names 'North Sea Germanic' and 'Ingvaeonic' do something very powerful: they conclusively establish a unique and direct line of descent between the language (singular!) spoken by the Germanic tribes before they reached Britain and the language that emerged there from the fifth century onwards. Referring to this new language, Gramley (p. 25) adds that

> although there were regional dialectal differences, there was such a high degree of similarity that the language spoken by the Anglo-Saxons was uniformly called *Englisc* by all four groups, which is perhaps indicative of a feeling of shared culture and identity.

Gramley doesn't say why and when the four groups decided to call their one language *Englisc* but what is important is that this name seals substantial linguistic and, significantly, socio-cultural uniformity. As Barber et al. (2009, p. 124) note, 'these groups were [. . .] closely related in language and culture, and eventually came to regard themselves as one people'. So, the picture that emerges quite clearly is one where not only did the 'Anglo-Saxons' speak fundamentally the same language, but they also saw themselves as one people.

The shared culture, identity and language of the *Englisc* is confirmed and reinforced by the fact that 'the beginning of [the] existence [of English] as a recognizably distinct language' (Hoad, 2012, p. 7) is commonly referred to as 'Old English'.

2.2.4 The story of 'Old English'

On the surface, the expression 'Old English' seems to possess a sort of natural and obvious face value. The modifier 'old' couldn't be clearer. More importantly, the noun 'English' is even more unequivocal, in that it uses the most basic and effective way – the same word – to suggest the fact that 'there is indeed a fair amount of continuity between Old English and Modern English' (Seargeant, 2012a, p. 17).

However, even a cursory glance at an actual language sample will at the very least induce readers to wonder just to what extent this can indeed be considered 'English'. If we consider, for example, the language of one of the oldest records of 'Old English', we would struggle to recognize it as 'English' at all. Figure 2.1 shows the text contained on the front panel of the *Franks Casket*, a chest made of whale's bone, dating back to the early eighth century (i.e. 300 years after the 'Anglo-Saxons' are believed to have arrived in Britain).

ᚠᛁᛋᚲᚠᛚᚩᛞᚢ ᚠᚻᚫᚠᚠᚩᛏᚠᛗᚱᚷ
ᛗᛏᛒᛗᚱᛁᚷ
ᛈᚫᚱᛈᚷᚠᛗᚱᛁᛚᚷᚱᚠᚱᛏᛈᚫᚱᚻᛗᚠᛏᚷᚱᛗᚢᛏᚷᛁᛗᛈᚠᛗ
ᚻᚱᚠᛏᛗᛗᛒᚱᛏ

FIGURE 2.1 *The runic inscriptions on the* Franks Casket.

This bears no obvious resemblance with modern English at all. Of course, part of the reason is the fact that it is written in runic script. However, even when transliterated into the Roman alphabet and split into words, its intelligibility doesn't improve much:

fisc flodu ahof on fergenberig;
warþ gasric grorn, þær he on greut giswom.
hronæs ban.

Even if two or three of the words in the transliterated text have fairly clear counterparts in Modern English, it is still completely impossible for a modern-English speaker to attempt an interpretation of this text without very specific knowledge not only of the runic alphabet but also, and more importantly, of ancient Germanic languages. According to Page (1995, p. 268), a possible translation into modern English could be:

The fish beat up the sea(s) on to the mountainous cliff. The king of ?terror became sad when he swam on to the shingle. Whale's bone.

Nor is the original text in the least comprehensible to modern English speakers when read aloud by people who have studied its likely pronunciation. The fact that any actual connection with modern English can only be explained by experts in the field confirms that the distance between what is commonly referred to as 'Old English' and modern English is very considerable indeed and is not appreciably smaller than, say, that separating Norwegian from English: 'the English we speak now does not look like the offspring of Old English at all' (Stockwell & Minkova, 2009, p. 54).

As Milroy (2002) has argued, from a purely linguistic point of view the texts that have survived from the 'Old English' period are much closer to texts in languages that, in the same period or even later, were used in the Continent than they are to texts in 'Middle English', let alone 'Modern English'. The question is: on what grounds is the choice of the noun 'English' justified when it applies to manifestly different languages like twenty-first-century English and what is referred to as 'Old English'?

An illuminating explanation for this terminological choice is given in a footnote by Baugh and Cable (2002, p. 45), who compare the use of the terms *Anglo-Saxon* and *Old English* to designate the language spoken by early Germanic people in Britain and claim that the former was 'logically less defensible' despite being 'amply justified by usage'. The reason being that '*Old English* . . . has the advantage of suggesting the unbroken continuity of English throughout its existence'.

The point made by Baugh and Cable is a crucial one. The 'logical' necessity to 'suggest' that English has always existed as one identifiable entity is seen as more important than the evidence provided by actual usage, which would surely undermine the very idea of the 'unbroken continuity of English'. But why should the notion of the unbroken continuity of English be put forward in the first place, especially if it can't easily (or at all) be supported by linguistic evidence? The only conceivable explanation is that such accounts must have aims that go beyond pure historical or linguistic reconstruction of facts. In this regard, Milroy (2002, pp. 16–17) critiques what he refers to as the 'efforts of language historians over the past 150 years' to produce a single narrative of the English language:

> In the historical dimension, we cannot define what is 'English' and what is not 'English' by internal analysis *alone*. We cannot demonstrate by internal analysis alone when 'English' began, or when one stage of English gave way to another. Nor can we demonstrate by internal analysis alone that Anglo-Saxon is the same language as modern English, or a different language which is its direct ancestor, or a related language which is not a direct ancestor. To answer these questions, we have to appeal to ideological positions.

The next section explores the ideological positions that Milroy alludes to.

2.3   Ideological motivations in the history of English

That history isn't, and can't be, an exact science in which facts are reported absolutely, objectively and impartially is of course a rather naïve observation and something that very few historians would dispute. This is first of all because what constitutes a 'fact' and 'the truth' has been radically challenged in the post-modern era (for a comprehensive overview, see Corthoys & Docker, 2010). As Foucault (1972) has influentially argued, knowledge and our understanding of the world are based not so much on direct observation and experience but on how things are represented in *discourse*, especially when these representations are repeated often enough so that they become institutionalized. So, if 'facts' derive from institutionalized discourse rather than from reality, the nature of history must also be seen from the same perspective. As Munslow (2006, p. 3) reminds us:

> the genuine nature of history can be understood only when it is viewed not solely and simply as an objectivised empiricist enterprise, but as the creation and eventual imposition by historians of a particular narrative form on the past: a process that directly affects the whole project, not merely the writing up stage.

What this means is that there are processes in motion that put forward interpretations of the past which later become conventionalized and accepted. This, in turn, generates more discourse echoing the same interpretations, which are eventually enshrined into canon and rarely disputed. So, it is entirely plausible that the mainstream 'history of English' has gone through exactly the same process. That is, to borrow Munslow's words, historical linguists have created and eventually imposed a particular narrative form on a period of the past that goes from the middle of the fifth century onwards. The term 'Old English' is part of that particular institutionalized discourse.

So, what are the ideological forces that produced the institutionalized discourse of the mainstream history of English? An answer to this question must be sought in the nation-state ideology that emerged and developed in Europe in the nineteenth century.

2.3.1   *Language and nationhood*

The nation-state discourse focussed very much on the indissoluble tripartite bond linking *one* people, *one* land and *one* language. As Hardt and Negri (2000) note, it was 'founded on a biological continuity of blood relations, a spatial continuity of territory, and linguistic commonality' (p. 95). In order for a nation-state to be fully legitimized, it was crucial that such a bond was seen as very old, dating back to the midst of time, or even simply part of the natural world. As S. Wright (2011, pp. 780–781) observes, '[l]anguage played a central role in all 19th century national(ist) movement' and, particularly interestingly for the present discussion, she also points out:

> The linguist was also of use, alongside the historian and the archaeologist, in establishing the long-standing existence of the group. If the language could be presented as dating back far into history, this suggested an ancient culture rooted in ancestral territory.

This is because '[l]inguistic affiliation bespeaks a community, perpetuates its heritage, and alienates outsiders. With few exceptions, a common language is felt to be a crucial criterion of nationhood' (Lowenthal, 1998, p. 69). That is why a language needs to be seen not only shared by a nation, but also as old as possible, since '[t]he "nation-state myth" – that basic view of the world as consisting naturally of nation-states – is bound up with an assumption that national languages are a primordial reality' (Joseph, 2004, p. 98).

The necessity to prove the existence of a primordial national language was particularly urgent in situations where political unification came rather late, as in Italy and Germany, for example, which became countries in the second half of the nineteenth century. It was imperative in those cases to demonstrate that a common ancestral language had existed for a very long time, to confirm the naturalness of the nation and hence justify the establishment of a political entity with authority over that nation's territory. This was especially important where the territory itself didn't have clear natural borders, as was the case of Germany: the area where it was possible to demonstrate that people spoke a common language could then be identified as belonging to the German nation. The relationship between language and national identity has remained the same over time. On 24 April 2014, for example, it was announced that the people of Cornwall will be officially recognized as a national minority group by the central UK government as well as the European framework convention for the protection of national minorities. Of course, an important part of the new status is the formal recognition of Cornish, a language that nobody speaks natively but that it is very important to promote and even display (e.g. on public signage) in order to cement a Cornish identity.

The context of the English language in nineteenth-century Britain, however, was different. Being an island, Britain had very clear physical borders while, politically, it had been united since the early eighteenth century. England had been a sovereign state since the tenth century. Yet, despite such significant differences, in the second half of the nineteenth century the national language began to be discussed in ways which were very similar to the discourse emerging on the Continent and derived from the same ideological drive that S. Wright and Joseph talk about.

Divisions were not political but social. As Crowley (1996, p. 149) explains, nineteenth-century Britain was 'a bitterly divided, contradictory, self-doubting and harsh place', principally as a result of the rise of the industrial proletariat and Chartism, which 'changed the nature of political discourse . . . by its positing of the people as the working class (with a consequent redefinition of the nation)' (1996, p. 152). Crowley goes on to note that the demands of those early working-class movements were met with 'force' and 'brute violence' but, interestingly, also with a strategy which sought to unify the population around a sense of national pride. He also suggests that the systematic study of 'the history of the language' was integral to that strategy:

> Not of course as a direct, panic response, but as one which attempts to think through and organise the basis of all sorts of crucial concepts such as the nation, loyalty, allegiance, that which we hold in common and which unites us, and so on. Chartism promised conflict and upheaval; 'the history of the language' belonged to the discourse of cultural nationalism which stressed continuity, that which is known, a sense of history, and gradual evolution. (Crowley, 1996, p. 152)

Significantly, Watts (2011, p. 32) points out that it was in that period that '"Anglo-Saxon" was discursively transformed into "Old English"', effectively creating what Milroy (2002) calls the *myth of the ancient language*, aimed to represent a language that had come a long way, fundamentally keeping the same identity through the centuries. Figure 2.2 shows the sharp rise in the use of the phrase 'Old English' at the end of the nineteenth century, according to *Google*'s 'n-gram' service.

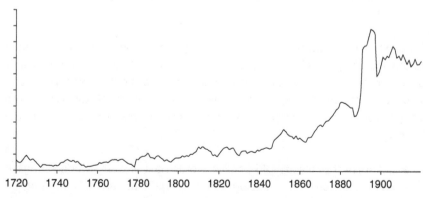

FIGURE 2.2 *The frequency of the use of the phrase 'Old English'.*

That was also a time when linguistics was emerging as a science and, as such, 'had to constitute an object of study that was stable and homogeneous' while 'the heterogeneous raw material of language activity had to be disciplined in order to make it stable enough for investigation' (Fleischman, 2000, p. 44). So, socio-political preoccupations merged seamlessly with academic ones.

It is now clear how the 'advantage' of suggesting the 'unbroken continuity of English throughout its existence' argued by Baugh and Cable and reproduced by most historical linguists in the twentieth century was not based on linguistic considerations but on political motives that were felt particularly strongly in the latter half of the nineteenth century. This, therefore, illustrates not only that interpretations of the past are often at the service of ideological and political motives of the present, but also that certain interpretations become part of institutionalized discourse and are elevated to the status of undisputed canon.

Furthermore, in Britain not only was the discourse of 'Old English' very similar to contemporary rhetoric on nation building elsewhere in Europe, but its roots could be traced as far back as the fifteenth century:

> The impact of language on nation formation was nothing new. In the early 1420s, when the term 'nation' was beginning to evolve from its technical, medieval function (describing groupings at church councils or universities) into its modern meaning of a people or race, it was 'peculiarities of language', rather than 'blood-relationship and habit of unity', that Henry V's ambassadors pronounced the 'most sure and positive sign and essence of a nation in divine and human law'. Language, in other words, was not solely a means of defining a nation: it was a means of creating one, overriding issues of blood or long-lasting alliances by its ability, on a practical as well as rhetorical level, to gather potentially disparate groups into one cohesive national community, using and understanding one tongue. (Shrank, 2000, p. 181)

It didn't take too long before the role of the linguist became of crucial importance to the necessity of defining a sense of national unity. Laurence Nowell was a sixteenth-century antiquarian who compiled the first Anglo-Saxon dictionary: *Vocabularium Saxonicum*, in which he translated Anglo-Saxon words into Early Modern English. With reference to his work, Brackmann (2012, p. 31) observes that

> a dictionary that places Old English words next to Early Modern English words is a logical way to explore the 'heritage' that Early Modern English had from its ancestor, and that its speakers had from the medieval period.

This makes clear that Nowell's concern with the English language's history and use is not simply 'academic' and antiquarian.

The idea of 'heritage' that Brackmann refers to is the one discussed by Lowenthal (1998), who defines it as 'a profession of faith in a past tailored to present-day purposes' (p. x). From this point of view, the entire discourse of 'Old English' can be seen as an effort not only to describe and document an ancient language, but also to contribute to constructing a national heritage, since 'language makes a link between the present and the foundational past of any culture, the past to which its larger-than-life predecessors belong, the heroic past' (Considine, 2008, p. 7).

Having discussed the ideological process whereby the mainstream history of English has developed and become established, in the next section I propose alternatives to some of the firmer myths about the 'history of English'.

2.4   Untidying history

What I have highlighted in the previous sections is that most histories of English follow a narrative line based more on ideological and political concerns than on rigorous, evidence-based accounts or, when evidence isn't easily available, argument-based hypotheses. The resulting representation of the sociolinguistic panorama of Britain in the fifth and sixth centuries tends to simplify reality to the extreme and to offer descriptions in which people, places and events are clearly identified and neatly named.

Consequently, there is the necessity to at least re-examine that particular interpretation of the past. In this section I revisit the three 'facts' about English listed at the beginning of this chapter, try to demonstrate their lack of validity and propose alternative readings. I must of course make clear that this is not an exercise in contrariness but an intellectual engagement that is of fundamental importance for the understanding of 'English', 'World Englishes' and language in general that underpins this book.

First of all, the very idea of a 'beginning', variously rendered metaphorically as the 'origin', the 'birth' or the 'roots' of English, can be challenged.

2.4.1   The 'birth' of the English language?

A beginning of something presupposes that there was a time when that something did not exist and a particular moment when certain factors caused it to begin to exist. But languages don't *begin* at any particular points in time. Rather, they are in a state of constant flux and evolution, following the societal and technological changes of their users, as well as their geographical movements. Any attempt to identify a 'start' for the English (or any other) language is therefore bound to be based on arbitrary decisions.

As was seen earlier, the arrival of the so-called Anglo-Saxons in Britain is the event that is most commonly indicated as marking precisely that kind of arbitrary and convenient 'origin' of the English language. Indeed, the word 'event' here is inappropriate and misleading. Bede's recount of Germanic invaders arriving in 'three long ships' in 449 is, at best, an extreme simplification. Germanic people began to cross the strip of water separating Britannia (as was called by the Romans) from the north-west shores of the continent since well before the fifth century, and the invasions that Bede recounts in a fairy-tale style 'were undoubtedly . . . a much more complex process' (Irvine, 2006, p. 35).

One starting point in addressing that complex process lies in the unpacking of such names as 'Angles', 'Saxons' and indeed the compound 'Anglo-Saxons'.

2.4.2   The 'Anglo-Saxons'?

The way these words are used in conventional histories of English suggests a level of certainty about their meanings that contrasts with the lack of actual historical evidence. The most cogent critique, in this regard, is offered by Reynolds (1985), who condemns a certain essentialist tendency among historians and linguists to a-critically accept names of 'tribes' in pre-Norman Britain as if they referred to groups neatly defined genetically, culturally and linguistically. Such names ('Angles', 'Saxons', 'Jutes', 'Frisians', etc.) are taken for granted despite the fact that we know virtually nothing about their use among the early Germanic people who settled in Britain:

> In fact we do not know how consistently the Germanic-speaking invaders of Britain behaved like a group or felt themselves to be a group during the fifth and sixth centuries. We do not know what they called themselves or what others called them, if indeed they had any collective name. (Reynolds, 1985, p. 401)

The origin of the name 'Anglo-Saxons' probably lies in the phrase *Angli Saxones*, which began to be used on the Continent only towards the ninth century 'to distinguish the Saxons of England from those elsewhere' (1985, p. 398). *Angli*, in that sense, acted as a premodifier of the noun *Saxones*. What the name 'Saxons', in turn, exactly referred to is unclear. There is no evidence to support that it may have indicated any ethnically defined tribe, while the most plausible hypothesis is that the word originated from a kind of short sword, the *seax*, which certain Germanic warriors used in battle, and so '[a]s long as a man carried a seax, he would be called Saxon, regardless of his ethnic or geographical origins' (Crystal, 2004, p. 18).

So the noun 'Anglo-Saxons' and the adjective 'Anglo-Saxon' can only be seen as convenient terminological shortcuts to designate, very loosely, the Germanic invaders who arrived in Britain in the fifth century. However, from a genetic or even linguistic point of view, virtually no justification remains to support the use of these names if one uses them to refer to the long period of English history that goes from those invasions to the Norman Conquest.

2.4.3   *Anglo-Saxon England?*

According to the conventional narrative, the might of the 'Anglo-Saxons' and their superiority as warriors were such that, soon after their mythical arrival, they exterminated the original Britons and forced them to retreat to the less hospitable and more remote parts of the island, such as present-day Wales and Cornwall. As a result, present-day England became, in the space of only a few generations, a purely Anglo-Saxon territory. This would both explain and be supported by the fact that Celtic languages have left virtually no visible trace in English.

However, the arrival en masse of very large numbers of 'Anglo-Saxons' and the consequent genocide of the Britons have been entirely discredited by archaeological, genetic and textual evidence (see, among others, Oppenheimer, 2006; Higham, 2007; Pattison, 2008). While it is very difficult to reconstruct exact historical details with confidence, there seems to be reasonable agreement about the following two main points:

1   migrations from the Continent, smaller in scale than previously thought, did cause a radical reconfiguration of the balance of power, undoubtedly through armed conflict, in favour of the Germanic invaders;

2   however, the indigenous population were not exterminated but lived side by side, and eventually assimilated into, the newcomers.

As the Germanic element maintained its prestige status, such assimilation was not culturally neutral. One consequence was that the very few who were able and needed to write, primarily clerics and legislators, did so in the more powerful languages, namely Latin and those that had attachments with Germanic culture. Non-prestige Celtic languages presumably continued to be spoken, even though their lower status meant that they eventually succumbed through contact with Germanic languages.

This brings the discussion to another widely accepted 'fact' that the English language is fundamentally Germanic and displays no evidence of influence from Celtic languages, whose only remaining contribution is in the form of place-names and a handful of words referring to land features.

2.4.4   *A purely Germanic language?*

English is generally believed to be a Germanic language whose vocabulary has been enriched by the introduction of new words from Viking languages first and, even more significantly, Norman French later. From this point of view, it is seen, metaphorically, as a river, whose tributaries have added new words to it but have not altered its Germanic identity. Similarly, it is also likened to a sponge, able to absorb lexical items from other languages while, again, retaining its core shape. These representations are underpinned by the ENGLISH IS A CONTAINER ontological metaphor. A container of words, primarily.

From this perspective, the absence of any visible lexical impact of Celtic languages into English is something that has been regarded as a 'puzzle', especially if one is willing to abandon the genocide myth mentioned earlier (see, e.g. Crystal, 2004, pp. 29–32).

However, in recent years there has been a significant body of research investigating what has been referred to as the 'Celtic hypothesis', according to which British Celtic languages had a much more significant impact on English than is commonly thought. Through close language analysis, researchers in this area are providing compelling evidence of the nature and the extent of this influence, at the levels of grammar, syntax, phonology and lexis (Tristram, 2006; Filppula & Klemola, 2009; Klemola, 2013). This work calls for a profound change in the way 'Old English' has been described, especially as regards the pure Germanic roots that it is often supposed to have.

In particular, the suggestion that aspects other than the vocabulary of English have been significantly influenced by other languages destabilizes one of the firmer tenets in the mainstream history of English, namely that the evolution of English can be understood metaphorically like a river into which a few tributaries have contributed a portion of its vocabulary. But to claim that the very structure and sound of the language have been modified as a result of contact with other languages upsets the canonical narrative at its core.

Not surprisingly, another aspect of the sociolinguistic situation of pre-Norman Britain that is hardly ever envisaged is the fact that there must have been a significant amount of language hybridity. Again, the paucity of data doesn't allow us to draw any conclusion, but observing the present may enable us to make fairly good 'predictions' about the past. If we consider present-day situations where two or more languages co-exist within the same speech community, it seems entirely plausible that forms of hybridity must have existed among the population in what we may more aptly call 'Anglo-Celtic' Britain. Of course, apart from the varieties of Celtic languages and Germanic languages, there was Latin, which hadn't simply disappeared with the withdrawal of the Roman Empire in the early fifth century.

Returning, once again, to the Franks Casket, the following string of letters appears on the top-right of the back panel:

hICFUGIαNThIERUΓαLIm

This part of the inscription is in Latin and uses mostly Latin characters, but maintains the absence of spaces between words typical of runic scripts. More conventionally, it would be rendered as:

HIC FUGIANT HIERUSALIM

The next word on the same panel of the casket is completely in runic characters:

ᚠᚠᛁᛏᚠᛏᚠᚱᛗᛋ

Transliterated into Roman characters, this word is AFITATORES, again a Latin word. The whole phrase is *Hic fugiant Hierusalim afitatores*, meaning 'Here the inhabitants flee from Jerusalem'. So the casket displays a clear example of language hybridity, blurring the borders between languages as well as scripts.

In fact, I'd like to suggest that the mixing in question goes even deeper. There are various aspects of it that can be observed. Beginning from the characters employed, are the runic and the Roman scripts really two distinct writing systems? Consider Figure 2.3, showing some runes alongside their corresponding Roman letters: do the two sets of characters really belong to different scripts? Aren't they simply very slightly different ways of representing

ᛒ	B
ᚠ	F
ᚺ	H
ᛁ	I
ᛗ	M
ᚱ	R
ᛋ	S
ᛏ	T

FIGURE 2.3 *Runes and Roman letters.*

the same phonemes? Of course, here I've hand-picked the runes that are most similar to Roman letters. Others are quite different. But the fact that about a quarter of the runes were near-identical to Roman characters at least indicates that the two scripts were less distinct than one might think.

Furthermore, on the Franks Casket three of Latin words were written in Roman letters and one in runes, exhibiting more intersecting layers of hybridity.

This is of course rather anecdotal, but it is significant that the earliest available piece of written 'Anglo-Saxon' should be so 'impure'. Also, by no means does the Casket represent an isolated example of mixing between vernacular languages and Latin. Schendl (2011), for example, has examined a corpus of texts consisting of the leases issued by Oswald of Worcester in the second half of the tenth century and has found extensive use of Latin together with what he simply calls 'English' in the same texts. He has identified as many as five different types of mixing between the two languages (p. 53) and shown that 'code-switching was consciously and systematically employed in some legal and administrative texts in the Anglo-Saxon period' (p. 89).

The key to understanding this linguistic border-crossing and apparent 'impurity' lies in seeing language as social practice. Latin and Germanic languages co-existed and were available to people and if Oswald's leases (and many other texts) made use of both languages, that was presumably because the 'lease' activity was best performed in that way. If we cease to see texts simply as artefacts and begin to see them as integral to some social action, then the co-presence of what we consider two (or more) languages shouldn't surprise us. The push to monolingualism is an oddity peculiar to the so-called modern age, especially in the Western world.

Whatever we may understand by the phrase 'Old English', one thing we do know is that it was much less 'pure' than ideologically driven narratives may want to portray it.

With regard to the idea of '(im-)purity', David Crystal (2003) offers an interesting perspective. On the one hand, with reference to the French words that entered the English language as a consequence of the Norman Conquest, he says that '[f]rom a lexical point of view, English is in fact far more a Romance than a Germanic language' (p. 8). On the other hand, he doesn't see the Normans to have had such an impact on Britain's language as to alter its quintessentially English character: there may have been a military conquest in 1066, but, he explains, '[t]here was no linguistic conquest' (p. 77). Similarly, Svartvik and Leech (2006, pp. 34–35) claim that since 'England never became a French-speaking country', English managed to survive during the Norman rule.

England may not have become a French-speaking country, but if we consider the language of two of the best-known texts in 'English' literature, the 'survival' of the language doesn't appear so obvious. The following two extracts are from *Beowulf* and *The Canterbury Tales*, respectively:

text 1
Þa wæs Hroðgare heresped gyfen,
wiges weorðmynd, þæt him his winemagas
georne hyrdon, oðð þæt seo geogoð geweox,
magodriht micel. Him on mod be-arn,
þæt healreced hatan wolde,
medoærn micel men gewyrcean
þonne yldo bearn æfre gefrunon,
ond þær on innan eall gedælan
geongum ond ealdum, swylc him God sealde
buton folcscare ond feorum gumena.

text 2
A KNYGHT ther was, and that a worthy man,
That fro the tyme that he first bigan
To riden out, he loved chivalrie,
Trouthe and honour, fredom and curteisie.
Ful worthy was he in his lordes werre,
And therto hadde he riden, no man ferre,
As wel in cristendom as in hethenesse,
And evere honoured for his worthynesse.
At Alisaundre he was, whan it was wonne.

The date of the surviving *Beowulf* manuscript is uncertain but it is probable that it was made between the tenth and the early eleventh century, that is, shortly before the Norman Conquest. This means that the gap between *Beowulf* and *The Canterbury Tales* may be of a little more than 300 years. By contrast, the time gap dividing Chaucer's *Tales* from our time is of nearly 700 years: twice as long. However, it is immediately apparent that the *linguistic* gap between the two texts is far greater than the one between Chaucer's language and contemporary English. To the point that while *Beowulf* is totally incomprehensible to someone who hasn't studied its language, the *Tales* can be read without too much difficulty. On what basis, other than political ones, can we argue that the language of *Beowulf* is fundamentally the same as the language of *The Canterbury Tales*? If the word 'conquest' sounds inconveniently unpatriotic, might 'revolution', at least, be a fitter alternative?

2.5   Varieties of 'Old English'?

Despite the assumption that 'Old English' was purely Germanic, traditional accounts don't necessarily suggest that it was also one, monolithic language. In fact, four regional varieties are identified in the mainstream history: Northumbrian, Mercian, West Saxon and Kentish. Figure 2.4 shows the way in which pre-Norman England is generally subdivided into four main dialects areas.

Like all dialects maps, the one in Figure 2.4 can only be interpreted as meaning that each of the four territories was inhabited by speakers of one particular variety. Each area, that is, is represented as internally linguistically uniform and, at the same time, distinct from the other areas. The lines neatly separating each division act very much like the borders delimiting administrative territories.

However, in the absence of strong processes of language standardization, for example, via explicit codification in mass-produced grammar books and dictionaries and/or via diffusion through media such as radio and television,

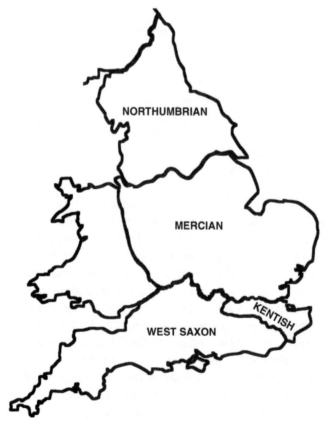

FIGURE 2.4 *'Anglo-Saxon' dialects map.*

the distribution of languages and dialects doesn't follow demarcation lines in the way that dialect maps indicate. Instead, the way people speak tends to vary, gradually, as one travels along an imaginary line, and the only real borders are encountered when there is a physical obstacle that interrupts the opportunities of communication between two communities, for example, a range of mountains, the sea and so on. This is the concept of *continuum*, which is completely ruled out by maps like the one in Figure 2.4.

For this reason, such a map *cannot* and does *not* represent the distribution of language varieties. With fairly negligible discrepancy in the exact location of the borders, what this map *does* represent is the areas of the kingdoms of Northumbria, Mercia, Wessex and Kent. As Schreier and Hundt (2013, p. 2) point out, this representation 'closely related to the way that the notion of "language" is commonly defined, namely with a strong sociopolitical grounding' and the result is that linguistic reality is

> somewhat simplified in two respects: first, the four major dialects are highly unlikely to have represented separate unities with their own characteristics, with features and properties that differed from others both quantitatively and qualitatively; second, the dialects were obviously not simply transplanted from the continent as such without undergoing any changes (externally) caused by contact with other migrant communities or the indigenous populations. (Schreier & Hundt, 2013, p. 2)

While significant variation is very likely to have occurred within what is now customarily called 'Old English', the description of such variation as being characterized by 'four dialects' doesn't seem adequate. As Crystal (2004, pp. 34–56) has demonstrated, textual analysis clearly shows much more *internal* and unsystematic variation than lines on a map are able to convey.

2.6   Conclusion

In this chapter I have argued that what I call the 'mainstream narrative' about the sociolinguistics of pre-Norman Britain tends to offer an extremely simplified interpretation of the past, without even contemplating anything that might upset the official storyline. The complexity of language change and language contact are glossed over in favour of the preservation of a discourse that dates back to Elizabethan times (Brackmann, 2012) and was reinforced and institutionalized in the late nineteenth century.

The firmest and most sacred axiom in that discourse is that, no matter how much change it has had over the centuries, the *object* of study is unquestionably *English*. The use of the noun 'English' is the single most powerful device that keeps the narrative together. It allows one to talk about the most extensive and profound changes without ever risking to subvert the narrative:

> English has undergone an enormous amount of change in the course of its development, more so than other Germanic languages . . . This is to a large extent due to invasion and conquest, which had an impact on all linguistic levels . . . (Fischer, 2013, p. 18)

Once given an undisputed name, 'English' becomes a *thing*, that is, it is reified and treated metaphorically as a physical object. This process is directly linked to Chomsky's and, ultimately, Saussure's conception of language as a 'system' (see Section 1.3.1). One of the properties of such an object is its capacity to withstand change or, indeed, to be enriched by it. The ENGLISH IS A CONTAINER metaphor mentioned earlier fits this purpose perfectly well.

If language is seen as social practice, integral to and inseparable from human activity, many of the well-established assumptions about the early history of English reveal themselves to be unfounded. In particular, the existence of neat boundaries between languages not only is unsupported by textual evidence, but also runs counter to the fact that people make use of the linguistic repertoire available to them as they see fit, that is, according to the activity in which they are engaged.

Finally, another way in which the objectification of English allows the preservation of its identity is through the idea of language *varieties*. In the same way in which markers such as 'old', 'middle' and so on identify varieties of the language that are defined on the basis of historical periods, words like 'Northumbrian' or 'Mercian' designate geographically defined varieties.

One running theme of this chapter has been the way in which scholarly enquiry about linguistic description seems to have made use of convenient shortcuts that have little or nothing to do with language. This concept will also underpin much of the discussion in the chapters that follow, beginning with the one examining 'new Englishes'.

Key reading

- Milroy, J. (2002). The legitimate language. In Watts, R. & Trudgill, P. (Eds), *Alternative Histories of English*, London: Routledge, pp. 7–25.
  This paper deals specifically with the myth of continuity in the ways in which the history of English is typically recounted.

- Watts, R. (2011). *Language Myths and the History of English*. Oxford: Oxford University Press. This entire book is dedicated to the topic of myth construction in relation to the history of English.

- A more traditional approach to the history of English is found in the majority of books on the topic. A classic one is Baugh, A. C. & Cable, T. (2012). *A History of the English Language*, Sixth Edition. London: Routledge.

3

New Englishes

I need a new language—something that comes out of my own body . . . I'm tired of borrowing inadequate terms from French critical theorists and British cultural workers.

JANE CHI HYUN PARK

Keywords

American English • Circles of English • postcolonial writing • spread of English • types of colonization

3.1 Introduction

The phrase 'new Englishes' (Pride, 1982; Platt et al., 1984) – a little old-fashioned now – refers loosely to varieties of English that have emerged outside the British Isles from the eighteenth century onwards as a result of colonialism. Like the mainstream narrative about the early history of English discussed in the previous chapter, the development of 'new Englishes' too has been described in ways which make heavy use of metaphor.

Some of these metaphors are the same as those used with reference to the early development of English in the fifth century. Indeed, one of the over-arching metaphors underpinning the representations of the 'new Englishes' phenomenon is ENGLISH IS A MOVABLE OBJECT, which is exactly the same as the one utilized to describe the 'arrival' of English in Britain. So, analogously, English 'travelled' or 'was brought' from Britain to the 'New World', Asia and Africa during the British empire, just like the 'Anglo-Saxons' took it with them to Britain: 'English has always been a highly mobile language, beginning with its arrival in the British Isles from Europe around the fifth century and its subsequent spread across the globe' (J. Smith, 2012, p. 197). Related to that,

ENGLISH IS A PLANT is also exploited, when the language is said to have 'set roots' or to have been 'transplanted' in this or that new place: 'English . . . grows from many roots' wrote Rushdie in an often-cited article in 1982.

In addition, ENGLISH IS A CONTAINER inspires much of the discourse on 'new Englishes': as it travelled and relocated in different parts of the world, English adopted a number of new words that would describe the new natural phenomena, cultural artefacts and social practices that it encountered. Also, 'English has over the centuries borrowed thousands of new words from the languages with which it has been in contact' (Crystal, 2003, p. 8).

This particular aspect has often been portrayed with enthusiasm and admiration as a great quality of the English language – its immense capacity to adapt to the different environments that surround it. In these descriptions, English acquires human-like attributes and is often the doer of some material action:

> It seems to me . . . that there is much to celebrate in the spread of English as a world language. Where over 650 artificial languages have failed, English has succeeded; where many other natural languages with political and economic power to back them up have failed, English has succeeded. One reason for this dominance of English is its propensity for acquiring new identities, its power of assimilation, its adaptability to 'decolonization' as a language, its manifestation in a range of lects, and above all, its provision of a flexible medium for literary and other types of creativity across languages and cultures. (B. B. Kachru, 1987, p. 222)

The word 'spread' is also very routinely used in this field, pointing at yet other metaphorical representations. The polysemy of the word allows different interpretations. One possible meaning is that English has grown and extended its reach well beyond the shores of Britain. Another interpretation is that the language has been 'distributed' or 'disseminated' in different places, and this can be seen positively, for example, for the opportunities that a global language provides, or negatively, in which case the 'spread' of English is similar to the spread of a killer disease, which destroys all the languages and cultures that it gets close to and infects.

The first part of this chapter is devoted to examining the 'spread' metaphor, some influential descriptive models that have been based on it, and a possible alternative to it. It then moves on to explore what I've called the 'prehistory' of World Englishes, that is the presence of embryonic forms of recognizably World Englishes principles in writings dating all the way back to the end of the eighteenth century. This chapter is finally concluded with some reflections on the pervasively political nature of much of the discourse on language.

3.2   The story of the 'spread' of English

3.2.1   *English everywhere*

English is now habitually considered a global or an international language. With varying degrees of fascination, such definitions are often accompanied by statistics showing the astonishing reach of the language worldwide. Estimates about the numbers of speakers of English are expressed comfortably in billions, while lists of countries where English is a (co-)official language occupy entire pages (e.g. Crystal, 2003, pp. 62–65). All these numbers are meant to point at the uniqueness of English, and comparisons with other 'big' languages, such as Mandarin Chinese, Arabic and so on, are used to demonstrate its unrivalled level of global expansion.

English, the story goes, has achieved this unique and unprecedented status for a number of reasons. First and foremost, the initial spread of the language took place when the British began to build their empire. Subsequently, when the empire started to crumble towards the middle of the twentieth century, the rise of the United States as a global power ensured that the language kept, and actually boosted, its prominent position as an international language. Finally, due to the fact that it has become such an important international language, hundreds of millions of people around the world now feel the need to learn it, increasing the ranks of those who speak English as an additional language. Accordingly, impressive pieces of statistics are cited to illustrate the extraordinary status of the English language, such as that 'non-native speakers far outnumber native speakers' (Seargeant, 2012b, p. 100), or that '[t]here may now be more learners of English in China today than there are native speakers of the language' (Sonntag, 2003, p. xi).

Indeed, in order to cope with such vastness, the omnipresent binary 'native speakers' and 'non-native speakers' is only one of the ways in which uses and users of English have been categorized. Terms and acronyms have proliferated. English has been called an 'international language' (EIL), a 'lingua franca' (ELF), a 'second language' (ESL), a 'foreign language' (EFL), an 'additional language' (EAL) and so on. Users of English, in turn, have been defined in relation to those labels, for example, 'speakers of English as a lingua franca' and so on.

Apart from individual terms, full-scale descriptive models have been developed in order to better understand the 'spread' of English in the world. The best-known and most influential of such models is Braj Kachru's *Three Circles of English*. In this model, B. B. Kachru (1985) identified 'three concentric circles representing the types of spread, the patterns of acquisition and the functional domains in which English is used across cultures and languages' (p. 12). The three parameters are conjoined, in the sense that to each of the three types of 'spread' correspond a pattern of acquisition and a function of the language.

The kinds of language spreads that Kachru refers to, in turn, are linked to two types of colonization: settler and exploitation. Before examining the 'circles' model more in detail, therefore, it will be useful to provide a brief historical overview of these forms of colonization.

3.2.2   *Two types of colonization*

By and large, British colonialism manifested itself in two types of colonization: (i) settler and (ii) exploitation. In the former type, territories were incorporated to the empire primarily in order for the 'new' lands to be occupied by settlers from elsewhere (principally from Britain, but not exclusively). In the latter, the principal objective was to acquire raw materials and, often, slaves from the colonies.

3.2.2.1   Settler colonization

Settler colonization followed the great exploration journeys that took place between the fifteenth and the eighteenth centuries, during which Europeans 'discovered' unknown (to them) lands that they immediately saw as 'available' to be claimed in the name of their respective European crowns. The fact that those lands were inhabited was dealt with by the use of violent coercion and genocide. Additionally, the elimination of the original inhabitants was accelerated by the diffusion of diseases brought by the Europeans for which the indigenous populations had no natural defence.

So, for example, as a direct consequence of the arrival of the British in 1770, in Australia the Aboriginal population was reduced to a fraction of its original size within a relatively short period of time. As people from Britain (mainly prisoners initially) replaced the Aboriginals, so the English language replaced the Aboriginals' languages, which had become drastically reduced in size or completely extinct. By and large, this happened in North America and New Zealand too, where the (near-)disappearance of the original population and their replacement by the settlers caused the same to happen to local languages.

When the British empire began to lose its pieces and the colonies to regain their independence, in countries which had been subject to settler colonization English remained the main (even if not necessarily the official) language of legislation, education, the media and every-day life for the majority of the population.

By contrast, in countries that had been at the receiving hand of exploitation colonization, the sociolinguistic situation was more complex.

3.2.2.2 Exploitation colonization

Exploitation colonization was aimed at procuring raw materials and cheap labour. There was no wholesale replacement of populations. The colonists sought to secure deals with local rulers that would bring financial gain to the formers and personal power to the latter. In this way, the British acquired a large number of territories mainly in Asia and Africa in the eighteenth century. English was primarily a vehicle of communication between the British and the local ruling classes. Local languages weren't replaced, even though their prestige was lowered.

In much European imperialism, especially British and Dutch, the actual conquest and appropriation of territories were often carried out by trading companies, which had powers conferred onto them by their respective governments. The raison d'être of these companies was to find and gain control of strategic locations, especially along coastal areas, that would enable them to have access to natural resources, raw materials, spices, gemstones, slaves and so on for trading purposes. Through the operations of such companies, European imperial powers gradually seized larger territories, until by the end of the nineteenth century virtually entire continents were under their direct or indirect control.

The following passage, from an article published in the London *Times* on 8 January 1897, is highly illustrative. In it, the name 'Nigeria' was first suggested, by a journalist and commentator called Flora Shaw, for the territory that the Royal Niger Company had acquired largely through bogus 'treaties' with local rulers:

In the first place, as the title 'Royal Niger Company Territories' is not only inconvenient to use, but to some extent is also misleading, it may be permissible to coin a shorter title for the agglomeration of pagan and Mohammedan states which have brought, by the exertions of the Royal Niger Company, within the confines of a British Protectorate and thus need for the first time in their history to be described as an entity by some general name. To speak of them as the Central Sudan, which is the title accorded by some geographers and travellers, has the disadvantage of ignoring political frontier-lines, while the word 'Sudan' is too apt to connect itself in the public mind with the French *Hinterland* of Algeria, or the vexed questions of the Nile basin. The name 'Nigeria' applying to no other portion of Africa may, without offence to any neighbours, be accepted as co-extensive with the territories over which the Royal Niger Company has extended British influence, and may serve to differentiate them equally from the British colonies of Lagos and the Niger Protectorate on the coast and from the French territories of the Upper Niger.

Nigeria, thus understood, covers, as is well known, a thickly-peopled area of about half-a-million square miles, extending inland from the sea to Lake Tchad and the northern limits of the empire of Sokoto, bounded on the east by the German frontier and on the west by a line drawn southwards from Say to the French frontier of Dahomey. The frontier lines have 10 years been the subject of discussion with our European neighbours on either side. The northern limit was definitely settled by the Anglo-French treaty of 1891; the eastern boundary was determined by the Anglo-German treaty of 1893; and certain vexed questions on the western frontier were for practical purposes brought to a close last year, when the Royal Niger Company completed in the neighbourhood of Bajibo the erection of forts which it judged necessary for the legitimate maintenance of its authority. Within these limits Nigeria contains many widely-differing characteristics of climate, country, and inhabitants. Its history is ancient and is not wanting in dramatic elements of interest and romance.

There are various elements of interest here. First of all, the invention of the name 'Nigeria' at the end of the nineteenth century by a journalist from another continent is already indicative of the fact that the genesis of the country was quite different from that of, say, Italy or Germany in the same period.

Secondly, the frontier-lines mentioned in the article were set by the British, the French, the Germans, in the same way as European colonial powers had done in the rest of Africa and in much of the rest of the world. So, the parties that must not be offended excessively by the coinage of the new name were Britain's European 'neighbours' that were engaged in the same looting of the African continent. The international conference held in Berlin in 1885 had precisely the purpose of settling disputes over borders dividing the various European possessions in Africa. The main preoccupation was to reach an agreement among colonial powers and, quite obviously, local African populations had absolutely nothing to do with the way their continent was being carved up in the heart of Europe. Ethnic, cultural and religious divisions were well known but were not taken into any account in what came to be known as the 'scramble of Africa'.

Significantly, the inhabitants of this newly defined and newly named territory of 'Nigeria' were described by Shaw as being of 'widely differing characteristics', just like the climate and the features of the land. Indeed, one of the distinctive marks in the ways in which the borders were drawn on paper by European colonizers was the inclusion, in the same territory, of people that were of different ethnicities, religions and, of course, languages.

Furthermore, the claim that Nigeria's history was 'ancient' was manifestly an attempt to legitimize this new entity as a country, *precisely* because Nigeria had in fact just been created. So, when the British empire began to shrink, the colonies that were now granted independence became sovereign countries for the first time. There was no Nigeria (or any other of the newly independent countries) before British and European colonization.

It is for this reason that, when the time came for these countries to establish their own sovereign governments and legislation systems, some difficult decisions had to be made concerning, among many other things, the national language. The typical situation was one in which many different languages co-existed within the same country but none of them was spoken by a proportion of the population that would be large enough as to be representative of the entire country. Selecting any of these languages was bound to be met with hostility from the sections of the populations that didn't speak it.

Obviously, it wasn't simply a matter of linguistic allegiance. Linguistic divisions were a reflection of socio-cultural and, frequently, ethnic and religious ones too. Tragic evidence of the depth of the disunity within populations that were suddenly part of the same country was the surge of civil wars fought by opposing factions that sought to achieve control and power in the country. Such wars, which continue to break out today, often led to secessions, like the Biafran war (1967–1970), in which the Igbo, in the south-eastern part of Nigeria, attempted (and, for a short while, succeeded) to establish a separate country for themselves.

It is evident how in such a situation the selection of one or another language as the national one would have meant granting special recognition to a particular group, with the inevitable strong resentment by the others. So, the policy makers of many governments ended up retaining the language of their former colonial masters. Accordingly, despite its cumbersome imperialist heritage, in most former British colonies English was at least seen as more neutral across the population than any other of local languages.

However, in this type of colonization English had been introduced in the colonies as an elite language, whose use was encouraged among, but restricted to, the higher classes, namely the top layer of society that the British dealt with directly. As Brutt-Griffler (2002, p. 89) explains:

> the British policy limited the number of students exposed to the formal teaching of English to meet the local demands for English-educated subjects of the empire. It left the bulk of the population to be educated in the local language or, at most, to acquire the rudimentary elements of the English language.

The poorer strata of the population had little or no access to English, which remained for them simply a foreign, unknown language. So this also meant that in the newly constituted countries, the national language was not really the people's language.

3.2.3   *The 'Three Circles of English'*

In relation to the two types of colonization described earlier, B. B. Kachru (1992a) coined the terms 'first diaspora' and 'second diaspora' describing the two ways in which English spread in the world. The former refers to the way in which English arrived and established itself as the national language in countries which were subject to settler colonization. The latter refers to the spread of English that occurred as a result of exploitation colonization, namely in countries where English became an additional (if elite) language, co-existing with local languages.

The Three Circles can be summarized as follows:

- The 'Inner Circle' refers to the 'traditional bases of English – the regions where it is the primary language' (B. B. Kachru, 1985, p. 12) for the majority of people; these include places like the United Kingdom, the United States, Australia and so on.

- The 'Outer Circle' refers to countries where English arrived through the 'second diaspora' – and hence exploitation colonization – and where it is often a (co-)official language, playing an important role in education, the media and legislation; these include India, Nigeria, Singapore and so on.

- The 'Expanding Circle' includes regions where the presence of English is more recent and not linked to colonization but primarily to its status as an international lingua franca; these include Germany, Brazil, China and so on.

In relation to each type of spread, which is the main variable determining the 'circles', English has a different function in each of them. This, in turn, can be expressed in terms of *depth* and *range* of use. In the Inner Circle, English is the main or only language for the vast majority of the population of all social classes and is used for all types of activities, from the most public and formal (legislation, education, etc.), to the most private and informal (family, friends). In the Outer Circle, the depth and range of the function of English is a little shallower and narrower. The language has unequal penetration in society, being used more commonly by the higher social classes and progressively less commonly by the poorer and less education strata of the population. Also, English tends to be limited to more official and formal situations, while local languages are more prevalent in more informal day-to-day activities. It is, therefore, a second or additional language. Finally, in the 'Expanding Circle' English has no historical presence in the society and is mainly used as a lingua franca for international communication. At the same time, the 'circles' are also associated to particular types of varieties of English. The Inner Circle comprises of *norm-providing* varieties, that is, varieties that 'have traditionally been recognized as models since they are used by "native speakers"' (B. B. Kachru, 1985, p. 16). The Outer Circle includes *norm-developing* varieties, in which 'the localised norm has a well-established linguistic and cultural identity' (B. B. Kachru, 1992c, p. 5), despite the inconsistency in the attitudes that speakers of such varieties have towards that norm. The Expanding Circle, finally, is *norm-dependent*, in the sense that no local norms exist and speakers of English in these settings rely entirely on Inner-Circle models such as British English or American English. As alluded to earlier, this has been by far the most influential model for the spread of English in the world. It is so well known and established that the terms designating the three circles have become standard phrases in the relevant literature and in academic conferences in the field.

The 'circles' model has important strengths. First of all, it has been an integral part of Braj Kachru's life-long academic endeavour to demonstrate the diversity of English. This is something that, especially in the earlier phases of his career, he often did in open contrast with other scholars in the field who maintained that it would be best for all speakers and learners of English to adhere to one of the two main varieties of the language: British or American (see Chapter 4). The three circles, in this sense, seek to represent the fact that English plays *different* roles and exists in *different* forms for *different* people in *different* places. The model symbolizes diversity, in opposition to rigid and immutable sameness.

Secondly, the clarity of the model has certainly contributed to its efficiency and immediacy. The *inner–outer-expanding* sequence is logical and memorable, while the circles are easily represented graphically. However, the simplicity of the model has also been the main source of the criticism that it has attracted.

3.2.4   *Criticism of the Three Circles model*

In one of the most frequently cited critiques that have been expressed about Kachru's model, Bruthiaux (2003) explains that its main limitation lies in the oversimplification of conflating too many variables that are not necessarily interrelated. In particular, Bruthiaux notes how the historical–geographical dimension of the spread of English is made to correspond to specific functions, varieties and speakers in a correlation that obfuscates sociolinguistic complexity and encourages 'broad-brush descriptions of manifestations of

English across all three circles' (p. 159). So, while it may be justified in geo-historical terms, the categorization in the model is not convincingly supported by sociolinguistic data.

This point can be illustrated by taking into consideration the example of neighbouring Malaysia and Singapore, both of which were part of British Malaya before they became independent. While their common colonial history firmly places both countries in the Outer Circle, their observable sociolinguistic reality is characterized by enormous diversity, not only *between* one country and the other but, more manifestly, *within* them. The different language policies adopted by the respective governments after independence have led to a situation where, to put it rather crudely, English is used quite clearly 'more' in Singapore than it is in Malaysia. However, what is really significant to note is that, to use Kachru's terminology, in both countries the 'depth' and 'range' of English varies from near-complete absence in people's linguistic repertoire all the way to its use as a native language in every domain of social activity.

The sociolinguistic diversity between and within Malaysia and Singapore is only one example. Similar observations can be made about virtually any other Outer-Circle country. The main problem, according to Bruthiaux, is that 'the Three Circles concept is a nation-based model that draws on historical events which only partially correlate with current sociolinguistic data' (2003, p. 172) and labels varieties of English 'on the basis of largely non-linguistic factors such as political boundaries' (p. 174).

Indeed, if we consider the fact that the genesis of the countries traditionally placed in the Outer Circle is rooted in exploitation colonization (Section 3.2.2), it becomes apparent how, while they may delimit territorial sovereignty very neatly, political boundaries can't be expected to map sociolinguistic realities with comparable precision. The use of English 'depends very much who you are: a well-educated Chinese Malaysian in Kuala Lumpur may speak English as a 'second' or 'first' language, while a rural Malay may know English only as a distant foreign language' (Pennycook, 2003, p. 519). It is for this reason that Yano (2009, p. 212) believes that a shift of focus is necessary, away 'from the geography-based model' and towards a 'person-based model of English speakers'. In other words, people's use of English should be described in ways that are completely independent from the country in which they happen to reside.

To be sure, Kachru's own description of the 'circles' does recognize 'significant variation within [outer-circle] varieties' (1985, p. 13) and as well the fact that '[t]he outer circle and the expanding circle cannot be viewed as clearly demarcated from each other' (pp. 13–14). However, the very postulation of the three circles inevitably presupposes that (a) within each circle the similarities of forms, functions and users of English must be more important than any differences among them and (b) between one circle and the next the differences must be more significant than any similarities that might blur the demarcations lines between the three categories. It is this, ultimately, that generates the 'broad-brush descriptions' that Bruthiaux refers to in his critique.

To sum up, the proposal of three separate categories of uses, users and forms of English in Kachru's model has been invaluable in putting forward a new approach to the study of English in the world – namely one which has moved away from monolithic Anglo-centric conceptions and has begun to take into serious account variation as a fundamental parameter. The ingenuity of the model is in its simplicity which, in turn, also delimits the scope of its action.

The 'three circles' model has helped push the boundary from singularity to plurality. It can be argued, however, that plurality isn't necessarily the end of the line. Indeed, the recognition and conceptualization of plurality is only the first stage in the journey from language as system to language as practice. This will be discussed more in depth in the next chapter. For the time being, I will briefly illustrate other two, more recent, models that seek to describe the very complex phenomenon of English in the world.

3.2.5 Schneider's Dynamic Model

Edgar Schneider's (2007) Dynamic Model is an attempt to generalize and describe the evolution of what he calls postcolonial Englishes, namely all varieties of English in the world with the sole exception of British English. Unlike the Three Circles model, the Dynamic Model makes no distinction between different types of colonization or 'diasporas' of English, since Schneider believes that they are 'not prime determinants of the outcome of the process of new dialect emergence' (2007, p. 25). Instead, taking into account colonization as a macro phenomenon, the model examines the development of postcolonial Englishes on the basis of the claim that 'there is a shared underlying process which drives their formation, accounts for many similarities between them, and appears to operate whenever a language is transplanted' (Schneider, 2007, p. 29).

The Dynamic Model defines such a shared underlying process in terms of a number of variables. The main factor determining the evolution of postcolonial Englishes is identified in the changing relationship between settlers and indigenous populations and, more specifically, in the ways in which identities are reformulated within that relationship. This gradual re-writing of identities, in turn, is considered within particular historical–political and sociolinguistic contexts, during which, as a result, certain features of lexis, syntax and so on emerge.

So, beginning from the initial arrival of the settlers in a new territory, each new variety of English has gone through the same process, which can be broken down into five phases:

1 Foundation: The phase during which British settlers arrive and English is first introduced to a new territory; the settlers still consider themselves fully part of the original nation; indigenous populations' identities are unaffected by the arrival of the newcomers.

2 Exonormative stabilization: English becomes established in the new territory especially for some official and administrative purposes, and begins to borrow words from local languages to refer to items that don't exist in Britain; the settlers' identity begins to distinguish itself from that of the original nation and begins to affect the identity of some members of the local people, especially those in position of power who are in direct contact with the British rulers.

3 Nativization: The settlers, and their offspring, are now inhabitants of the new territories and the cultural link to Britain has substantially weakened; the identity of the indigenous population is more significantly influenced by the settlers' culture; English continues to borrow lexical items from local language but begins to undergo some alterations at other linguistic levels too, such as accent and, to some extent, structure.

4 Endonormative stabilization: The two groups, settlers and indigenous population, see themselves as one nation, wholly separate from Britain; the features of the new variety that has emerged become stable and codified internally, without reference to the norms of British English.

5 Differentiation: This is the most advanced phase, during which cultural and regional diversification begins to develop among the younger members of the new nation; dialects, or sub-varieties, emerge as a consequence.

All models are, by definition, reductionist in nature. That is, they necessarily operate a degree of simplification in order to be able to extrapolate general features occurring in a complex phenomenon. In many ways, descriptive models like B. B. Kachru's 'circles' or Schneider's Dynamic Model act just like a metaphor: they reduce a complex phenomenon to something more tangible. The idea of evolution of varieties is much more comprehensible if it is mapped onto the domain of a journey that is broken down into stages.

Of course, one possible drawback of this approach is that certain differences may be downplayed excessively. The re-writing of identities that took place in the United States since the arrival of the British was significantly different from that which characterized West Africa or Southeast Asia, just to name two examples. That is because the relationship between settlers and indigenous populations was of a markedly different nature.

In North America and in Australia, the emergence of new national identities was based primarily on an increased sense of autonomy, independence and distance that the descendants of British settlers felt towards Britain, and was largely unaffected by the cultures of indigenous people, who were nearly wiped out from their land. Similarly, in New Zealand, despite the fact that the proportion of the people we now call 'Maoris' is greater (and this is reflected in the handful of Maori words in New Zealand English), the 'kiwi' identity is only very marginally and tangentially influenced by original local cultures. Tellingly, one of the most frequent comments made by British visitors to New Zealand today is that it 'looks like "Britain in the 60s"' (Frost, 2013). By contrast, in parts of the world involved in exploitation colonization there was little or no settlement as such and it was mainly intellectuals in the indigenous populations that developed a feeling and urgency of self-determination.

Another potential problem with Schneider's model is that its notion of phases of development may be lend itself to being (mis-)interpreted as being a distant echo of the nineteenth-century discourse in which the 'diachronic stages of humanity's evolution toward civilization were . . . conceived as present synchronically in the various primitive peoples and cultures spread across the globe' (Hardt & Negri, 2000, p. 126).

However, the kind of generalization offered in the Dynamic Model has indubitable advantages, since it helps us realize that what pertains to, say, English in Singapore is not wholly different to the 'story' of English in other parts of the world, such as India or Zambia, for example. It allows us to see similarities where other parameters (e.g. different geography, history, culture, etc.) might lead us to believing that varieties of English are exclusively characterized by difference and distinction. A different approach is that adopted by Melchers and Shaw (2011). Instead of trying to combine variables together, they consider each one of them individually since, as they say, 'the same cake can be cut up many different ways for different purposes' (2011, p. 32).

3.2.6   Melchers and Shaw's classification

One of the problems with B. B. Kachru's Three Circles model and, to some extent, the Dynamic Model, is the attempt to combine too many variables together within each circle or within each phase of development. For this reason, Melchers and Shaw, who otherwise follow Kachru's main categorization as the basis for the organization of their book, propose a classification system that treats each variable as a separate entity: varieties, texts, countries, speakers as well as the situations in which these use the language.

Thus, Melchers and Shaw don't actually devise an all-encompassing model as such. They argue that each aspect involved in the large phenomenon that we call 'English' can be classified according to certain parameters. So, for example, in terms of linguistic form, English varies according to adherence to certain norms, the perception of standardness, the level of codification and the degree of prestige attached to each variety. The texts produced in any variety can be classified in terms of their function and level of standardization. Speakers can be categorized on the basis of language acquisition patterns (e.g. native speakers, non-native speakers) or scope of proficiency, that is, their ability to communicate with different types of speakers in different types of situations. These, in turn, can be described according to the types of speakers involved.

What Melchers and Shaw's classifications begin to show is not only that variables can, and should, be taken into account individually, but also that they intersect in complex ways. A 'situation', for example, may well involve speakers who have different degrees of competence and 'scope proficiency', use varieties to which different levels of recognition is accorded, produce texts adhering to different norms and are based in countries where English plays different roles. All of this, of course, may not have any incidence at all on how successfully such speakers carry out the particular activity they are engaged in.

Despite their inherent differences, the Three Circles model, the Dynamic Model and Melchers and Shaw's classification are all based on one basic premise: that the English language spread around the world with the expansion of the British empire and subsequently went through a process of local adaptation out which different varieties of English emerged. This concept appears to be eminently obvious and is generally uncontested. It is underpinned by ontological metaphors such as ENGLISH IS A PHYSICAL MOVABLE OBJECT, ENGLISH IS A TRAVELLER and ENGLISH IS A SPREADABLE SUBSTANCE. Or, even more fundamentally, ENGLISH IS A THING. If, however, English, and language in general, is seen as *social practice*, then the 'spread' scenario may not seem so self-evident. The next section explores an alternative interpretation.

3.3   Beyond the 'spread' metaphor

Practice is much more complex than a *system* regulated by self-sufficient internal rules. That is because practice is integral to its social context and therefore tied to contextual variables such as the purpose of an activity and participants in it. From this point of view, the question of what is linguistically 'correct', for example, becomes futile and leaves space to the more pertinent question of *how successfully language contributes to the activity at hand*.

Drawing from this general view of language as social practice, Alastair Pennycook has in recent years proposed a radically alternative interpretation to the 'spread' metaphor. His main tenet is that the presence of English as a global language doesn't have to be seen as the result of its expansion outwards from a central point (Britain), and that we need to 'engage instead with the possibility of multiple, co-present, local origins of English' (Pennycook, 2010b, p. 208).

In doing this, Pennycook uses a rather unconventional metaphor: ENGLISH IS HIP HOP. He refers to various hip-hop artists around the world who claim to have not simply appropriated an American style of music and singing, but that hip hop is not fundamentally dissimilar to local styles, which have been around for a long time and that, therefore, hip hop actually *is* and *has always been* Aboriginal, Turkish, West African and so on.

In this respect, Australian hip-hop artist Vulk Makedonski is cited:

> hip hop is the culture of people that were oppressed at one stage, and a lot of cultures have songs about oppression in their folk tales. To me, that's hip hop . . . . Hip hop . . . is too powerful to be modern, that's why I believe it's more ancient. It's an ancient culture, with a new name. And the new name is hip hop, that's the modern name, but the elements that come out of hip hop go back – way, way back. (Pennycook, 2010b, pp. 196–197)

The *social practice* of expressing one's feelings about oppression via music and song is something that has always existed everywhere. 'By analogy', Pennycook reasons, 'instead of assuming that English has spread and taken on new characteristics, . . . the argument would be that what we are looking at are, in fact, old cultural and linguistic practices with a new name' (p. 197). Similarly, 'rather than trying to sort out the local from the derived, or even trying to see how English has been appropriated locally, we can start to consider that English is only a name given to something that has always been local' (pp. 203–204).

But there are a number of important questions to address at this point. First of all, what are these 'old cultural and linguistic practices' that have been given the new name 'English'? To what extent are they similar to hip hop? What is, exactly, hip hop anyway?

To try and answer this last question is key. Is hip hop a particular style of music? Only very superficially so. In this sense, it would be defined as a set of features such as a 4/4 rhythm, heavy bass lines, rap vocals, breakdance and so on. But, as Vulk Makedonki's words earlier allude to, it can be argued that hip hop is much more than the use of a combination of stylistic features. In his excellent *It's Bigger than Hip Hop*, M. K. Asante, Jr (2008) refers to hip hop with phrases such as 'the cultural expression of young Black America' (p. 6), 'art, culture and community' (p. 7), 'a revolutionary cultural force that was intended to challenge the status quo and the greater American culture' (p. 8), and 'a form of aesthetic and sociopolitical rebellion against the flames of systemic oppression' (p. 9).

Specific features of music style appear to be of secondary importance. Asante, Jr's book is very much about how the success of hip hop has in the new millennium been channelled by music corporations into a mainstream and lucrative commercial enterprise, which, with themes like misogyny and Black-on-Black violence, has turned the earlier revolutionary drive on its head. So, while many contemporary bands make use of hip hop's music features, they are engaged in a *social practice* that is profoundly different from that of hip hop.

Significantly, in an interview with the online magazine *Anonymous* (2013), Public Enemy's Chuck D. commented that hip hop 'should be along the lines of Bob Marley, it should be along the lines of Bob Dylan, and also it should be along the lines of Bobby Womack', all of whom have made music that is, formally, very different from hip hop. This suggests that, ultimately, the essence of hip hop isn't necessarily in its rhythm or singing style, but in socio-political rebellion expressed through music, without regard to where it happens or the ethnicity of who does it.

So, how does all of this help answer questions about English being an old practice with a new name? In the same way in which hip hop is one way of realizing socio-political rebellion through a set of musical resources, so, in a bigger scale, English is one way of realizing social activities via a set of linguistic resources. The 'origin' of English, in this sense, is completely irrelevant, just like the ethnicity of those who speak it, whether they speak other languages too or whether they 'mix' these other languages with English. Also, from this point of view, 'features' of English, phonological, syntactic and so on don't matter very much, as they don't alter the essence of English as a manifestation of language as social practice.

However, from certain points of view, great importance is attached to aspects of language which would otherwise appear to be entirely insignificant in terms of social practice. Orthographic conventions such as the *-ise* or *-ize* spellings, the use of the apostrophe and so on may be the subject of heated and passionate debate. One typical domain where this tends to happen is in the circles of those who see themselves as language guardians. The argument in these quarters is always the same: various culprits (young people, technology, other languages, etc.) are identified as corrupting a particular language and urgent action is invoked in order to preserve its beautiful and elegant forms.

In an online blog of the British newspaper *The Daily Telegraph*, for example, commentator Gerald Warner (2010) calls for 'an Academy of English to save our beautiful language'. He alerts readers that while French, Spanish and Italian all have academies to maintain their purity, 'English has been left to fend for itself at a time when it is under unprecedented attack'. In order to highlight the severity of the problem, the author mentions 'the current pandemic misuse of the subjunctive' as only one of the perils threatening the beauty of English. These kinds of admonitions have of course been expressed throughout history and about all languages. Three hundred years ago Jonathan Swift worried about the 'continual corruption of our English Tongue' in very similar terms. Language purism is nothing new and the 'attack' on the purity of English is certainly not 'unprecedented'.

One of the sources of such attacks is the influence of varieties of English deemed inappropriate. In March 1995, *The Times* reported that Prince Charles gave a speech on the occasion of the British Council's *English 2000* project, 'intended to protect the country's £500 million share of a global growth industry' (O'Leary, 1995). In it, he urged British people to defend the English language from the very corrupting influence of the American variety:

> We must act now to ensure that English, and that to my way of thinking means *English* English, maintains its position as the world language well into the next century. . . . People tend to invent all sorts of nouns and verbs, and make words that shouldn't be. I think we have to be a bit careful, otherwise the whole thing can get rather a mess.

Members of the royal family aren't generally held as authorities in linguistic matters and their citation index isn't particularly high in sociolinguistics. Yet, in many ways, Prince Charles's preoccupations concern the same aspects of language that the study of world Englishes has focussed on, albeit generally from the opposite ideological viewpoint. As mentioned earlier, underpinned by the 'spread' metaphor, much of this work has concentrated its attention on grammatical, phonological and lexical alterations that the language has undergone in its *code* as a result of its geographical expansion. The next section explores how this is connected to what we may call the 'prehistory' of World Englishes.

3.4 The 'prehistory' of World Englishes

Perhaps, the essence of the broad research area of World Englishes is in the pluralization of the noun 'English' (when referring to the language). The suffix *-es* encapsulates the spirit of this entire scholarly enterprise: there are more than one English in the world and they all deserve to be studied.

Although the genesis of World Englishes as an academic area can be traced towards the beginning of the 1980s (with earlier embryonic forms dating back to the 1960s), the focus of this section is on what I call the 'prehistory of World Englishes'. This is because I wish to demonstrate how the 'seeds' of this broad school of thought can be found much earlier than the time when academic publications related to it started to flow.

3.4.1 *American English sets the scene*

One of the first (or, possibly, *the* first) recorded appearance of the noun 'Englishes' was in the headline of an article published in the *Baltimore Evening Sun* by American journalist and commentator Henry Louis Mencken, in 1910. The article was entitled 'The Two Englishes' and dealt with the differences between the American and the British varieties of the language. A few years later, between 1919 and 1921, Mencken published *The American Language*, one of the earliest quasi-sociolinguistic accounts of the American variety of English (Mencken, 1921). The introductory chapter of that book included a very useful review of attitudes towards American English expressed at the time by American and British observers, both academic and not. What is particularly interesting is that the views reported by Mencken, as well as his own discussion of them, contain all the main ingredients of the debates, reflections and research that would later form the core of the World Englishes academic field.

Mencken relates two competing positions. One regarded American English as a corruption and degradation of the English language, and its users guilty of blatant disregard of its fundamental rules, purity and grandeur. The other saw it as an entirely natural evolution of the language, resulting from the new environment in which it had been transplanted.

Among the proponents of the former position, Mencken cites Thomas Hamilton, a British writer who recounts his travels in the United States at the beginning of the nineteenth century and describes, among other things, the language he finds there:

> The amount of bad grammar in circulation is very great; that of barbarisms enormous. . . . the commonest words are often so transmogrified as to be placed beyond the recognition of an Englishman. . . The Americans have chosen arbitrarily to change the meaning of certain old and established English words, for reasons which they cannot explain, and which I doubt much whether any European philologist could understand. . . . The privilege of barbarizing the King's English is assumed by all ranks and conditions

of men. . . . I feel it something of a duty to express the natural feeling of an Englishman, at finding the language of Shakespeare and Milton thus gratuitously degraded. Unless the present progress of change be arrested, by an increase of taste and judgment in the more educated classes, there can be no doubt that, in another century, the dialect of the Americans will become utterly unintelligible to an Englishman, and that the nation will be cut off from the advantages arising from their participation in British literature. If they contemplate such an event with complacency, let them go on and prosper; they have only to 'progress' in their present course, and their grandchildren bid fair to speak a jargon as novel and peculiar as the most patriotic American linguist can desire. (Hamilton, 1833, pp. 232–235)

The classic ingredients of language prescriptivism and purism are all present in this citation. First of all, the use of the word 'barbarism' is possibly the most iconic. The sense of the word has always (i.e. not just in 'English') been associated to anything foreign and alien by reference to unintelligible speech, where of course 'foreignness' and 'unintelligibility' are both perceived from the subjective point of view of the person who refers to someone else as a 'barbarian'. In Hamilton's mind, the 'transmogrified' words that have become 'beyond recognition' to 'an Englishman' make Americans barbarians.

Hamilton clearly accuses them of unilaterally and unreasonably tainting something that isn't theirs, but is the property of the English people, of their king and of the nation's greatest poets. Indeed, his comments are about language only rather superficially. One key word stands out spectacularly: *patriotic*. What does (bad) grammar have to do with patriotism? Indeed, was Hamilton himself being profoundly patriotic in his tirade against American English? This adds two more elements that are recurrent in this type of rhetoric: language ownership and nationalism.

A third classic component in the discourse of language purism is a sense of fatal consequences looming in the near future if immediate action isn't undertaken to remedy the situation. Hamilton seemed to want to warn Americans that if they continued to modify the English language senselessly, they might end up linguistically isolated and no longer able to benefit from the privileges that came from sharing the language of British literature.

With regard to the second position, namely that the American variety of English was the consequence of natural evolution in a new territory, Mencken cites Thomas Jefferson who, a century earlier, in a letter dated 13 August 1813, wrote:

I am no friend . . . to what is called Purism, but a zealous one to the Neology which has introduced these two words without the authority of any dictionary. I consider the one as destroying the nerve and beauty of language, while the other improves both, and adds to its copiousness. I have been not a little disappointed, and made suspicious of my own judgment, on seeing the Edinburgh Reviews, the ablest critics of the age, set their faces against the introduction of new words into the English language; they are particularly apprehensive that the writers of the United States will adulterate it. Certainly so great growing a population, spread over such an extent of country, with such a variety of climates, of productions, of arts, must enlarge their language, to make it answer its purpose of expressing all ideas, the new as well as the old. The new circumstances under which we are placed, call for new words, new phrases, and for the transfer of old words to new objects. An American dialect will therefore be formed; so will a West-Indian and Asiatic, as a Scotch and an Irish are already formed. (Bergh, 1903, p. 340)

Jefferson's words are strikingly congruous with the central ethos in World Englishes. This is particularly evident in the idea that English acquires new forms as it naturally adapts to different environments and that, accordingly, 'purism' is a concept which doesn't easily apply to language. What is even more remarkable is that his open-mindedness about regional variation in the English language allows him to predict the emergence of dialects in parts of the world that would later be categorized as Outer Circle and become the central concern in World Englishes literature. He continues:

But whether will these adulterate, or enrich the English language? Has the beautiful poetry of Burns, or his Scottish dialect, disfigured it? Did the Athenians consider the Doric, the Ionian, the Aeolic, and other dialects, as disfiguring or as beautifying their language? Did they fastidiously disavow Herodotus, Pindar, Theocritus, Sappho, Alcaeus, or Grecian writers? On the contrary, they were sensible that the variety of dialects, still infinitely varied by poetical license, constituted the riches of their language, and made the Grecian Homer the first of poets, as he must ever remain, until a language equally ductile and copious shall again be spoken. (Bergh, 1903, pp. 340–341)

Jefferson's ideas about language were incredibly modern in the way he regarded as enrichment what others would see as 'adulteration'. He was an intellectual but was, first of all, a politician. He was one of the 'Founding Fathers' and the third president of the United States as an independent country. His defence of the American variety of English, therefore, was inspired not only by his refined erudition and knowledge of other languages, but also, undoubtedly, by his profound convictions concerning the independence of the new country.

Indeed, Mencken's own book was itself a political statement as well as a linguistic account. Its very title, *The American Language*, which did without the word 'English' altogether, was unmistakably political.

That political independence had to be accompanied by linguistic independence was expressed extremely clearly by one of Thomas Jefferson's contemporaries: Noah Webster, the compiler of the *American Dictionary of the English Language* and popularly known as the 'Father of American Scholarship and Education'. As a lexicographer, Webster felt that it was necessary to reform the English Language, both to suit the American environment in which it was now found and to regularize its orthography. The way in which he expressed this necessity displayed a seamless mixture of linguistic and political concerns: 'As an independent nation, our honor requires us to have a system of our own, in language as well as government' (Webster, 1789, p. 20).

A few lines later, he elaborated on the divergent paths that the American and the British versions of English were on:

. . . several circumstances render a future separation of the American tongue from the English, necessary and unavoidable. . . . These causes will produce, in a course of time, a language in North America, as different from the future language of England, as the modern Dutch, Danish and Swedish are from the German, or from one another: Like remote branches of a tree springing from the same stock; or rays of light, shot from the same center, and diverging from each other, in proportion to their distance from the point of separation. (Webster, 1789, pp. 22–23)

Making use of the LANGUAGE IS A PLANT metaphor, Webster emphasized both the same origin of American and British English and the different branches that they now represented. Again, it wasn't just a matter of linguistic distance:

Great Britain, whose children we are, and whose language we speak, should no longer be our standard; for the taste of her writers is already corrupted, and her language on the decline. But if it were not so, she is at too great a distance to be our model, and to instruct us in the principles of our own tongue. (Webster, 1789, p. 21)

Here, besides the inextricable link between political and linguistic autonomy, Webster interestingly uses the 'corruption' argument *against* Britain and British English. What he advocates, therefore, is not only that a separate American variety of English should be documented and codified, but also that this was made even more urgent in order to preserve the language from the decline that it was subject to on the other side of the Atlantic.

Indeed, Webster was himself a purist. In his view, American English had to be not only distinct from the distant and inexorably corrupt British English, but also as internally uniform as possible, and hence devoid of any variation. It was important, therefore, to 'demolish those odious distinctions of provincial dialects, which are the objects of reciprocal ridicule' (1783, p. 5) and to 'diffuse an uniformity and purity of Language' (p. 11).

3.4.2   Seeds of World Englishes in postcolonial writing

As we saw in Section 3.2.2, in places that had been affected by exploitation colonization, linguistic independence was a more complicated matter. The retention of the former colonizers' language was a forced choice that stemmed from the socio-political impossibility of selecting a local national language. English was an elite language, and access to it was restricted to the ruling classes and those who were rich and privileged enough. It is for this reason that in the post-independence period it was mainly creative writers who became the champions of localized varieties of English.

In India, for example, even before independence, writer Raja Rao commented on his use of the English language:

> The telling has not been easy. One has to convey in a language that is not one's own the spirit that is one's own. One has to convey the various shades and omissions of a certain thought-movement that looks maltreated in an alien language. I use the word 'alien', yet English is not really an alien language to us. It is the language of our intellectual make-up, like Sanskrit or Persian was before, but not of our emotional make-up. We are all instinctively bilingual, many of us writing in our own language and in English. We cannot write like the English. We should not. We cannot write only as Indians. We have grown to look at the large world as part of us. Our method of expression therefore has to be a dialect which will some day prove to be as distinctive and colourful as the Irish or the American. Time alone will justify it. (Rao, 1938, p. vii)

It is clear in Rao's words how the choice of using English came with the necessity to mould a variety of English that would be distinctively Indian. This later became a leitmotif in the debate about language that emerged among postcolonial writers a few decades later. Nigerian writer Gabriel Okara, for example, believed that English, or any other European language, needed to be consciously *made* African in order to express African ideas and values:

> As a writer who believes in the utilisation of African ideas, African philosophy and African folk-lore and imagery to the fullest extent possible,

I am of the opinion that the only way to use them effectively is to translate them almost literally from the African language native to the writer into whatever European language he is using as his medium of expression. (Okara, 1963, p. 15)

Just like Rao had made references to the American and Irish varieties of English in justifying the existence of an Indian one, Okara used the same argument to claim that there was no reason why African varieties couldn't develop too:

Living languages grow like living things, and English is far from a dead language. There are American, West Indian, Australian, Canadian, and New Zealand versions of English. All of them add life and vigour to the language while reflecting their own respective cultures. Why shouldn't there be a Nigerian or West African English which we can use to express our own ideas, thinking and philosophy in our own way? (Okara, 1963, p. 16)

In the same period, Chinua Achebe, another Nigerian writer, who had acquired worldwide fame through his novels, expressed very similar ideas about the use of English in African literature:

The price a world language must be prepared to pay is submission to many different kinds of use. The African writer should aim to use English in a way that brings out his message best without altering the language to the extent that its value as a medium of international exchange will be lost. He should aim at fashioning out an English which is at once universal and able to carry his peculiar experience. . . . I feel that the English language will be able to carry the weight of my African experience. But it will have to be a new English, still in full communion with its ancestral home but altered to suit its new African surroundings. (Achebe, 1965, pp. 29–30)

It was clear that what Rao, Okara and Achebe were talking about was independence. Again, linguistic independence is a vital component of political independence. The alterations to be made to the English language were symbolically important. They were meant to create a language that would be Indian or Nigerian in much the same way in which Webster had advocated for an American brand of English almost two centuries earlier.

The fundamental importance of decolonizing the language in decolonized countries was even more explicit, years later, in an article that Salman Rushdie wrote for the *Times*:

The old colonies are not wholly free. The British, as every schoolboy knows, gave the world cricket, parliaments, sun hats, boundary commissions, legal systems, roads, mission schools and the English language. But they also left us, disguised as freedom, this dominion of spoons. And the English language, like many of the other bequests, is tainted by history as a result. . . . The language, like much else in the newly independent societies, needs to be decolonized, to be remade in other images, if those of us who use it from positions outside Anglo-Saxon culture are to be more than Uncle Toms. (Rushdie, 1982)

Like the other writers mentioned earlier, Rushdie emphasized the fact that English could be appropriated in postcolonial settings just like it had been in other Anglophone countries: *not* English:

The phenomenon has occurred before. Earlier escapees from colonialism, in America and Ireland, made similar assaults upon the classic frontiers of the language . . .

Now it is happening again, and on a more global scale than ever before. English, no longer an English language, now grows from many roots; and those whom it once colonized are carving out large territories within the language for themselves. (Rushdie, 1982)

Postcolonial writers' efforts to decolonize and claim ownership of the English language is something that has directly fuelled much of the discussion that unfolded in World Englishes, as we will see more in depth in the next chapter.

3.5   Conclusion: Language and politics

One way in which this chapter, and indeed this whole Part One, could be summarized is through John Joseph (2006)'s statement that 'language is political from top to bottom' (p. 17). In particular, what I have sought to demonstrate is that the discourse *about* language is immanently political. The very name 'English' is entirely political, in that it refers not only to a language, but also to a nation. *Eng*lish is also the language of *Eng*land, the country.

I have sought to show how this idea pervades the discourse of the early history of English as well as that of 'new Englishes'. In the former, which was part of a widespread nationalistic rhetoric in nineteenth-century Europe, the idea of 'Old English' had the function of cementing the bond between nation and territory instrumentally by fabricating the myth of a very old language that has always been 'English' at its heart. The ideological drive was so strong that it managed to disregard very conspicuous and substantial differences between languages that were only few centuries apart and to construct a narrative which, by contrast, told a story of continuity and fundamental one-ness in the relatively smooth development of the language that the 'Anglo-Saxons' brought with them to Britain. This was then codified in textbooks and the story was simply replicated without significant departures.

The proto-discourse of 'new Englishes' was based on the same conception of languages bound to nations and to territories. Many of the key ingredients in World Englishes principles were already contained in preoccupations about the language in post-independent America at the end of the eighteenth century. The discussion was all about political autonomy. When the United States gained their independence, the role of the language which bore the name of their former colonizers was problematic. The reforms put forward by Webster were aimed at fashioning a language that would be as distinctly American and un-British as possible. Significantly, Mencken's book, a hundred years later, was entitled *The American Language*, the word 'English' having completely been dropped.

Some postcolonial writers in Africa and Asia were engaged in very similar efforts in the second half of the twentieth century to mould English in such a way as to make it able to express their African and Asian experiences. The academic field of World Englishes has always been very strongly inspired by the linguistic endeavours in postcolonial literature to liberate English from its Anglo-centric cultural straitjacket. This is, in essence, the central idea: English is not one, but many, because its relocation in different parts of the world has made it capable of expressing different national identities: American, Australian, Indian, Malaysian, Nigerian and so on.

Paradoxically, however, the idea of *many* Englishes isn't fundamentally different from that of *one* English. Webster wanted to codify a language that was at one time distinct from British English *and* uniform internally. American English was to become another language. Another *one*. Similarly, the idea of plural Englishes entails the same principle: many *ones*. If there is one English for the English, there can be one for the Americans, one for the Singaporeans, one for the Ghanaians, one for the New Zealanders and so on. One plus one plus one plus one. This is, through and through, based on the conception of language as system.

In the discourse of old and new Englishes, language takes a back seat. Its instrumental role in the nation-territory bond is never questioned and, consequently, its nature, its essence, never really investigated. But if we take the view, as I do, that language is first and foremost social practice, then we may begin to see other possibilities besides the 'pluralisation of singular entities' (Otsuji & Pennycook, 2010, p. 247) encapsulated in the -*es* of Englishes. This will be discussed more in depth in Part Two.

Key reading

- Crystal, D. (2003). *English as a Global Language*, Second Edition. Cambridge: Cambridge University Press.
  This book provides an accessible overview of how English has become a 'global' language. Despite some criticism that it has received (see, e.g. Section 6.1), and the consequent critical standpoint from which it should be read, the book remains a useful introduction.

- Braj Kachru's model of 'three circles' of English is explained in many textbooks in the field. The following paper has his own early description of the model:
  Kachru, B. B. (1985). Standards, codification and sociolinguistic realism: the English language in the outer circle. In R. Quirk & H. Widdowson (Eds), *English in the World: Teaching and Learning the Language and Literatures* (pp. 11–30). Cambridge: Cambridge University Press.

- One of the most cogent critiques of the 'three circles' model can be found in:
  Bruthiaux, P. (2003). Squaring the circles: issues in modeling English worldwide. *International Journal of Applied Linguistics*, *13*(2), 159–178.

- Edgar Schneider's Dynamic Model is explained in:
  Schneider, E. (2007). *Postcolonial English: Varieties around the World*. Cambridge: Cambridge University Press.

- The 'language spread' metaphor has been criticized by Alastair Pennycook in a number of publications. The following book contains a thorough discussion of this and other issues:
  Pennycook, A. (2010). *Language as a Local Practice*. London: Routledge.

PART TWO

Language

4

Understanding World Englishes

We are equal because of our differences, but not so different from each other that some could regard themselves as more human than others.
LEOPOLDO ZEA

All animals are equal, but some animals are more equal than others.
GEORGE ORWELL

Keywords

codification • diversity • equality • feature • nativization • variety

4.1 Introduction

In the previous chapter, I illustrated the 'prehistory' of World Englishes, namely how the ideas that became the fulcrum of this academic area can be found in the writing of scholars and politicians from previous centuries. In this section, I examine the 'history' of World Englishes, that is, the ways in which fundamental principles have been discussed in the body of literature that has grown since the late 1970s.

4.2 The egalitarian matrix of World Englishes

It is often very difficult to identify a precise paper or book that can be said to mark the beginning of a research field. In the case of World Englishes, however, this task is perhaps a little easier. This is because the origin of the field can be located in an article that Braj B. B. Kachru wrote in 1976 as a risposte to a previous paper by the American sociolinguist Clifford Prator. Prator's (1968) piece, in turn, was a diatribe against what he described as 'heresy', namely the idea that scholars should begin to consider and study varieties of English beyond the confines of Britain and America.

Such a 'heretical' thought had been expressed in the middle of the 1960s by Halliday et al. (1964, p. 293):

> Where the choice used to be between American (in a few marginal cases) and British English, now it is between American, British, Australian or other regional variants. English is no longer the possession of the British, or even of the British and the Americans, but an international language which increasingly large numbers of people adopt for at least some of their purposes . . . and this one language, English, exists in an increasingly large number of different varieties.

In Prator's view, this position was completely untenable, and since those culpable of promoting it were primarily British linguists discussing the relationship between linguistics and the teaching of English, he named it the 'British heresy in TESL'. In his paper, Prator expressed exactly the same kind of language purism mentioned in the previous chapter. He forcefully accused the three British linguists of illogically wanting to promote varieties other than 'mother-tongue' ones as viable teaching models, since the practice would inevitably lead to 'a tongue caught up in a process that tends to transform [English] swiftly and quite predictably into an utterly dissimilar tongue' (1968, p. 464).

Prator didn't believe varieties of English that emerged in the former British colonies were on a par with 'mother-tongue' ones. In order to prove his point, he made particular reference to the variety of English in India, which, in his view, was 'a certain linguistic phenomenon that is often popularly and impressionistically labelled "Indian English"' (1968, p. 464):

> After 20 years of testing the English of hundreds of incoming foreign students semester after semester at the University of California, I am firmly convinced that for the rest of the English-speaking world the most unintelligible educated variety is Indian English. The national group that profits least from the University's efforts to improve their intelligibility by classroom instruction also seems to be the Indians; they can almost never be brought to believe that there is any reason for trying to change their pronunciation. It is hard to doubt that there is a direct connection between these conclusions and the fact that the doctrine of local models of English

is championed more often and more vehemently in India than anywhere else. (p. 473)

The mention of broad categories such as 'the English-speaking world' and 'the Indians' were evidence of the fact that Prator's comments went well beyond linguistic considerations and turned into glaringly sweeping statements tinged with gross stereotype and quasi-racism.

Braj Kachru, originally from India, responded to Prator's paper in 1976. Using the same religious metaphor, he characterized Prator's purism and intolerance as 'sins' which, he claimed, were 'nurtured by several educated native speakers and educators of English' (1976, p. 222). His position was that 'third-world varieties' – as he called them – had their own validity as expressions of the socio-cultural environments in which English had relocated. In the conclusion to his paper, B. B. Kachru (1976, p. 236) explains:

It will . . . be appropriate that the native speakers of English abandon the attitude of linguistic chauvinism and replace it with an attitude of linguistic tolerance. The strength of the English language is in presenting the Americanness in its American variety, and the Englishness in its British variety. Let us, therefore, appreciate and encourage the Third World varieties of English too. The individuality of the Third World varieties, such as the Indianness of its Indian variety, is contributing to the linguistic mosaic which the speakers of the English language have created in the English speaking world. The attitude toward these varieties ought to be one of appreciation and understanding . . .

In many ways, this concept laid the foundation of World Englishes, before the term was even coined. It expounded notions that would soon become core in the field: (a) that the formal differences observable in 'non-native varieties of English' in postcolonial settings had come about as a result of the different context-bound functions that the language played in those contexts (and not as a consequence of imperfect acquisition), (b) that such localized varieties were capable of expressing different cultures and, consequently, (c) that they deserved the same degree of appreciation as those in the developed world.

Before writing this paper, Kachru had already distinguished himself for his research on the forms and functions of English in India (1965, 1966, 1971, 1975), and his work had been greatly influenced by the analytical paradigm centred upon the concept of *context of situation*, introduced by Bronislaw Malinowski (1923) and further developed by J. R. Firth (1957). Consequently, Kachru's philosophy places great emphasis on the inextricable relationship between local context and language.

In the same period, Kachru's colleague Larry Smith expressed very similar views:

> It is important to note that there is a single English language but many varieties. The language of the United States is American English. Certainly speakers of American English are identifiable by their pronunciation, intonation, stress, rhythm, and some vocabulary items but the language (the general orthography, lexicology, semantics, syntax – the grammar, if you will), is English. It is the same English that is spoken in Singapore, however; Singapore English speakers are also identifiable by their pronunciation, intonation, stress, rhythm, and some vocabulary items. (L. E. Smith, 1976, p. 38)

Again, these were soon to become central points in the World Englishes, where one of the central ideas is that specifiç linguistic features characterize distinctive varieties of English which, in turn, are associated to their respective countries.

There was, therefore, a clear debate between those who held conservative views about English and tended to regard the existence of too many varieties of the language as disadvantageous and those persuaded that plurality was a defining characteristic of English in the world. It was, as Bolton (2004, p. 368) observes, 'an evident concern with monocentrism versus pluricentrism, i.e. one English (with all its geographical and social varieties), or multifarious Englishes (deserving consideration and recognition as autonomous or semi-autonomous varieties of the language)'.

It was a debate destined to continue through time.

Meanwhile, pluricentrism began to gain momentum in the early 1980s, as important book-length publications appeared. B. B. Kachru's first edition of *The Other Tongue* (1982), John Pride's *New Englishes* (1982), Bailey and Görlach's *English as a World Language* (1982) and Platt et al.'s *The New Englishes* (1984) all examined the characteristics of Englishes in different parts of the world, with particular emphasis on postcolonial settings.

In one of the reviews of Bailey and Görlach's volume, Pride (1985, p. 384) asks: 'Just as the language spreads and its study grows, will a new academic discipline naturally take shape?' The launch of the journal *World Englishes* in 1985 was a clear sign that a new discipline was indeed taking shape. Having succeeded to William Lee as editors of the journal *World Language English* and changed the title of the periodical to *World Englishes*, Braj Kachru and Larry Smith explained that the use of the plural 'Englishes' represented 'the functional and formal variation in the language, and its international acculturation'. With reference to the journal, Tom McArthur later commented that its acronym *WE* represented a 'club of equals' and a 'democratization of attitudes to English everywhere on the globe' (1993, p. 334).

This was also the time when Kachru was developing the Tree Circles model (see Section 3.2.3), in order to provide a description of the uses and the users of English which would move away from the idea of one monochrome English and begin to demonstrate the reality of the diversity of English in the world.

But the controversy went on. Kachru's interlocutor was now Randolph Quirk, who criticized what he felt was a fashionable trend among linguists to embrace principles of tolerance and equality towards all varieties of English and to disregard any advantages in trying to maintain a stable standard of English. His disagreement with such a liberal propensity was based on his belief that outside the Inner Circle, 'the relatively narrow range of purposes for which the non-native needs to use English (even in ESL countries) is arguably well catered for by a single monochrome standard form that looks as good on paper as it sounds in speech' (Quirk, 1985, p. 6). Therefore, Quirk argued that it was best for English to be kept as uniform as possible so as not to impede the primary function of a world language, that is international communication.

The debate between Quirk and Kachru continued, a few years later, on the pages of the journal *English Today*. In even more unequivocal terms, Quirk (1990) expressed his opinion about the ill-judged tolerant attitudes towards varieties of English which, he claimed, stemmed from 'liberation linguistics' and amounted to no more than a 'half-baked quackery'. In a prose that was reminiscent of Prator's, Quirk made it very clear that what was in certain quarters seen as evidence of distinctive varieties of English was in fact deviation from standard English. Such departures from standard English did more harm than good, especially for those learners who needed to acquire an international language that would give them concrete advantages in terms of employment and so on and a laissez-faire attitude would be irresponsible:

> No one should underestimate the problem of teaching English in such countries as India and Nigeria, where the English of the teachers themselves inevitably bears the stamp of locally acquired deviation from the standard language ('You are knowing my father, isn't it?') The temptation is great to accept the situation and even to justify it in euphemistically sociolinguistic terms. (Quirk, 1990, pp. 8–9)

He also pointed out that it wasn't simply a matter of a personal opinion and that the existence and the validity of varieties of English in what he called 'non-English-speaking countries' was questioned by the very people who lived in those countries:

> Put at its simplest, the argument is this: many Indians speak English; one can often guess that a person is Indian from the way he or she speaks English; India is a free and independent country as Britain is or as America

is. Therefore, just as there is an American English . . . and a British English
. . . so there is an Indian English on precisely the same equal footing (and
of course a Nigerian English, a Ghanaian English, a Singaporean English, a
Filipino English, etc., etc.).

No one would quarrel with any of this provided there was agreement within
each such country that it was true, or even that there was a determined
policy to make it true. So far as I can see, neither of these conditions
obtains, and most of those with authority in education and the media in
these countries tend to protest that the so-called national variety of Enghsh
is an attempt to justify inability to acquire what they persist in seeing as
'real' English. (Quirk, 1990, p. 8)

This was an important move by Quirk since, although his article was very
anecdotal, the reference to the views of people from countries outside the
Inner Circle corroborated and provided more objectivity to his argument.

In his response, B. B. Kachru (1991) reiterated the points that he had been
making for nearly 20 years. In particular, he stressed how the 'linguistic,
sociolinguistic, educational and pragmatic realities' in the Outer Circle were
far more complex than Quirk appeared to recognize and that only a deep
understanding of such complexity would allow one to operate a paradigm
shift in the way postcolonial Englishes were seen, that is, no longer as
'deficit' versions of the language but as varieties that were the result of the
and acculturation of English in many different parts of the world.

The '*English Today* debate' has since then been cited numerous times and
become a 'classic' in World Englishes literature. One aspect that I consider
particularly important in that debate is B. B. Kachru's explicit mention of
ideology as underlying the positions being expressed:

In Quirk's paper, there is a presupposition that liberation linguistics has an
underlying ideological motivation, an articulated philosophical and political
position. . . .

Quirk does not use any ideological terms for his concerns; that does
not, however, mean that his position cannot be related to an ideological
position. After all, it is rare that there is a position without an ideological
backdrop. (B. B. Kachru, 1991, p. 4)

Indeed, it can be argued that the substance of the ideological drive in
Quirk's stance was fundamentally the same as that which underpinned
the purist views expressed by Prator as well as those cited in the previous
chapter. Hamilton's concern about the 'barbarisms' he found in the
language spoken by Americans in the early eighteenth century was the
same as Prince Charles's worry about Americans 'making up new words',

Prator's fear of English turning into 'an utterly dissimilar tongue' and Quirk's anxiety over the effect that 'locally acquired deviation' might have upon the English language. The linguistic aberrations that were evident in 'non-native varieties' of English represented a stamp of takeover of property. For those expressing purist positions it was, therefore, quite clearly a matter of re-claiming ownership of a language that others wanted to appropriate and that some of those who ranked among its rightful owners seemed inexplicably willing to give away.

As we saw in Part One, language can be a powerful symbol of nationhood. Clearly, therefore, the moment English ceases to be just *English*, it loses that symbolic power, which dissipates irrecoverably. Hence the anxiety. But it's not simply a matter of national identity. English is also an important national asset. The millions of people around the world who learn the language sustain the enormously remunerative TESOL industry. From this point of view, the continued role of English as *the* international language is of crucial importance. It is significant that Quirk's invocation for an end to 'liberation linguistics' was not just to the benefit of those who learn English as a foreign language:

> . . . the effort is worthwhile for those of us who believe that the world needs an international language and that English is the best candidate at present on offer. Moreover, the need to make the effort is something for which we must bear a certain responsibility – and in which we have a certain *interest*. (Quirk, 1990, p. 10, my emphasis)

From this point of view, the international status of their language is something that the English may be proud of but also, importantly, something that turns it into a very profitable export. In an article in which he recommends that Britain lose its 'imperial swagger', former British Member of Parliament Chris Huhne (2014) recently said: 'Our strengths are our language, literature, law, industry, culture, inventiveness, civil society, science, architecture and the arts. They should be the source of pride, just as they can be a source of soft power'. The possessive *our* is obviously indicative of the fact that the items that Huhne lists are all seen by him as precious commodities. Again, if ownership of the language is shared, then the exclusivity of the advantages and the 'soft power' that comes with it are lost.

To sum up, the origins of the academic field of World Englishes lie in a self-perpetuating debate which, on the surface, is between plurality and singularity but, more deeply, is about (in-)equality. Not only among varieties of English but also, and more importantly, among *users* of English and the countries where they live. On the one hand, purist positions are never about language alone. The preservation of a particular 'standard' variety of English symbolizes the preservation of identity and, more prosaically, the preservation of a valuable piece of property that must not be shared freely. On the other hand, the recognition of equal validity and dignity of all varieties of English inherent in the World Englishes ethos is inspired directly by the ideas about language that were expressed by prominent postcolonial writers, whose aim was to liberate the language from its colonial heritage by re-forging it and infusing it with local Asian, African and Caribbean meanings (see Section 3.4.2).

The endeavours in this first phase of World Englishes scholarship have therefore been extremely important and valuable. They challenged and destabilized a set of pre-conceived ideas about English and its users around the world and promoted a new paradigm which considered difference and variation no longer as faults but as organic to the relocation of English in parts of the world outside its Western, Judeo-Christian base.

Within this frame, difference not only is re-evaluated as a result of productive processes of the evolution of English, but also becomes the actual defining trait of 'third world' varieties of English. This means that their very existence rests upon their distinction from, primarily, British English. Something is a variety of English if it can be demonstrated to possess characteristics that are sufficiently different from 'standard' English.

This has lead to a considerable amount of attention being paid to the description of such difference on the basis of linguistic *features*. The way in which these features are understood is in terms of distinctiveness from norms that are considered to have broader currency and that are, generally, associated with British and/or American English. However, the focus on difference may have turned out to be a limitation for the World Englishes paradigm, for a number of reasons.

4.3 Limitations in the paradigm

4.3.1 Equality in diversity?

First of all, there is a difficulty in reconciling the idea of *different* Englishes with that of *equal* Englishes. The concept of 'equality in diversity' is rather insecure in a world where power and wealth are very unequally distributed, with 'the top 10% of the world population owning 86% of global wealth' (Credit Suisse, 2013, p. 4). This will be discussed more in depth in Part Three, but in a situation where the Inner Circle has more than 30 per cent of the planet's wealth and only 6 per cent of its population and where the figures for the Outer Circle are exactly reversed – 30 per cent of the word's population owning 6 per cent of the word's wealth – presupposes a 'hierarchy of Englishes, some of which are more equal than others' (Parakrama, 2012, p. 113).

In addition, emphasis on difference necessitates a benchmark for comparison and in the vast majority of cases world Englishes are described on the basis of the extent to which they deviate from more established (and more powerful) varieties, namely American and British English. This, unwittingly but inevitably, produces a division that, again, tends to oppose 'first-rate' Englishes to 'second-rate' ones. In other words, it is difficult to sustain the argument that world Englishes are qualitatively equal if they are defined by how much they diverge from varieties that are considered 'standard' by virtue of having been codified in the Inner Circle. The distinction between a 'feature' and an 'error' is thus a very precarious one.

Methodologically, a research agenda that sets out to look for difference has an in-built deficit, in that it is programmed to ignore similarity, regardless of how pervasive it may be, and ends up tracing a potentially very partial picture of world Englishes.

4.3.2 How different are Englishes allowed to be?

Another way in which the 'full picture' may be obstructed if analysis is conducted from the particular point of view adopted in the traditional World Englishes paradigm is that linguistic differences can only be of a fairly limited scale before the varieties they define cease to be 'of English'. This creates a paradoxical situation in which difference is fundamental in the definition of world Englishes but also needs to be kept under relatively strict control before a variety escapes into the realm of unintelligibility and non-English and, consequently, under the researchers' radar.

One of the classic tenets in World Englishes is that different varieties of English have emerged as a result of the language having spread and set new roots in settings where it has come into contact with other languages (see the previous chapter). So, a common way in which linguist innovations are thought to have come about is through the influence of these languages as well as the cultures of which they are expressions. However, this phenomenon tends to considered in terms of forms of 'exoticization' of English, through the introduction of (mainly) lexical and phonological patterns that are said to have 'transferred' from local languages. English, in this way, acquires Nigerian, Malaysian, Indian and so on flavours while retaining its solid and recognizable original backbone.

But the relocation of English in different sociolinguistic milieus has done much more than spice it up. As it has become part of local linguistic repertoires, English has merged into, and broadened, existing semiotic resources that people draw from in their daily activities. In this way, the language they produce may not conform to the very European notion of discrete and separate languages. As English seamlessly amalgamates within such repertoires, the tradition idea of 'variety' dissipates and needs to be replaced with something else.

4.3.3   *What about the Expanding Circle?*

Finally, the focus on the Outer Circle and on intranational communication is one more factor that has, to some extent, limited the scope of World Englishes research. As mentioned in Chapter 1, a growing amount of attention has been devoted, in recent years, to Expanding Circle regions especially in East and Southeast Asia, particularly China (see, among many others, Kirkpatrick & Xu, 2002; Bolton, 2003a; Hu, 2005; He & Li, 2009; Bolton & Graddol, 2012; Shi, 2013), Japan (Seargeant, 2009, 2011; McKenzie, 2010; Hino, 2012), South Korea (Lee, 2004; Lawrence, 2012; Hadikin, 2014) and so on. However, the forms and functions of English as an international lingua franca in the Expanding Circle have traditionally featured comparatively rarely in World Englishes literature, despite the fact that, statistically, this major role of English has been on an upward trend for some time now, boosted by tightly connected forces in global economy, trade and movements of people. For this reason, a 'cognate' field of research focussing specifically on ELF began towards the beginning of the century and has since gained considerable momentum. This will be discussed more in depth in Section 4.5.

4.4   The 'spot the difference' approach

With reference to varieties of English that emerged in postcolonial settings as a result of contact with local languages and cultures, B. B. Kachru and Nelson (1996, p. 72) stress that 'although these contemporary Englishes have much in common, they are also unique in their grammatical innovations and tolerances, lexis, pronunciations, idioms and discourse'. According to them, therefore, it is important that sociolinguists go beneath the apparent similarity among these Englishes and are able to detect and describe less obvious, but significant, differences:

> If you glance at the front pages of, say, the *New York Times*, the London *Times*, the *Times of India*, and Singapore's *The Straits Times*, you will probably notice more similarities than differences; that is, you will have little trouble reading and understanding the headlines and news stories before you. In fact, the front pages of major English-language dailies in other parts of the world bear striking resemblances to one another, *although close reading may reveal some unfamiliar features*, depending upon the reader's origin. (1996, p. 75, my emphasis)

So, a serious account of the various forms of English in the world cannot overlook those 'unfamiliar features' and it is the job of sociolinguists to carry out 'rational analysis' in order to provide 'descriptive categorizations' of varieties of English which can in turn offer a 'cogent insight into the way language actually works, as opposed to prescriptive declarations of the way one or another group of individuals wishes language to work' (1996, p. 77).

As an illustration of this, B. B. Kachru and Nelson take an extract from a Pakistani English-language newspaper and, in it, identify expressions such as *shuttling in the region* and *adamantly evasive to comment* as examples of unusual collocations. These, according to them, must be seen as evidence of a different variety of English rather than violations of fixed rules set outside the socio-cultural context of this particular variety of English.

4.4.1   'Errors' or 'features'?

Essentially, therefore, it is a matter of perceiving particular linguistic phenomena no longer as *errors* but as *features*. The argument being one of acceptability: in the same way as it is acceptable that 'American speakers say "path" and British speakers say "pahth"' (B. B. Kachru & Nelson, 1996, p. 74), either pronunciation being simply a feature of different national varieties of English, so there is no reason why it shouldn't be acceptable for Pakistani speakers to say 'adamantly evasive to comment'.

As B. B. Kachru (1983) had clarified years earlier, a distinction must be made between *mistake* and *deviation*. While both are different from the norm, the latter

> is the result of the new 'un-English' linguistic and cultural setting in which the English language is used; it is the result of a productive process which makes the typical variety-specific features; and it is systemic within a variety, and not idiosyncratic. (p. 159)

This basic principle has informed much scholarship in the field, where phonological, lexical, grammatical and syntactic peculiarities are meticulously singled out and displayed as proofs of the ways in which new varieties of English have evolved. The identification method is based on the extent to which a 'feature' departs from an established norm. This, in turn, is often measured in terms of *unexpectedness*. So, for example, with reference to a passage from a Ghanaian newspaper, Melchers and Shaw (2011, p. 165) mention the expression *because it will be partisan affair* and note that 'one might expect *a partisan affair*' (i.e. with the inclusion of the indefinite article *a*) and suggest that this 'reflects a local, or unsystematic, use of articles'.

To stay, for a moment, on the (non-) use of articles (a common topic in the relevant literature), it is interesting to notice the terminology with which it is discussed. With reference to Singapore and Malaysian Englishes, for example, Low (2010, p. 238) mentions 'article deletion' as a common feature of the two Southeast Asian varieties. In the same collection (Kirkpatrick, 2010b), McLellan (2010, p. 430) describes how the presence of a Malay word within a particular English phrase in Malaysian English 'causes deletion of the required English indefinite article'.

Indeed, the word *deletion* is conventionally used in sociolinguistics to describe situations when a bit of language (e.g. an article, a preposition, the verb *be*, etc.) is 'missing' in the place where it is expected to be. For example, the following phrase taken from an online forum shows an instance of what might be regarded as deletion of the auxiliary *will*:

. . . in your 2nd semester you probably be busy . . .

Such phenomena are described in detail in a branch of sociolinguistics sometimes called 'contact linguistics', which studies situations where different languages come into 'contact' with one another, generally as a result of significant numbers of people moving from one territory to another, for example, via migration flows, colonization and so on. The general phenomenon is one in which the language of the newcomers and that of the original inhabitants are used in the same territory and influence each other. Often, one of the two languages is more powerful than the other, carries more prestige and its use offers better opportunities for higher social standing. This language is called the *superstrate* and the less powerful language is called the *substrate*.

In colonial and postcolonial settings, English is often the superstrate, and the ways in which it has been influenced by different substrates has been the subject of much World Englishes scholarship. Mesthrie and Bhatt (2008), for example, provide a comprehensive analysis of varieties of English fundamentally from the point of view of language contact. In doing so, they highlight both similarities and differences in the linguistic features that have developed in individual varieties. At one point in their description, Mesthrie and Bhatt distinguish between 'deleters' and 'preservers', namely 'varieties that favour deletion of elements and those that disfavour it' (2008, p. 90).

Within this frame, elements are said to be deleted or preserved with reference to standard versions of the language. In an earlier paper, Mesthrie (2006) suggests that varieties of English can be placed along a cline of (un-)deletion, where on one end are varieties, such as Singapore English, that tend to delete everything that they can afford to without compromising intelligibility, and on the other end are varieties, such as Black South African English, that do the opposite, namely restore anything that can be, and often is, deleted both in standard English and in other varieties of English. What is significant to the present discussion is that unexpected or unusual collocations, omissions, (un-)deletions and so on are all markers of some alterations made to the standard code which clearly suggest (more or less deliberate) departures from established norms. Standard English is thus the frame of reference against which all varieties of English are described. I will now illustrate this phenomenon further with particular reference to research on English in Singapore.

4.4.1.1 English in Singapore

Singapore is a city state of 5 million people on a small island just off the southern tip of peninsular Malaysia, in the middle of Southeast Asia. It is one of the postcolonial territories that have been talked about most often and in depth in World Englishes. There are three main reasons why Singapore has attracted so much interest in sociolinguistics. First of all, as part of the language policy adopted by the government since independence, English has been actively promoted as the de facto national language, especially within the education system, where it is the medium of instruction at all levels. As a consequence, Singapore has probably the greatest proportion of habitual English speakers among the countries in the Outer Circle, with a significant number of households where English is the primary language. Secondly, English is part of a rich linguistic repertoire and coexists with a number of other languages: Mandarin, Hokkien, Teochew, Malay, Tamil and others. English, Mandarin, Malay and Tamil are all recognized as official languages and, by law, each Singaporean is assigned a 'mother tongue' exclusively according to their ethnicity and regardless of their ability to speak it. So, each of the three main ethnic groups has a mother tongue: the Chinese have Mandarin, the Malays Malay and the Indians Tamil, while English cuts across all three groups. The third reason why Singapore has been discussed so much is that its small size means that it is easier for researchers to produce relatively comprehensive sociolinguistic accounts.

Within a broad World Englishes perspective, research in this area has focussed on what is generally termed 'Singapore English' (SgE). In one of the most recent studies to date, Leimgruber (2013) provides a very useful overview of the various analytical models that have been devised over the years to describe SgE. He divides these models into 'old' and 'new' (Table 4.1).

TABLE 4.1 Analytical models of SgE

Old models	New models
Continuum	Cultural orientation
Diglossia	Indexicality
Polyglossia	

All these models, old and new, attempt to describe variation in SgE. The following is a summary of their basic principles:

Continuum – Every instance of SgE can be placed on a particular *lectal level*, ranging from *basilect* to *acrolect*, with *mesolect* somewhere in the middle. Basilectal forms characterize Colloquial Singapore English (CSE), or 'Singlish', and acrolectal ones pertain to Standard Singapore English (SSE). A speaker is able to move along the lectal scale according to their level of education and socio-economic position, so that the higher their position, the greater their ability to shift between the two ends of the cline.

Diglossia – This model considers the same sub-varieties at the ends of the continuum: CSE as the L(ow) sub-variety, acquired natively, and SSE, the H(igh) sub-variety acquired through formal education. It postulates that the choice of H or L depends on functional factors (e.g. religion, education, family, etc.) rather than just speakers' level of education and/or their socio-economic standing.

Polyglossia – This model takes into account the multilingual environment of Singapore. In this way, language varieties are placed along a scale of prestige according to the domains of use and individual speakers' attitudes towards them. Thus variation between SSE and CSE is positioned within a wider frame encompassing other languages (and their varieties) in the local repertoire.

Cultural orientation – In this model, speakers of SgE vary their use of English between Singlish and Standard English according to how they orient themselves towards the two broad dimensions of localism and globalism. The former 'is associated with informality, familiarity, equality, membership in a community and socio-cultural capital', while the latter 'necessarily implies formality, distance and authority and is associated with educational attainment and economic value' (Alsagoff, 2010a, pp. 345–346).

Indexicality – In this model, variation between an H and an L sub-variety of SgE may be an index of 'one or more social meanings, understood by the speaker and addressee consciously or unconsciously'

(Leimgruber, 2013, p. 20). Indexes are multilayered, so that in a single utterance there may be several social meanings simultaneously produced. So, manifestations of H or L aren't necessarily distributed across speakers, situations or even utterances, but may fluctuate *within* each instance of language use.

One significant difference between the 'old' and the 'new' approaches is the capacity for the latter to account for more complex types of variation. In particular, there has been a move away from the idea that speakers were able to select one sub-variety at a time and much more attention has been paid to variation as *choice* and the significance that it has in terms of pragmatics, group identity, stance in the hybrid linguistic manifestations that it produces. Yet, despite these important differences, one crucial aspect seems to remain unchanged: variation is identified, measured and described in terms of deviation from a 'standard' version of the language which is taken as a universal yardstick.

4.4.2   British and American English as yardsticks

As Baker (2010, p. 82) points out with reference to research conducted on corpora of regional Englishes, much attention has been devoted to difference from norms codified in Britain or America:

> Many of the researchers who have examined these 'regional' corpora of English have focussed on grammatical variation, either within the genres or subcategories of a particular corpus, or by comparing it against other corpora (particularly British and American English, which are normally implied to be a kind of 'default' for 'standard' English). Thus, a typical research question in such studies would be something like 'How does use of grammatical or linguistic feature *x* differ in English variety *y* when compared against British (or American) English?

The practice of comparing world Englishes to some idealized 'standard', variously referred to with or without a geographical attribute (typically 'British'), is a well established one, even though the need to move away from it and to examine world Englishes as autonomous entities has also been expressed for a long time. Again with reference to Singapore English, Lim (2012, p. 284) notes:

> Only a decade after independence, in Tongue's (1974) pioneering work, we find the first suggestion that one could talk of features of Singapore English that were different from standard English but could be considered standard within the Singapore context.

However, in actual fact, the comparative method has been predominant. In the now classic account of English in Singapore and Malaysia, Platt et al. (1983) introduce their description of the two varieties of English by stating that 'SgE and MalE vary from Standard British English in a number of ways' (p. 12) and, indeed, that same preface is more or less applied to most of the studies that followed. As Gupta noted in the middle of the 1990s, '[v]irtually all analyses of [it] in the past . . . have analysed Singapore English comparatively, using British Standard English as a benchmark' (Gupta, 1994, p. 9). However, Alsagoff and Ho (1998) a few years later remarked that an approach that would comprehensively avoid comparisons with (British) Standard English was still unrealistic for a new variety of English, since 'there has to be a great deal of work done before a grammar of Singapore English can be written that does not make reference to any exonormative standard' (Alsagoff & Ho, 1998, p. 133).

Even in recent approaches, which aspire to a 'more fluid and dynamic understanding of language variation' (Alsagoff, 2010b, p. 110), the frame of reference remains 'standard English', and names such as 'SSE' are little more than re-localized versions of the same concept. The way in which Leimgruber (2013, p. 64) describes the challenge one encounters in documenting SgE, for example, is particularly illuminating:

> When describing a variety such as Singapore English, the first question that arises is: which Singapore English? The Singlish used by the lesser-educated hawker is quite unlike the polished Standard English employed by a minister when addressing parliament. . . . And yet both have to be considered instantiations of Singapore English, as they are, obviously, English, and used by Singaporeans. This variability is omnipresent. . . .

Significantly, the phonology of SgE is described with reference to Received Pronunciation (RP) and so, inevitably, 'features' are catalogued on the basis of their divergence from it and referred to through names such as *absence* (of phonemic length distinction), *collapse* (of minimal pairs into a single vowel), and what does *not* happen, such as the aspiration of plosives (pp. 64–65).

To be sure, in sociolinguistics, such alterations are conventionally not openly judged in terms of correctness and, in fact, the opposite is more often the case. Mesthrie (2006), for example, prefaces his description of Black South African English by clarifying that 'far from being a problematic and error ridden dialect, with a miscellany of non-standardisms . . . BlSAfE can be seen as a coherent system' (p. 115). Generally, indeed, differences observed in varieties of English tend to be viewed neutrally or positively in World Englishes, where much of the discourse has been shaped by early debates against a 'deficit' view of varieties of English (see Section 4.2 earlier).

Take, for example, the following passage about Indian English:

> While largely in tune with the codified rules and norms of standard English, IndE users do take the freedom to modify *their* English to extend the range of their language and enlarge its possibilities whenever a communicative need to do so should arise. (Sedlatschek, 2009, p. 311)

And yet, despite such declarations of attitudinal neutrality, there is a sense that the possibility of a 'deficit' view is always there, just below the surface of discourse, making its looming presence felt through words like *omission*, *deletion*, *unusual*, which are used against words like *norms*, *required*, *rules*, *standard*. This is very similar to the ways in which the histories of non-Western countries are 'cast in terms of irrevocable principles of failure, lack, and absence, since they are always already measured against the West' (Dube, 2002, p. 337).

In fact, it can be argued that the 'deficit' position and what I've called the 'spot the difference' approach are inseparable. This is because by engaging in the same exercise of measuring departures from standard English, much World Englishes discourse becomes trapped in a sort of dead end where it finds itself dealing with precisely the same conceptualization of languages as coherent bounded systems that the 'deficit' stance subscribes to. And *feature* and *error* end up being simply sides of the same coin, which is susceptible of being flipped at any moment.

The following passage illustrates this particularly well. Here, with reference to the features of Singapore English observed in a study primarily based on the speech of one single speaker, Deterding (2007) comments on the fact that the concern of 'falling standards' often voiced in Singapore may be unfounded:

> Of course, the data from Hui Min . . . are not representative of all speakers in Singapore, and it is certainly true that we could offer many samples of speech that would be largely incomprehensible for people from elsewhere, so it must be acknowledged that plenty of young people in Singapore continue to have a poor command of the language. However, if listeners agree that the speech of Hui Min is clear and articulate even though it includes so many features of Singapore English, maybe we really do not have so much to fear about falling standards, at least for trainee teachers. And indeed, there are many features of the speech discussed here that are distinctly Singaporean but do not interfere in any way with intelligibility. In conclusion, then, it is quite possible to sound Singaporean but still be easily understood in the rest of the world, and it seems that a mature variety of educated Singapore English is indeed emerging. (Deterding, 2007, p. 92)

The coin flips several times here. On one side of it, we find 'clear and articulate' speech and a reassurance dispelling fears over the standards of English in

Singapore. On the other side, we find the 'largely incomprehensible' speech of many young Singaporeans due to their 'poor command of the language'. Somewhere in the middle, perhaps on the edge of the coin, is the observation that Hui Min and other educated Singaporeans like her can be perfectly intelligible *despite* the presence of distinctly Singaporean features in their speech.

A 'feature', then, is necessarily something that is constantly on the verge of trespassing into the unknown territory of 'incomprehensibility'. In order to avoid that, it mustn't taint the English linguistic code excessively. This is a firm point in classic World Englishes literature, and one that even Chinua Achebe made when, in the 1960s, he argued that African writers needed to forge a new English that, while being able to express *Africanness*, would remain 'in full communion with its ancestral home' (see Section 3.4.2). The fact that the focus of attention tends to be on educated speakers of varieties of English is indicative of this basic principle.

4.4.3   'In full communion with its ancestral home'

That's why, despite their socio-culturally motivated deviations, varieties must maintain their overall recognizably English identity in order to merit the 'of English' modifier. This creates a tension between 'deficit' and 'innovation'. It's not just a matter of giving the same thing a new name. It's a matter of *legitimacy*. The distance that 'features' can travel in their deviations from established norms is short. Beyond a certain limit, they are disqualified and degraded into a bundle of terms like *basilect, colloquial variety, uneducated variety, pidgin English*, various *-nglish* compounds ('singlish', 'manglish', 'inglish', etc.) or, simply, 'poor command of the language'. These, presumably, are no longer in communion with the ancestral home of the English language.

This is a point that has been made by other scholars too. Pennycook (2007a), for example, has produced one of the strongest critiques of this aspect of the World Englishes framework, which he calls an 'exclusionary paradigm' where 'divergences from the core are viewed as "localizations" so long as the overarching system remains intact' (p. 22). He adds:

> A core system of English is assumed, with deviations from this core that destabilize the notion of system discounted. The world Englishes paradigm, while attempting to achieve sociolinguistic equality for its varieties, is not epistemologically different from this model of core, variation and exclusion: for a world English to be such, it must adhere to the underlying grammar of central English, demonstrate enough variety to make it interestingly different, but not diverge to the extent that it undermines the myth of English. (2007a, p. 23)

The – unintended – exclusionary effects of the conceptualization of 'variety' in World Englishes is also underlined by Canagarajah (2013), who observes that 'the normed nature of local varieties excludes many domains' and '[t]he varieties recognised by WE require a level of stability that leaves out other creative and emergent uses that are still meaningful and functional in local contexts' (p. 59).

A number of important questions must be asked at this point. Which, exactly, are the 'norms of standard English' against which 'features' of varieties of English are identified? Who sets such norms? Who decides what the 'core system of English' is?

4.4.4 *The norms of English*

Semantically, the word *norm* is a very interesting one. There are two closely interrelated senses to it. One refers to what happens most frequently, is most usual, most common and is, therefore, *normal*. The other relates to patterns of acceptable behaviour and conduct which, too, are seen as *normal*. In this second sense, 'norm' becomes a near-synonym of 'rule'. The two senses are so inextricably linked that it is sometimes difficult to use, or understand, the word *norm* only in one of them.

The representation of homosexuality is a case in point. Those who say they object to same-sex relationships typically do so on the basis of such relationships being 'ab-normal', clearly conflating something that could be seen as a statistical dimension – there are fewer homosexual couples than heterosexual ones – with a more moral one – homosexuality is wrong. There seems to be a cause–effect connection between un-common and un-acceptable in this kind of argument. What is less frequent tends to be seen as less natural, and this in turn makes it unacceptable.

The link between the statistical and the moral dimensions of the word 'norm' works in both directions. Namely, while something that happens most frequently is more likely to be considered morally acceptable, something that is consistently *represented* as normal, natural and right is more likely to become standard practice. As is often the case, one aspect reinforces the other. So, while heterosexuality is considered normal, its *representation* as such also influences actual manifestations of different sexual orientations. In societies that are particularly repressive about non-heterosexual orientations, people are not only less willing to display them, but also crucially less inclined to question their own sexuality. As Foucault (1977) discussed at length, this two-way relationship between the two sense of 'norm' has always been exploited by those in positions of power. Legislation is often precisely about controlling, minimizing or even completely eliminating certain patterns of behaviour on the basis of their being 'abnormal'. When applied to language, the concept of 'norm' is understood in similar ways and produces similar effects. There is a very fine line between *description* and *prescription*. A language norm may refer to established lexical, grammatical, phonological patterns but the process whereby that pattern becomes established in the first place may be largely prescriptive and, hence, related to power (im-)balances. This is one of the principles in language standardization. Milroy and Milroy (2012) have pointed out how the main idea behind wanting to standardize a language is that 'everyone should use and understand the language in the same way with the minimum of misunderstanding and the maximum of efficiency' (p. 19). In concrete terms,

> this means preventing variability in spelling and pronunciation by selecting fixed conventions uniquely regarded as 'correct', establishing 'correct' meanings of words . . ., uniquely acceptable word-forms . . . and fixed conventions of sentence structure. (2012, p. 19)

Of course, as Milroy and Milroy as well as a number of other scholars (see, e.g. Bex & Watts, 1999; Holborow, 1999; Locher & Strässler, 2008; Hickey, 2012) have observed, beyond the functional aim, the notion of a standard language is also of clearly ideological and political inspiration. The selection of 'correct' forms, for all languages, has always been made in the centres of power. In the case of English, standardization has historically been based on educated models in the London area and the south-east, while ways of speaking in other parts of the country (e.g. the north and the west) have been regarded as distinctly *non*-standard.

4.4.5   *The power of codification*

Codification is a process in which patterns of language use are, in a sense, turned into a linguistic 'code of conduct'. This can take place in various ways, more or less explicitly. In some countries, dedicated 'academies' have the task of establishing the rules of the national language, and stipulating what is permitted and what is not. In France, for example, the Académie Française operates 'with all the possible care and diligence, in order to give our language clear rules and to make it pure, eloquent and capable of treating the arts and the sciences' (Académie Française, my translation). The activities of an institution such as the Académie, which has similar counterparts in Spain and Italy, aren't the only ways in which languages are codified. In fact, such academies have now become less relevant and influential than they used to be.

Codification is implemented via many other means. Dictionaries and grammar books play a very important role. The *OED*, for example, is generally thought of as the ultimate authority as regards the vocabulary of English. The role of such publications is always on the verge between description and prescription. Dictionaries document language use but also serve as reference, setting rules and boundaries. People consult dictionaries to check the meanings and the spelling of words. So, the functions of reporting what language users do and determining what they *ought* to do merge into one. Describing and prescribing language use become the same thing. This can have very powerful effects in the process of language standardization.

It is said, for example, that the phonology of standard British English is non-rhotic, which means that *r* is not pronounced before consonants (as in *part* and *corn*) or after vowels if at the end of a syllable (as in *car* and *sister*). In terms of actual diffusion, however, the standardness of this particular feature is relatively recent. Historically, non-rhoticity is a deviation from the standard rhoticity (i.e. *r* always pronounced) of English which originated in eighteenth-century London (Beal, 2010, p. 15). While in contemporary British accents rhoticity is found mainly in the south-west of England, in Wales and in Scotland, until about the first half of the twentieth century it was common in very large areas of England too. Not only, but the non-pronunciation of *r* was explicitly condemned as wrong. The widespread shift from rhotic to non-rhotic accents is so recent that in some areas, such as around the border between West Sussex and Hampshire, the accent of some older people is rhotic while that of *all* younger speakers isn't.

As Mugglestone (2003) points out, the establishment of non-rhoticity in standard RP was largely a matter of prestige, given that its geographical base was the London area. By the beginning of the twentieth century non-rhoticity became codified into a norm, especially through Daniel Jones's *English Pronouncing Dictionary* in 1917, and the short step from description to prescription was made, which resulted in this feature rapidly spreading in most parts of England, where rhoticity, which used to be the 'correct' form, is now seen as a sign of rustic or uncultivated speech.

Not only does this show the arbitrariness of what is considered (in-)correct, but it also demonstrates how codification and standardization are transient and highly contextualized in specific socio-political settings. Importantly, in this sense, while it may be prestigious in England, non-rhoticity sits on the opposite end of the prestige scale in America, where dropping one's *r*'s is considered incorrect. Ultimately, therefore, the 'codified norms of standard English' that Sedlatschek (2009) refers to are actually the products of relationships of power and prestige which may be completely irrelevant in the various parts of the world where English has a presence in the local linguistic repertoire.

At this point, I will, for a moment, draw a parallel with an example of discourse coming from a different domain and, fortunately, a different time: the discourse of scientific racism.

4.4.6   *Varieties of language and varieties of race*

Why . . . have men repeatedly thought and acted as if a few superficial differences were evidence of biologically distinct races? The superficial answer is that people swallowed a lot of 19th-century pseudo science: the idea of biologically distinct races was able to reproduce itself far more successfully than the distinct races it claimed to identify. (Ferguson, 2006)

The nineteenth-century pseudo-science that Ferguson refers to was central in the theorization of the existence of distinct 'peoples' within the discourse of the nation-state. As Hardt and Negri (2000) explain:

Two fundamental kinds of operations contribute to the construction of the modern concept of the people in relation to that of the nation in Europe in the eighteenth and nineteenth centuries. The more important of these are the mechanisms of colonial racism that construct the identity of European peoples in a dialectical play of oppositions with their native Others. The concepts of nation, people, and race are never very far apart. The construction of an absolute racial difference is the essential ground for the conception of a homogeneous national identity. (p. 103)

As it became such a fundamental concept, 'race' was also exploited, at the height of European imperialism, to try and demonstrate scientifically that the 'white race' was biologically superior to all other races and, especially, that of the 'negro'. This was part of a more general and broader discursive construction which, by invoking Christianity and other forms of 'civilizing mission', sought to provide a kind of moral justification for such imperial activities as genocide, looting and slavery.

The proof of the superiority of 'white' people was argued on the basis of purportedly biological and physiological 'features' which were presented as scientific facts. In an early twentieth-century essay entitled 'The Psychology of American Race Prejudice', George Washington Ellis explained how the discourse of the inferior Negro had been constructed in the nineteenth century. I believe the following long passage quoted offers more than one stimulus for reflection.

ADOPTION OF FALSE ETHNOLOGICAL STANDARD

The Gobineau and Ammon school adopted the best form of the white race as the standard of measurement and judged all other race varieties as they approximated or diverged from it. As the Negro presented apparently the widest physical divergence, they assigned to this race the lowest intellectual and moral estate in the genus homo. Because of differences in the Negro's color, hair and the weight of the brain; because of differences of the angle of the cephalic index and the general anatomical structure of his organism, as compared to that of the white standard, scientists not only condemned the Negro to the lowest human plane, but they exaggerated these differences, gave to them meanings and interpretations which are not and never were true. In the zest of their cause they overlooked the additional facts that the standard they adopted is not representative of the white races, whose differences among themselves are quite as substantial as from the Negro.

ADOPTION OF THE FALSE NEGRO TYPE

As representative of the Negro they selected the ugliest type, and after exaggerating its deformities, they held it up to the white mind of the reading world, in striking contrast to the white standard, to give permanence and stability to the false doctrine of natural Negro inferiority . . . . [T]his false Negro type was circulated with this perfect white standard to impress the rising generations of all nations against the black, and to solidify with the sanctity of science that natural antipathy which always attends the initial contact of unassimilated individuals or groups . . . .

FEATURES OF ABNORMAL NEGRO TYPE

The picture of the Negro as set forth by the ethnological type is the next thing in order to the ape family. Types corresponding to it, however, are to be found in all races . . . . In word and picture [European and American writers in the fields of science and literature] taught the world that the true Negro was less than human, with an oval skull, flat forehead, snout-like jaws, swollen lips, broad, flat nose, short, crimped hair, calfless legs, highly elongated heels, and flat feet. (Ellis, 1915, pp. 301–302)

Setting aside the obviously different intents and purposes of those so-called ethnological writers, as well as their absurdly grotesque 'scientific' descriptions denounced by Ellis, there are some unexpected similarities here with the ways in which 'features' of varieties of English are presented that it is worth dwelling upon. I would in fact argue that a surprising amount of this citation bears striking relevance for the discourse of 'varieties of English' to the point that some of the concepts can almost be mapped onto one another. As an intriguing exercise, two extracts from the passage can be paraphrased slightly:

original

The Gobineau and Ammon school adopted the best form of the white race as the standard of measurement and judged all other race varieties as they approximated or diverged from it. As the Negro presented apparently the widest physical divergence, they assigned to this race the lowest intellectual and moral estate in the genus homo.

modified version (changed words emphasized)

The *World Englishes* school adopted the best form of *British English* as the standard of measurement and *described* all other varieties *of English* as they approximated or diverged from it. As *colloquial uneducated forms* presented apparently the widest *linguistic* divergence, they assigned to them the lowest *position in the lectal scales*.

original

In the zest of their cause they overlooked the additional facts that the standard they adopted is not representative of the white races, whose differences among themselves are quite as substantial as from the Negro.

modified version (changed words emphasized)

In the zest of their cause they overlooked the additional facts that the standard they adopted is not representative of *British Englishes*, whose differences among themselves are quite as substantial as from *postcolonial Englishes*.

The similarities are remarkable and difficult to ignore. The entire argument for the superiority of the 'white race' rested upon the identification, description and magnification of 'features' in the 'negro' that would demonstrate how *different* the two 'races' were. The list of such 'features' at the end of the passage is significant. Not only are they glaringly derogatory and degrading but, crucially, they are clearly defined in terms of an idealized 'white' standard. Lips can only be described as 'swollen' if the description is in relation to an idealized norm based on the 'standard' lip size of those who have set that norm in the first place.

Analogously, articles can only be described as 'missing' or 'redundant' (Hung, 2012, p. 127) in a local variety of English if this is judged against idealized British or American norms of article usage. Exactly in the same way as 'the histories of India or Mexico or Venezuela come to be cast in terms of irrevocable principles of failure, lack, and absence, since they are always already measured against the West' (Dube, 2002, p. 337). It is difficult, within this frame, to avoid suggesting inferiority of postcolonial Englishes, even when equality is the postulated remit. It is difficult to convincingly claim the equal status and dignity of an entity that is constantly being judged against a notional standard. In his essay, Ellis quite rightly pointed out that racist ideology tended to ignore similarity among races. In a racist view of ethnicity, similarity must be downplayed and difference amplified.

This is also the discursive practice which generated what Said (1978) called *orientalism*, 'a way of coming to terms with the Orient that is based on the Orient's special place in European Western experience' (p. 1). Within this frame, the 'Orient' was represented as 'alien', 'foreign', 'unknown' and 'exotic'. In other words, it was 'otherized'. As Hyam (2010, p. 5) explains, '"[o]thering", at its simplest, is the attempt to understand the actions and thought-worlds of communities perceived as culturally alien, often by comparing them with a supposed "norm"'. So, even when interpretations of assumed 'superior' or 'inferior' varieties is explicitly antagonized, as is the case of World Englishes literature, the possibility of 'othering' non-Inner Circle varieties is always implicit.

So, even in domains that have nothing to do with racism, or where an egalitarian stance is explicitly adopted, the step between *non*-standard and *sub*-standard is extremely small. Rubdy, McKay, Alsagoff, and Bokhorst-Heng (2008, p. 48) explain this very well:

> The traditional practice of describing New Varieties of English (NVEs) in the Outer Circle with reference to Inner Circle native-speaker norms tends to characterize Outer Circle speakers' usage in wholly negative terms with regard to their general proficiency level, the credibility of their intuitive judgements, and their overall authority over the language in terms of their confidence and sophistication in the use of English. This is because most descriptions of these varieties have tended to use difference as a means of defining them.

In introducing syntactic features of Singapore English, Low (2012, p. 48), for example, observes that 'the syntax of Standard SingE generally tends to resemble other standard varieties of English, such as BrE or AmE' and so she informs her readers that in her description 'only examples that are uncommon in standard BrE or AmE will be highlighted'. But then, once again, the same conflation of 'feature' and 'error' is always very likely and almost inevitable. So, for instance, she points out how 'the tendency for subject–verb agreement to take place with the noun nearest to the verb instead of with the head of the noun phrase . . . may be found amongst users of Standard SingE, [but] is not accepted as grammatically correct' (p. 48).

A little later, Low reprimands another feature/error of Singapore English, namely the use of adverbs such as *actually* and *basically* and, with reference to two examples, explains how this might be confusing for British or American speakers:

> In both these sentences, the use of *basically* and *actually* do not add to their meaning. The meaning might even be distorted! For example, in the sentence, *My name is actually Sarah*, the speakers of BrE or AmE might (understandably) misunderstand her intended meaning and presume that

Sarah has all along been using another pseudonym and is clarifying this point to her interlocutors. (Low, 2012, p. 49)

There is a very clear assumption here that British and American people are imagined to be the sole judges of the 'distortions' produced by the hundreds of millions of other speakers of English in the world. But, more importantly, Low's own use of subject–verb agreement according to the noun nearest to the verb in 'the use . . . do not add' from the citation earlier seems to do two things: (i) it confirms that this feature is indeed common in Singapore English, including in formal domains, perhaps even more so than Low is prepared to recognize and (ii) it indicates that perhaps it might be useful to stop examining Englishes within a comparative frame which induces a Singaporean linguist such as Low to evaluate her own variety of English from the point of view of imagined British and American 'native speakers' who stipulate what is or is not acceptable.

Finally, all of this may also have to do with the fact that 'people tend to find differences more noteworthy than similarities' (Baker, 2010, p. 83), because 'it is *difference* that most often stands out in marking one's identity' (Kumaravadivelu, 2012, p. 10). This is related to what, paraphrasing Urry and Larsen's (2011) *tourist gaze*, I call the *linguist gaze*.

4.4.7 *The linguist gaze and dominant discourses*

Generally speaking, the study of language relies heavily on research data coming from actual manifestations of language, produced by people in a wide range of situations and for a wide range of purposes. Different types of language analysis take into account the social context in which discourse is produced to varying degrees. In corpus linguistics, for example, social context is only of marginal relevance, the main concern being on how chunks of language 'behave' in certain *textual* environments. At the other end of the scale, in sociolinguistics context generally plays a more central role. However, even when context is taken into consideration, the linguist's perspective tends to remain *external* to the social activities that generate linguistic data.

The position of the linguist outside the social activity isn't necessarily unfavourable. In fact, it can be a definite advantage, as it guarantees greater detachment and objectivity which, in turn, can produce more rigorous analysis. However, there are cases where an external vantage point *is* limiting. One of such cases is when the researcher does not share the linguistic repertoire of the people whose language use is analysed and/or does not have sufficient 'insider knowledge' of the sociolinguistic, cultural and historical environment under scrutiny. In this situation, linguists will tend to look at this environment through the lens of patterns of behaviour that are more familiar to them. Metaphorically, this isn't dissimilar to what tourists do when they visit a place for the first time. The things that they notice first and are most fascinated by are those that stand out for being different from 'home': features of landscape, architecture, urban layout, food, social etiquette and all the infinite elements that are usually subsumed under 'culture'. This is what Urry and Larsen (2011) call the *tourist gaze*:

> People gaze upon the world through a particular filter of ideas, skills, desires and expectations, framed by social class, gender, nationality, age and education. Gazing is a performance that orders, shapes and classifies, rather than reflects the world.
>
> . . .
>
> What makes a particular tourist gaze depends upon what it is contrasted with; what the forms of non-tourist experience happen to be. The gaze therefore presupposes a system of social activities and signs which locate the particular tourist practices, not in terms of some intrinsic characteristics, but through the contrasts implied with non-tourist social practices, particularly those based within home and paid work. (Urry & Larsen, 2011, pp. 2–3)

Gaze is an active process which *defines*, rather than simply photographs, what is being observed. This means that the 'feature' status of certain aspects of landscape and so on is created by the tourist's subjective viewpoint. Of course, features that appear out of the ordinary to particular groups of tourists will be unremarkable and unnoticeable to local, non-tourists. With reference to the Italian region of Apulia, for example, D'Egidio (2014, p. 69) points out how olive trees, which abound there, are considered particularly interesting to English and German tourists:

> Since such landscapes are not to be found in Britain or Germany, olive groves and trees are perceived as something 'out-of-the-ordinary' and 'unfamiliar', and for this reason they are worth gazing at. This idea is conveyed in particular by adjectives . . . such as gnarled, endless, old and wonderful.

It is the English and German tourists' gaze that defines fields of olive trees with those adjectives, not, normally, the inhabitants of the area. In a similar fashion, language 'features' can be almost fetishized as an object of desire for the linguist who goes around the world documenting interesting linguistic anomalies just like the tourist in search of little-explored idylls off the beaten track.

The following description, made by an American blogger living in Spain, of when Andalucian people have their evening meals is also illustrative:

> Eating out in Andalucia is fantastic. Eating times are late. Get to a restaurant in the evening during the warmer months at 9pm and you may be the only person there. I'm serious. It'll feel weird. (Huxham, 2013)

Clearly, eating after 9 p.m. is 'late' only from the point of view of someone who normally has dinner at 6 p.m., but it's nothing 'weird' to an Andalucian, who won't even find 'eating time' something to comment on in the first place.

Significantly, however, in his blog post Huxham doesn't address fellow American readers, nor is the blog site (ask.metafilter.com) in any way explicitly located in the United States. Also, there is no indication that Andalucian eating times are 'late' in comparison to North American norms – the description is simply offered in a way that appears to bear a sort of inherent universal validity. This is because the American blogger's description of Andalucia is not just the opinion of a single expat living in a foreign country but is expression of a *dominant discourse* which has the power to *normalize* the representations that it produces. So, dinner at 6 p.m. is 'normal' while dinner at 10 p.m. is 'late'.

Clearly, this particular discourse is dominant because it is produced in part of the world, the United States, which has a dominant position in the world. Of course, representations of the world produced, more generally, in the West have become dominant as a result of centuries of European imperialism which has created and imposed descriptions of the world that have been enshrined and institutionalized to the point of being considered 'universal'. With reference to history, for example, Chakrabarty (1992, p. 1) notes:

> . . . insofar as the academic discourse of history . . . is concerned, 'Europe' remains the sovereign, theoretical subject of all histories, including the ones we call 'Indian', 'Chinese', 'Kenyan', and so on. There is a peculiar way in which all these other histories tend to become variations on a master narrative that could be called 'the history of Europe'. In this sense, 'Indian' history itself is in a position of subalternity; one can only articulate subaltern subject positions in the name of this history.

The academic discourse about language may find itself in a similar position. Especially in the broad academic areas of applied linguistics, sociolinguistics and discourse analysis, dominant discourses have traditionally emanated from the Inner Circle (mainly the United States, Britain, Australia). Accordingly, conceptualizations of language that are generally accepted tend to be those held in those parts of the world. The normalizing effect of these dominant discourses can be so powerful that even researchers who operate *within* a non-Inner Circle sociolinguistic environment may feel compelled to follow representations that are defined by a gaze originating from well outside that very environment. As Kumaravadivelu (2012, p. 17) notes, 'studies by periphery-based researchers on pragmatic (in)competence, that is, how EIL [English as an International Language] learners fail to perform certain speech acts in a way that is acceptable to the native-speaking community, are indeed numerous'. This can explain, for example, why Low adopts an American–British perspective in describing Singapore English.

Again, this coincides with Chakrabarty's analysis of what he sees as a paradoxical situation, in which scholars in non-Western regions of the world seem unable to shake off representations of those very regions emanating from the West:

> For generations now, philosophers and thinkers shaping the nature of social science have produced theories embracing the entirety of humanity. As we well know, these statements have been produced in relative, and sometimes absolute, ignorance of the majority of humankind – i.e., those living in non-Western cultures. This in itself is not paradoxical, for the more self-conscious of European philosophers have always sought theoretically to justify this stance. The everyday paradox of third-world social science is that *we* find these theories, in spite of their inherent ignorance of 'us', eminently useful in understanding our societies. (Chakrabarty, 1992, p. 3)

Finally, the tourist-like fascination with 'out-of-the-ordinary' features ultimately produces very partial descriptions. With reference to her 'revised' notion of Standard English, Gupta (2010) makes the point that too much emphasis has been put on differences while the overwhelming similarity has been downplayed:

> Sociolinguists have a choice whether to focus on shared features and uses of Standard English across the English-using world, or to focus on the differences. There are both political and linguistic issues here. We have spent too much time focussing on the rare features that distinguish the Standard English in one region form that in another, and too little time in the much more widespread features that unite Standard English all over the world. (Gupta, 2010, p. 60)

More in general, an exclusive focus on difference also creates a serious methodological problem. As Taylor cogently points out, there are two reasons for this:

> The first is simply that, by focussing on difference, we effectively create a 'blind spot'; this means that, rather than aiming for a 360-degree perspective of our data, we are actually starting out with the goal of achieving only a

180-degree visualisation. . . . [The second is] that by setting out to look at difference, the analyst is likely to find and report on difference. Such findings are potentially highly misleading as it may be that in quantitative terms. . . similarities. . . considerably outweigh. . . differences. (Taylor, 2013, p. 83)

So, while spotting the difference might be interesting or even exciting, setting it as a research aim can only lead to findings that ultimately don't tell us anything particularly useful. Achieving balance between what we may find interesting and what actually corresponds more closely to reality in the particular context of enquiry is a very common challenge in research. While no research can be said to take place in an ideological void, the very awareness that this is the case should at least encourage us to not shy away from the 360-perspective, especially in an area so vast and complex as that of World Englishes. If that challenge is not taken on, the very real risk is that we end up sketching pictures from a point where our view is deliberately obstructed and the resulting descriptions too partial, as shown, metaphorically, in Figure 4.1.

4.5   Spotting differences in ELF

Towards the beginning of the century the field of ELF began as a ramification of World Englishes and rapidly developed into a full-fledged research area, in which some of the main contributions include Jenkins (2000), Jenkins (2006a, 2006b, 2007, 2009a, 2013), Seidlhofer (2001), Seidlhofer (2004, 2006, 2009a, 2009b, 2011), Mauranen (2012), Mauranen and Ranta (2009), Kirkpatrick (2010a), Prodromou (2010), Dewey and Jenkins (2010), Jenkins et al. (2011), Cogo and Dewey (2012).

The 'official' start of ELF research can be said to have been marked by Barbara Seidlhofer's (2001) seminal article calling for the closing of a

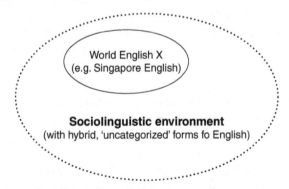

FIGURE 4.1 *A narrow view of world Englishes.*

'conceptual gap' between the descriptions of varieties of English available within the traditional World Englishes framework and a new analytical orientation that was necessary in order to document the uses of English as an international lingua franca.

Coming primarily from a pedagogical standpoint, Seidlhofer shared World Englishes scholars' preoccupation that learners of English around the world needed models that would be more culturally relevant for them than British or American English. She contended that somebody learning English in, say, continental Europe, or Japan, Brazil and so on should no longer have to acquire linguistic norms emanating from a very restricted set of socio-culturally distant locations. However, she also felt that, while British and American English didn't represent suitable pedagogical models, Outer-Circle varieties, with primarily intranational diffusion and roles, were equally inappropriate for learners in the Expanding Circle. An Italian learner of English, for example, wouldn't directly benefit from the availability of norms that apply to Singapore English or Indian English, which would be just as 'alien' as those that pertain to British English. Given the fact that such a learner is likely to be using English in international contexts with other people who don't share the same first language, the most suitable model would be one which reflects this specific function of English used as an international lingua franca.

It is for this reason that Seidlhofer advocated a description of ELF that would be as precise as possible – to establish what it looked and sounded like and then to codify it into an actual pedagogically sound model. In this sense, the research aims envisaged in her paper were explicitly complementary to, and built on, those in World Englishes, with which they shared the projection towards a full recognition of non-Inner Circle varieties of English, be them national or international. In the same way as national varieties of English were in the process of being codified, so too a form of international English needed to be codified.

The research agenda delineated by Seidlhofer was in part inspired by Jennifer Jenkins's (2000) pioneering work on the phonology of English as an international language. Jenkins's study had highlighted the fact that there were certain phonological features of English that were 'core' and affected intelligibility if pronounced differently and others that were 'non-core' and their mispronunciation wasn't problematic since meaning was easily recoverable from the context. This had pedagogical implications since it demonstrated that learners didn't have to focus their attention excessively (or not at all) on 'core' features and it wasn't necessary for them to make efforts to try and adhere to models such as RP of General American. So Seidlhofer intended to expand this same principle to vocabulary and grammar:

As a first research focus, it seems desirable to complement the work already done on ELF phonology and pragmatics by concentrating on lexico-grammar and discourse, in an investigation of what (if anything), notwithstanding all the diversity, might emerge as common features of ELF use, irrespective of speakers' first languages and levels of proficiency. (2001, p. 147)

It was thus important to describe the 'common core' of ELF to be able to arrive at a full model that would include phonological, lexical and grammatical norms that could be realistically alternative to British or American ones: 'What I propose, then, is . . . to explore the possibility of a codification of ELF with a conceivable ultimate objective of making it a feasible, acceptable and respected alternative to ENL [English as a Native Language] in appropriate contexts of use' (p. 150). Such a description would also provide clues as to how people should use English in international contexts:

anyone participating in international communication needs to be familiar with, and have in their linguistic repertoire for use, as and when appropriate, certain forms (phonological, lexicogrammatical, etc.) that are widely used and widely intelligible across groups of English speakers from different first language backgrounds. (Jenkins, 2006a, p. 161)

So, quite clearly, '[t]he early focus of ELF-oriented research was the sociolinguistic description of language forms (phonological, lexical, grammatical and pragmatic) of English in lingua franca interactions' (Cogo & Dewey, 2012, p. 2).

Methodologically, ELF research has historically employed corpus linguistics tools, the main idea being that it is only through the analysis of a sufficiently large dataset that one can reliably attain a description of features that are salient among ELF users. The VOICE (Vienna and Oxford International Corpus of English) was set up at the University of Vienna with precisely this aim (www.univie.ac.at/voice/). Similarly, the ELFA (ELF in Academic Settings) was created at the University of Helsinki (www.helsinki.fi/englanti/elfa/) with the more specific objective of describing features of English as an international academic language.

4.5.1   ELF versus ENL

Within that frame, the identification of linguistic features that are typical of ELF use follows the same comparative principle adopted for the identification of distinctive national varieties of English, in that Inner-Circle English is the benchmark against which such features are identified. Again, the same tension between 'feature' and 'error' is re-proposed:

ELF distinguishes between difference (i.e. from ENL) and deficiency (i.e. interlanguage or 'learner language'), and does not assume that an item that differs from ENL is by definition an error. It may instead be a legitimate ELF variant. (Jenkins, 2009a, p. 202)

This is a point that is repeated in virtually identical terms in most ELF publications. Cogo and Dewey (2012), for example, state that they 'regard variability away from English as a native language (ENL) in the expanding circle as a legitimate manifestation of the language, resulting in the emergence of innovative linguistic and pragmatic forms' (p. 19).

In this regard, with reference to findings in the early phases of research done on the VOICE corpus, Seidlhofer (2004) listed a number of such 'features'/'errors':

- Dropping the third person present tense -*s*

- Confusing the relative pronouns *who* and *which*

- Omitting definite and indefinite articles where they are obligatory in ENL, and inserting them where the do not occur in ENL

- Failing to use correct forms in tag questions (e.g., *isn't it?* or *no?* instead of *shouldn't they?*)

- Inserting redundant prepositions, as in *We have to study about . . .*

- Overusing certain verbs of high semantic generality, such as *do, have, make, put, take*

- Replacing infinitive constructions with that-clauses, as in *I want that*

- Overdoing explicitness (e.g. *black color* rather than just *black*) (Seidlhofer, 2004, p. 220)

The words 'confusing', 'omitting', 'failing' and so on clearly indicate a deficit here, although in a recent publication Jenkins (2013, p. 33) reveals that 'scare quotes . . . were mistakenly removed' by the publisher in the original paper. This is a significant point, not so much because it restores the truth about Seidlhofer's 'scepticism towards the pejorative terms' (p. 33), but because it confirms how quick and almost ineffable the semantic shift between 'error' and 'feature' is when the concept is so clearly based on departure from Inner-Circle norms.

Within this analytical frame, establishing the status of such departures isn't straightforward, as this 'depends on factors such as systematicity, frequency, and communicative effectiveness' (p. 33). Researchers, therefore, need to make decisions based on those factors and, inevitably, these will be an element of subjectivity: how frequently or systematically does an item need to occur before it can be 'upgraded' from error to feature status? How is communicative effectiveness measured from a point of view external to the context in which language is used?

In addition, this fine distinction is tied to another one: while it's important to stress that differences aren't necessarily errors, '[t]his does not mean, however, that all ELF speakers are proficient: they can also be learners of ELF or not fully competent non-learners, making errors just like learners of any second language' (Jenkins, 2009a, p. 202). So, this means that whether something is a 'feature' or not also depends on the status of the person who uses it: the more proficient they are, the more likely it is that they would use 'features' rather than make 'errors'. Of course, as I commented elsewhere (Saraceni, 2010, p. 96), determining ELF users' degree of proficiency is extremely problematic, especially if one considers the thorny issue of what might constitute 'full competence'.

In general, even if its speakers aren't taken as ideal models, the constant reference to 'ENL' produces a situation similar to the one described earlier regarding the focus on difference in the identification of national varieties of English. The analysis gets tangled in knots and the object of the analysis, be it ELF or world Englishes, struggles to breathe freely, as it were, suffocated by the perpetual comparison with ENL, Standard English and the 'ancestral home' of English. It must be said, however, that the research aims in ELF have changed over the last few years, in line with recent developments in sociolinguistics that are discussed more in detail in the next chapter. In particular, the emphasis on 'features' seems to have diminished, and 'ELF is not a variety of English with clearly demarcated formal linguistic properties to be set against some institutionalized norm of the so-called standard language, but as the variable exploitation of linguistic resources' (Seidlhofer, 2011, p. 110).

4.6   Conclusion

In this chapter, I have first of all recounted the genesis of the World Englishes framework and explained its egalitarian motives. I have subsequently critically discussed the emphasis of much World Englishes research on the identification of linguistic features that characterize differences between postcolonial varieties of English and those that are generally held as reference, that is, British English and American English. In doing so, I tried to point out the pitfalls in the 'spot the difference approach':

- it is difficult to reconcile the special emphasis devoted to difference in World Englishes with its general ethos which promotes equality;

- the distinction between 'error' and 'feature' is a very fine one and it is unclear who has the right to decide which is which or on what criteria are; ultimately, it is little more than a difference in name if both derive from a comparison of world Englishes to established varieties such as British and American English;

- this approach ends up excluding significant portions of language that is either to unremarkably familiar or simply too deviant to fit the 'variety' paradigm.

So, the question is: how can we move on from an analytical approach which (a) privileges difference defined in terms of departures from norms codified in distant socio-cultural settings and (b) disregards departures that are considered to be too distant from those very norms? One possible way forward is to be a little bolder about the localization of English around the world and be prepared to sever the umbilical cord between local manifestations of English and idealized notions of an 'ancestral home'. This proposition is taken into account in the next chapter.

Key reading

- The most comprehensive description of World Englishes as an academic and research field can be found in:
  Bolton, K. (2006). World Englishes Today. In B. Kachru, Y. Kachru & C. Nelson (Eds), *The Handbook of World Englishes* (pp. 240–269). Oxford: Blackwell.
  The Handbook also includes a range of chapters covering all the main aspects and issues in World Englishes.

- A more recent similar edited volume is:
  Kirkpatrick, A. (Ed.) (2010). *The Routledge Handbook of World Englishes*. London: Routledge.

- A good overview of English as a lingua franca is:
  Seidlhofer, B. (2011). *Understanding English as a Lingua Franca*. Oxford: Oxford University Press.

5

Untidying Englishes

I grew up in South Africa in a mixed family, well, with me being the mixed one in the family. My mother is a black woman . . . My father's Swiss. But they didn't care. . . . So they got together, and they had me, which was illegal. So I was born a crime.
TREVOR NOAH

Keywords

language hybridity • linguistic repertoire • metrolingualism • super-diversity • translanguaging

5.1 Introduction

In the previous chapter, I've highlighted how definitions, descriptions and analyses of varieties of English with respect to their deviations from 'standard English' are unsatisfactory for two main reasons. First of all, this approach isn't able to shake off the notion that such varieties are somewhat deficient, no matter how forcefully one declares that the opposite is the case. Secondly, this frame of analysis disallows all those instances of language practice which can't easily be categorized neatly into recognizable varieties of English.

In this chapter, I begin to examine alternative approaches to the study of localized Englishes which attempt to gain useful distance from the concept of norms that are 'standard' in contexts far removed from where language practice takes place.

5.2　Cutting the umbilical cord with the ancestral home

The question is: if Singapore English is a fully 'transplanted' English, with roots in its own soil, how much work is necessary before it (or any other world English) can be analysed independently? With reference to his Dynamic Model (see Section 3.2.5), Schneider (2007, p. 160) contends that 'Singapore has clearly reached phase 4 of the cycle', which is the 'endonormative stabilization'. The question, then, seems to be a particularly relevant one.

It must be noted, however, that Schneider's assessment isn't universally accepted. L. Tan (2011), for example, openly disagrees with it and points out how Singapore English 'has clearly not developed its own norms' (p. 6). In his article, L. Tan identifies a series of grammatical, lexical and syntactical 'divergences' from Standard English found in the national press and concludes that these 'non-standardisms' should however be seen as 'features' of Singapore English rather than 'errors', for a number of reasons: (a) it is normal for varieties of English to differ from one another, just as American English and British English do, (b) features of 'New Varieties of English' tend to regularize the complex and often illogical grammar and syntax of English, (c) such 'non-standardisms' don't impede comprehensibility but (d) they, instead, contribute to forming a national linguistic identity (pp. 16–17). L. Tan therefore hopes that such features become officially recognized and codified so that Singapore English 'ceases to look elsewhere for its own norms' (p. 18). The argument, however, is still fundamentally entrenched in the old 'spot the difference' approach, and the issue is still the same: there seems to be a contradiction in wanting to establish endonormativity and linguistic autonomy on the basis of incessant reference to the very norms from which such independence is sought.

An additional problem is that as long as exonormative models continue to be the framework for the analysis of linguistic data pertaining to world Englishes, discussions of research findings can never go beyond trying to fit such data within those external models. It is, in many ways, the same situation in which the grammar of English has been for centuries described within the framework of Latin grammar and not fully on its own terms. This has produced very awkward 'rules' that forbid things like 'split infinitives' or 'ending sentences with prepositions'. But infinitives may be regarded as 'split' only from the point of view of languages in which they are expressed by single words. From the point of view of English, the notion of a 'split infinitive' is nonsensical, since infinitives are expressed via *two* words: *to* plus the base form of the verb. There is absolutely nothing remarkable about that. It's only a 'feature' if judged from the point of view of Latin. The invention that there should never be any intervening word between *to* and the base form originates from trying to force one language into the shape of another.

Describing Singapore English, or any other world English, on the basis of the norms of another variety ultimately leads to the same results. All one is able to do is ponder over dilemmas about the bits that don't seem to fit in the frame too well: are they 'errors' or 'features'? Also the most radical option available is to say that they're 'features'.

Additionally, there is often a certain degree of uncertainty about the status of such 'features'. Deterding (2007), for example, notes how, in his findings, '[m]any of the features that are discussed are ones that sometimes occur, but there is no suggestion that they are always found' (p. 12) and provides a possible explanation for this:

> The indeterminate occurrence of some of the features may partly arise because of the emergent status of Singapore English: it is still developing into a mature variety with its own standards which have yet to become fully established, and this may result in an extra element of instability. (Deterding, 2007, p. 12)

So, the only logical possibility envisaged within this frame of analysis is that if observed features don't seem to be stable enough, that's because the variety itself isn't yet stable enough.

In a paper presented at the 18th Conference of the International Association for World Englishes, Alsagoff (2012) made precisely this point and set out to demonstrate that the perception of 'seemingly inconsistent patterns of use of certain grammatical forms' in Singapore English is the result of the 'incorrect assumption that the grammars of new Englishes are organized along the same grammatical principles as those of standard varieties . . . when in fact other underlying patterns prevail'. So she posited that 'new Englishes must be examined as autonomous linguistic codes in their own right'.

In her paper, Alsagoff analysed three aspects of Singapore English grammar: (i) nouns and noun phrases, (ii) patterns of past tense marking and (iii) caretaker constructions. In this regard, she showed how patterns that looked inconsistent were actually not so, but was, instead, simply following different sets of rules. Nouns and noun phrases, for example, were considered in terms of the use of the suffix -s to mark plurality and the use of determiners. So, in Singapore English, words like *furniture, luggage* and *equipment* sometimes take the -s suffix to mark plurality and other times they don't.

If we attempt to force the description of grammatical patterns of SgE into the frame of British English, words like *furnitures, luggages, equipments* will be among the bits of language that don't quite fit, unlike the singular versions of the same words, which would fit more comfortably. The presence of both singular and plural will be taken as evidence of instability. That's because in British English, as well as in many other Englishes, a distinction is made between countable and uncountable nouns and so, if judged on this basis, marking the plural in a word like *furniture* would be seen as an 'error', 'feature', 'deviation', 'non-standardism' and so on.

However, if we examine this independently, namely if we disregard the (un-)countable 'rule' completely, then we open up new possibilities for analysis that takes the autonomy of Singapore English more seriously. So, Alsagoff shows that the SgE rule is that nouns and noun phrases are marked as plural or not depending on whether they are specified or general. That is what underlies the following two examples:

> All our *furnitures* are on sale this Christmas (specified)
>
> Cheap and good *furniture* is not easy to find (general)

This rule governs the use of number (singular or plural) regardless of countability, and applies to the following other two examples too:

> Some of my *customers* wait five minutes (specified)
>
> Offer valid for new female *customer* only (general)

Adopting the same approach, Alsagoff examines the other aspects of the grammar of Singapore English mentioned earlier and shows the local rules that underpin grammatical patterns. This represents an important step away from traditional comparative methods which constantly debate over 'errors' or 'features', and towards a type of analysis where world Englishes are more seriously examined in their localities.

This new approach, in turn, entails new and exciting challenges. One of them involves re-visiting the relationship between English and the languages that it coexists with.

5.3 Dealing with English and other languages

So far, this has been predominantly been considered within the 'contact' frame, within which the main tenet is that world Englishes have developed distinctive features largely as a result of the influence exercised onto them by substrate languages (page 82). According to this paradigm, some of the characteristics of local languages have 'transferred' into English and manifest themselves in phonological, lexical, grammatical, syntactic and discourse patterns.

So, for example, one of the most visible forms of such influence is the regular use in world Englishes of certain lexical items coming from local languages. Traditionally, such words are called 'borrowings' or 'loanwords'. In the case of Singapore English, *kiasu* is one of the many loanwords that are used routinely by virtually all speakers, in all contexts. The word refers to the attitude of people who are obsessed with succeeding in everything they do and are equally obsessively frightened of failure. 'Kiasu parents', for example, would be those who want their children to always be the best at, for example, school, learning to play musical instruments and so on. Here's a short passage from a letter written to Singapore's national newspaper *The Straits Times*:

> Come the school holidays, it is not difficult to spot a Singaporean family overseas. Just witness the telltale sign of kiasu parents lugging along an assessment book or two for junior to dutifully complete during any down time. (Koh, 2012)

One interesting question, and one that I always ask students taking my World Englishes course, is whether or not *kiasu* is an English word. The reason why I ask it is because out of such a seemingly simple 'yes/no' question, a more profound and more philosophical discussion often ensues. Generally, none of my students will have ever seen the word, which will appear decidedly 'strange' and 'un-English' to them. So, their first interpretation tends to be that it is a 'foreign' word that has found its way into an otherwise English text – a word that has been 'borrowed' from another language.

5.3.1 *Borrowing words?*

Indeed, *borrowing* is a classic concept in sociolinguistics, which describes the process in which a 'bit' of one language is replicated in another. The 'bit' is often a word or phrase, but it can also be an element of phonology, grammar or syntax.

However, there is a great deal of uncertainty and disagreement over the exact nature of a 'borrowing'. First of all, the term is 'semantically misleading from the start, since it implies that the source language relinquishes a form in lending it temporarily to the target language, which is expected to return the form later' (Heath, 2001, p. 432; the same problem has been discussed in sociolinguistics for a long time, see, e.g. Hockett, 1958, p. 402). Secondly, and more importantly, 'there is by no means any clear consensus as to how borrowing should be defined' (Winford, 2010, p. 170).

In an effort to disambiguate the term, some distinctions have been made, for example, between 'borrowing' and 'imposition' (see Van Coetsem, 1988) and between 'borrowing' and 'code-switching' (see Heath, 2001). In the first distinction, while a 'borrowing' is a kind of transfer that takes place into a speaker's first language, the concept of 'imposition' has been introduced in order to describe cases in which 'the speaker . . . transfers features of the [source language] into the [recipient language] *in which the speaker is less proficient'* (Winford, 2010, p. 171, my emphasis). 'Imposition', therefore, typically involve language learners who transfer features of their first languages into a language that they are in the process of learning.

The second distinction is more a matter of degrees: while a 'borrowing' is a single item that becomes part of a 'host' language, code-switching has more to do with situations where speakers quite literally 'switch' between one language and another during the same instance of communication. As Heath (2001, p. 433) explains:

> a borrowing is (ideally) a historically transferred form, usually a word (or lexical stem), that has settled comfortably into the target language, while code-switching is (ideally) a spontaneous, clearly bounded switch from sentences of one language to sentences of another, affecting all levels of linguistic structure simultaneously.

However, Heath also notes that 'borrowing and code-switching are not always so clearly distinct', precisely because the terminological opposition is a graded one: 'borrowings may resemble code-switches in retaining a foreign status and/or a discernible internal structure, while code-switches often resemble borrowings in brevity (words, short phrases) and in being fitted into another language's syntax'.

Additionally, 'settled comfortably' and 'spontaneous' don't represent easily measurable dimensions. How long does an item need to be used in a language before it can achieve the 'borrowing' status? Also, can it ever become so established as to qualify as a full member of the recipient language, without being considered a 'borrowing' anymore? If so, how does that happen? If we accept, for example, that '"money" is a thirteenth-century borrowing from French' (Heath, 2001, p. 433) and that 'English has borrowed *face* and *river* from French and *give*, *shy*, and even the pronoun *they* from Old Norse' (Millar, 2007, pp. 27–28), where do we draw the line between words that have been borrowed and those that haven't? Similarly, what are the criteria for spontaneity in the use of chunks of two different languages in the same piece of discourse for the practice to be regarded as 'code-switching'? Most importantly, who decides what the answers to these questions are?

The idea that certain words have entered Language A coming from Language B is underpinned by the LANGUAGE IS A CONTAINER metaphor (see Section 2.4.4). The statement that 'well over half of the words in [the dictionary] are taken from other languages' (Millar, 2007, p. 22) allows for considerable communication between 'containers' and doesn't challenge, but actually reinforces, the metaphor as well as the view of language as bounded system in which the metaphor itself is firmly grounded.

But if over half of the words in English really come from other languages, this presents a paradox: on what basis can the language continue to be called

'English'? Perhaps, it could be said that the identity of a language is given by its syntactic structure rather than by its vocabulary. But then even from this point of view the argument doesn't hold, since the 'English language' has undergone radical structural changes through its history, especially if we accept, for a moment, the notion of the 'unbroken history' of English discussed in Chapter 2 which places the 'origins' of the language with the arrival of the 'Anglo-Saxons'. The only way in which the paradox can be resolved is by taking the container metaphor very seriously indeed.

A language, that is, needs to be understood as an actual material place, a physical space, which encloses a collection of words. But what, exactly, is this space? The following citation is revealing:

> The vocabulary of English is not an unchanging list of words. New words enter the language every day, words acquire or lose meanings, and words cease to be used. The online *Oxford English Dictionary* (*OED*) is updated quarterly with at least 1,000 new and revised entries. (Stockwell & Minkova, 2009, p. 5)

Quite clearly, the *OED* represents that space. The dictionary that I've already referred to as the ultimate repository of English sets the boundaries of the language by concurrently de- and pre-scribing its code.

At one point in the discussion with my students about the status of *kiasu*, I tell them, anticipating the pleasure in seeing their surprised reactions, that the word can be found in the online *OED*. This crucial piece of information puzzles them, unsettles their points of view and makes them reconsider their initial opinions regarding the question: is *kiasu* an English word? Gupta (2010, pp. 70–71) sees the inclusion of *kiasu* in the *OED* as an important step for the word in its becoming fully part of Standard English (a stage that will be attained, in her view, when *kiasu* is no longer used exclusively with reference to Singapore or Singaporeans). She also suggests that 'the agency of standardization is obscure' (p. 71). Indeed, this is a crucial point.

Agency is often attributed to language itself or to elements of it. The word *language* routinely appears as the subject of material processes (physical actions) expressed through verbs like *evolve*, *vary*, *change*, *move*, and so on while human agency tends to be obscured. When people *are* mentioned, they tend to be referred to as members of specific groups defined by the languages they speak. In this way, they are 'speakers of Language A' or 'speakers of Language B', who perhaps take words from each others' languages. So, it is more common to discuss, as I initially do with my students, whether or not a word like *kiasu* may have 'entered' the English language, than to talk about what people *do* when they use that word.

The exchange of words between languages is then a fascinating area of enquiry, which sheds light into the ways vocabulary items 'travel' through time and space, reveals irresistibly intriguing facts about their tortuous itineraries and lends itself well to a conception of linguistics as measurable accumulation of information about language(s). However, what happens if we abandon the view of languages as enclosed spaces? If we operate the switch from *language as bounded system* to *language as social practice* that recurs throughout this book, the entire phenomenon of borrowing and loaning words and switching between languages can be seen from a radically different point of view. Can the question of whether or not *kiasu* is an English word be answered by explaining its irrelevance?

5.3.2   *Language across borders*

In order to begin to explain the irrelevance of deciding whether or not *kiasu* is an English word, I ask my students to consider the following two passages taken years ago from the Thai newspaper *Bangkok Post*:

1   Police said yesterday they could find no motive for the killing but said that Mr Prapruet had a minor wife who lived in the same soi as his family

2   Offering food to the monks in the morning so that they are able to eat makes sense from any perspective, but what about the custom of placing food in front of Buddha images for the images to eat? Viewed from the scientific standpoint it seems odd, but it is part of the Thai system of Buddhist religious beliefs. Most Thais see it as an important opportunity to make merit for the household.

I initially ask similar questions about *minor wife* and *soi* from the first extract and *make merit* from the second extract. Are they English? At this point, my students tend to be more hesitant, so I steer the discussion towards a more productive approach, namely to see how these expressions are used. I usually tell them that *soi* is just another way to say *street*. Regarding the other two phrases, the small amount of context in the two passages provides some initial clues about their uses, and this can be complemented by concordance lines (Tables 5.1 and 5.2) extracted from the latest, and probably the largest, English corpus available, called *enTenTen*, which can be accessed through the SketchEngine web interface (www.sketchengine.co.uk). About *minor wife*, the concordance lines clarify that it is used to indicate a sort of 'secondary', younger wife, mainly with reference to Thai society or ancient Egypt. In Buddhist societies people are said to *make merit* when they perform some especially good, more or less ritualistic, deeds that would earn them better chances of attaining liberation through a series of incarnations.

TABLE 5.1 Concordances for 'minor wife'

when I get a raise I should get a mia noi (**minor wife**) and set her up in an apartment . . . but

II, who had a son, Thutmose III, by a **minor wife** . When Thutmose II died in 1479 B.C. his

II was the son of Thutmose III and a **minor wife** , Hatshepsut-Meryetre . Amenhotep was

fact that he was the son of Pharaoh by a **minor wife** may well accord with the Bible record that

the risk that he will take on a mia noi, a **minor wife**). Since prostitution in Thailand acts as

a minor. The victim was the defendant's **minor wife** from an arranged marriage, which is common

died prematurely, Thutmosis' son by a **minor wife** , was legitimised by marriage to his half

resources! April 4, 2007 Fill out as **minor wife** scholarship strategies as you can find,

is appeased and worshipped. She was a **minor wife** of a Shan king whose magic powers frightened

favorite daughter of the ChaoKhun and a **minor wife** , both whom passed out from the picture

will frequently keep a 'mia noi' (**minor wife**)on the side and set her up in an apartment

course, no wealthy man would even take a **minor wife** who was not a virgin. The minor wife bit

a minor wife who was not a virgin. The **minor wife** bit came into fashion when polygamy went

that included Smenkhkare, his son (by a **minor wife**) and son-in-law, and Tutankhaten, his nephew

Plot: Calvino agrees to follow the " **minor wife** " of a Thai politician and report on her

impose a severer punishment for rape on a **minor wife** . 3. If the Parliament considers it

made it acceptable to have a major wife, **minor wife** , a formalized mistress, and hostess or

His mother Tiy had also died as did his **minor wife** , Kia. That combined with the loss of his

was son of either Akhenaten himself by a **minor wife** , or possibly his father Amenhotep III.

to a customer, at least to become a " **minor wife** ".They are considered a degree above bar

TABLE 5.2 Concordances for 'make merit'

their people, they should not be allowed to **make merit** and wipe their crimes away. As we marched

officials and local people turned out to **make merit** by offering monks food and alms. Tak Bat

Others will visit their local temple to **make merit** either on New Year's Eve or New Year's

go to the temple early in the morning to **make merit** . Then they will be back in the evening

a large Buddha's footprint. Local people **make merit** by giving flowers to the monks. The flower

time out to visit their local temples to **make merit** and also to pour rose scented water over

also go to their local temple to pray and **make merit** for dead ancestors. The ashes of these

with little thought apart from the need to **make merit** . However, others pull out all the stops

food to give to the monks in order to **make merit** . Strictly speaking, to make the most merit

hoping that the Buddhists will also want to **make merit** by giving some spare change to them. Not

the monk to come over so that they could **make merit** . Some of the monks had people rowing for

needed to build a place where persons could **make merit** and learn the teachings of the Buddha.

become less noisy, firstly, you need to **make merit** by doing good deeds for others this

patience, time, effort and generous action to **make merit** , and a sacrifice – the sacrifice of one

effect), and the good causes one has made to **make merit** , it is possible to understand and make

interest in the Dhamma. People also came to **make merit** on Monday and Tuesday and they included

holiday people attend their local temples to **make merit** and perform Wian Tian, a candlelit

gathered in the early morning of 1st January to **make merit** in an annual religious ceremony attended

against all profanity, or from the attempt to **make merit** out of what should have been the free

that it would be possible to enjoy wealth & **make merit** . What if I were to disavow the training

From a classic World Englishes perspective, the regular presence of such words and phrases in English-language texts in Thailand is seen as evidence of an emerging Thai English. More specifically, according to traditional classifications, *soi* would be an example of 'borrowing' and *minor wife* and *make merit* would be examples of 'imposition'. Trakulkasemsuk (2012, p. 103), for example, says that Thai people's variety of English 'shows some distinctive characteristics which have been transferred from their first language background, culture, rhetorical styles, and norms of communication' and describes 'several common language contact processes affecting ThaiE, namely transfer, translation, shift, lexical borrowing, hybridization and reduplication'.

All of this not only presupposes the retention of clear borders between languages, but also sets its own boundaries on two levels. First of all, the identification of a local variety of English draws a demarcation line within the local linguistic repertoire: some of it is English, some of it isn't. Secondly, a variety of English called 'Thai English' is set apart from other similarly labelled Englishes, and another border is thus erected between this variety of English and all the others. I will now discuss these two types of divisions.

5.3.3   *English and non-English*

The identification of 'Thai English' as an emerging variety of English establishes that in the local linguistic repertoire some uses of language are 'in English' and some others aren't. Importantly, what earns such manifestations of 'English' the attribute 'Thai' is the presence of precisely the kinds of words and phrases mentioned earlier. For example, in an article he wrote for the *Bangkok Post*, Bolton (2003b) talked about the rising number of Asian people using English to communicate with one another and noted how '[w]hen they do this they may borrow words and expressions from their own languages'. With particular reference to Thai English, he brought to the readers' attention the fact that the compilers of the *Macquarie Dictionary* were in the process of adding words such as *acharn* ('university teacher'), *farang* ('a foreigner of European ethnic origin'), *klong* ('canal'), *sanuk* ('fun') and many more as items to be labelled 'Thai English'.

So, effectively, what happens is that certain Thai words 'make it' into 'Thai English' and this is, ironically, codified by the compilers of an Australian dictionary. One immediate question, however, is: how many Thai words are allowed to enter 'Thai English' before it ceases to be 'English' altogether? Let's consider the following snippets of language produced by the same person on an online social network:

1   very nice, I love it

2   never change na!

3 Perfect Mom มั้ย

4 Happy birthday คุณอาด้วยค่ะ

5 cheesecake ที่ banyan tree เทียบกับของผี่ สุไม่ได้ชักนิ้ด

6 ถ้าขอแนไปซื้ออหมวก shut down ที่เวที่อโศก แมจะให้ไปมั้ยนภาาา

Such a small amount of language generates a string of questions. Which ones of these would qualify as 'Thai English'? Does the use of Thai characters make a difference? Is this a speaker of 'Thai English'? In the classic World Englishes framework, line 2 would be most likely to be considered a good example of 'Thai English', as it is very recognizably English but has a certain Thai 'flavour' given by the particle *na*, while more orthodox linguists might even comment on the 'absence' of the subject *you*, which might be seen as an additional Thai ingredient. What about line 1? Is it not sufficiently Thai, perhaps? Are items 3, 4 and 5 *too* Thai, as they include words in Thai script? Are they, therefore, disqualified? Who is to decide, and on what criteria? Intelligibility is sometimes invoked as a possible test, but the problem doesn't really go away: whose intelligibility? It is reasonable to assume that the participants in the particular social activity of which the small extracts of language earlier are part understand each other perfectly well. That's because they are drawing from a pool of linguistic resources that they share. So, should intelligibility be measured by someone outside the instances of communication under scrutiny? Even so, the variables are still too many to control. Different individuals may have different backgrounds, mental schemata, experiences or also pre-conceived ideas as to what counts as intelligibility. In addition, the exercise would be a very artificial one due to the utter unnaturalness of 'guessing' the meaning of de-contextualized chunks of language and their correct amount of Thainess. Within this frame, the question of whether or not *soi* or *minor wife* is 'in English' or 'in Thai' clearly loses significance. So, another way of looking at the same phenomenon is to abandon the idea that languages have pre-fixed boundaries. Instead of necessarily thinking in terms of separate, bounded languages which allow the 'intrusion' of sporadic 'foreign' elements that are otherwise untranslatable, we can think of shared linguistic repertoires made up of linguistic resources that people draw from in their daily activities. Instead of imagining words travelling from one well-defined language into another, we could see them simply as part of a large pool of linguistic resources that people have at their disposal as they carry out those activities.

If we adopt such a perspective, languages as enumerable discrete entities don't matter so much anymore. In Bangkok, people refer to streets as *soi* because that's the most common way of doing so in the shared linguistic repertoire, and it doesn't matter whether a piece of discourse is 'in English' or 'in Thai'. *Soi* is standard, while saying *street* would sound awkward and foreign – it would be marked as a sign of unfamiliarity with the context or it would *index* (Blommaert, 2005) foreignness. Similarly, expressions such as *minor wife* and *make merit* are entirely standard in the same context. Alternative forms, for example, 'secondary wife', 'concubine', 'mistress' for *minor wife* or 'do good' for *make merit*, would be not only unnecessary but also fundamentally misleading and, again, awkward (see also L. E. Smith, 2009, p. 22).

A shared linguistic repertoire is much more fluid and border-less than the rather artificial concept of 'a language'. Crucially, also, it is very flexible, as its scope as well as its content depends on the participants, real or envisaged, and how they negotiate it in each individual act of communication. In other words, a shared linguistic repertoire isn't an entity that exists a priori to speakers, but is something that is dynamically defined *by* speakers as they engage in various social activities. In fact, the term 'speaker' itself is inherited from the language-as-system stance. Linguists tend to see people primarily as 'speakers', often *of* this or that language, in a rather crude, ad-hoc characterization which presupposes that the act of speaking is people's primary function, divorced from social practice. But if we see language as part of social practice, we're forced to take a different perspective. Let's consider the brief exchange between two Thai friends, whom I'll refer to by the names of Fon and Nut, on the same online social network, shown in Figure 5.1.

███████ ███████ Why you take your picture alway beside ?
June 27, 2013 at 3:44pm · 👍 5

███ ██████ Because it looks good than the reality , ha ha ha
June 27, 2013 at 3:45pm · 👍 5

███████ ███████ Oh I see .
June 27, 2013 at 3:45pm · 👍 2

███ ██████ เชิด เกือบสวย แต่ไม่หยิ่งค่ะ 5555
June 27, 2013 at 3:46pm · 👍 2

███████ ███████ เป็นงัย เจอภาษาปะกิด ของ วิตวะ เช้าใจก่อ
June 27, 2013 at 3:46pm · 👍 1

███ ██████ I do understand kaaa ha ha ha
June 27, 2013 at 3:46pm · 👍 1

███████ ███████ Geschätzter Freund
June 27, 2013 at 3:49pm · 👍 1

███ ██████ Du bist auch mein Freund !
June 27, 2013 at 3:51pm

FIGURE 5.1 *How many languages?*

What language are these two individuals 'speakers' of? Are they multilingual? Maybe but, again, this short dialogue can be considered from a different viewpoint. Rather than trying to decide what Fon and Nut *are* with regard to the languages they *speak*, we could focus on what they are *doing*. In which case we can say that they are chatting and reinforcing their friendship and, in doing so, they are making use of linguistic and other semiotic resources they share. Some of these can be given recognizable names: 'Thai', 'English', 'German'. Language purists might perhaps even feel compelled to remark on the 'quality' of the 'English' on display here, but their comments would be out of place, since there is no evidence that the social activity in question has been in any way impeded by non-compliance to the 'rules' codified in grammar books. At the same time, one could speculate that the use of German, not a widely used language in Thailand, might be a conscious attempt of the two friends to exhibit their cosmopolitanism, modernity, education, sophistication and so on but that is a conjecture that falls outside the scope of this discussion. What is important is that, regardless of the labels we may choose to affix to bits of their dialogue – 'Thai', 'English', 'German' – Fon and Nut are exploiting *their own* linguistic repertoire. Their chatting is multilingual or hybrid only to the extent that we, from our external point if view, consider it to be so.

5.3.4   *Switching languages?*

Or, again from a point of view which insists on seeing language as divided up into separate entities, the extracts seen in this section could be called examples of code-switching, which Muysken (2011, pp. 301–302) defines as 'the use of more than one language during a single communicative event'. Despite the straightforward definition, Muysken immediately adds that '[s]ince many switches in a sentence involve a single word, a major difficulty is how to distinguish code-switching from borrowing' (p. 302) and, after reviewing a number of criteria that are generally adopted in drawing a distinction between the two phenomena, comes to the conclusion that 'it is virtually impossible to distinguish code-switching from bilingual borrowing' and asks: 'do we really want to?' (p. 303).

Indeed, the notion of people 'switching' languages is too neat and doesn't quite capture what goes on in the dialogue between Fon and Nut. There seems to be more seamless mixing than switching and, additionally, the two friends in the dialogue also use other semiotic resources at their disposal. The elongated 'ka' represents the way this particle is often pronounced by Thai people at the end of utterances. The use of multiple '5' symbols is standard among Thai young people to represent laughter, as the Thai word for *five* sounds like 'ha'.

Seargeant et al. (2012) investigated the linguistic behaviour of Thai students on the same social network and, in particular, on their use of English alongside Thai. One of their aims was to gain an insight into '[w]hat motivates switches between the two languages' (p. 511). Having thus started from a relatively traditional frame of analysis, it is significant that they came to the conclusion that 'to the participants involved, their language use is less about choosing to switch from one language system to another, but rather about drawing in various ways on a shared set of semiotic resources' (p. 528).

If code-switching is an inadequate representation of the language practice under scrutiny, the concept of 'Thai English' is even more ill-equipped to deal with it. 'Thai English' requires a degree of stability and uniformity that is obviously at odds with this kind of language. This is the reason why the sources of data illustrating varieties of English tends to be texts from newspapers, novels and so on, and, if spoken interactions are included, they typically involve 'educated' speakers in situations where English isn't *too* mixed with other languages, thus ensuring that the language analysed is sufficiently 'clean' and 'features' can be spotted in relative comfort.

In this way, however, the scope of investigation is considerably restricted. Such a limitation is even more evidently the case in settings with a colonial past (Thailand was never colonized) and where, consequently, English has had more time to amalgamate within the local repertoire. The three texts in the Table 5.3 below were taken from the same online social network. Here, the participants are Malaysian, and it is evident how Malay and English are so tightly amalgamated that it becomes impossible to separate them from one another.

TABLE 5.3 Language Amalgam

TEXT 1	
A:	Ejaat . . . Off topic. Hafizul masuk newspaper eh? Haha
B:	Haha x sure. But da pernah masok da dulu. U mean today's npaper?
A:	Dok bc newspaper kosmo smlm. Then ada page nasi arab. Trigt d arab cafe. Zoom in sikit eh hafizul tersenyum berbaju putih haha
B:	Hahaha oh really? didnt know that. Haih bila la nak dapat berlegoland dgn uols
A:	Haha . . . ada . . . ada. Feels like knowing a celebrity plk :)) tc apens, eeiiihh

TEXT 2	
A:	ni yang hari tu korang nak tngok tak dapat ^^ lol misai is shaved!
B:	Haha . . . sound tu yg aku menyirap tu aritu . . . nk tdo pon susah
C:	Haha shave jugakkk finally ^^
D:	hahahahahhaha! made my day
E:	with or without the moustache, you look like snoop dogg
F:	the sound of shaver klakar gile. siap boleh break2 tu last2
G:	menyirap aku denga musik background tu . . .
H:	hahaha . . .NICE!!
I:	Haha . . . I'm trying to imagine if this vid is played backwards . . . Nway semua ok . . . Except for the two 'Tocangs' (>.<) lol
J:	ko nak aku share video ko nih keh? nanti trending kat facebook plak!
K:	rambut kau xle bla ==" haha but it was a cool vid haha
L:	haahaha siriyes! nice video (^_^)

TEXT 3	
A:	*B* has the pemantau come to ur school yet?
B:	Yeah . . . He told me to get BM tuition from *A* XP
A:	ur pemantau very cekap la bro . . . hahahaha . . . hws png bro? is *C* still fetching u with ur abm all??
B:	Nah bro . . . But I hear he smoke and Fly . . . *C*
A:	smoke and fly hahahahahahahaa . . .
C:	sometimes only la *B*. cannot always fly. nnti kna hijack
A:	hijack ka?? hahaha . . . hijack ngan bini je la brooo . . . *B* dun work too hard in ur school
B:	I tak work hard bro . . . I think I'm the one with paling kurang tugas . . . setakat ini,,,
A:	relak *B* . . . after tis u mmg work hard la . . . wei i come png i roger u la

In Text 1, two friends are chatting jokingly about a common friend who has appeared in a newspaper, in Text 2 several friends are commenting on a photograph that one of them posted showing his recently shaven moustache, while in Text 3 a group of friends are sharing their experiences as their teaching careers have just begun. From a linguistic point of view, these certainly aren't just a matter of code-switching, as the points where the participants 'switch' between languages, especially, in Text 1, aren't always obvious, or the 'switches' are simply too frequent to be understood in these terms. From an outsider's point of view, these may therefore appear to be examples in which English is mixed with another language, something that is often called *code-mixing*, or *code meshing* as Canagarajah (2006) and Young et al. (2014) prefer to call it. Code-mixing may be, to some extent, 'messier' than code-switching, the main difference between the two being that 'mixing' involves the use of two codes *within* the same utterance/sentence while 'switching' occurs *between* utterances/sentences.

But it can be argued that even 'code-mixing' (or 'meshing') may be inadequate in describing the language being used here. It is evident that the concept of 'English' as a separate code is simply not tenable, as there are no obvious reasons why the friends in the three Texts would choose to use two separate codes together in such a way which exhibits no recognizable patterns. Words, both lexical and grammatical, to which we may still attach the labels 'English' and 'Malay' are used in a level of *togetherness* that escapes systematic descriptions. In order to deal with this degree of linguistic amalgam, therefore, we have to resort to a different paradigm. To this end, language *hybridity* has been invoked in recent years, and a discussion on this concept can take us to the kind of terrain where the World Englishes framework can usefully and healthily re-generate.

5.4   Delving deeper into language hybridity

Hybridity goes beyond the idea of two (or more) codes being switched, mixed or meshed, by questioning the usefulness of positing language boundaries when describing situations such as those in the Table 5.3. In a recent collection entirely dedicated to the subject, Rubdy and Alsagoff (2013, p. 9) contend that 'hybridity is a helpful concept because it provides a profoundly reflexive perspective in transcending binary categories'.

However, the term is not necessarily a straightforward one. In the introductory chapter to their volume, Rubdy and Alsagoff identify – and negotiate – potential problems with the concept. One of them relates to a fundamental question posed by Hutnyk (2005, p. 81): 'to what degree does the assertion of hybridity rely on the positing of an anterior 'pure' that precedes mixture?' The point being that describing something as 'hybrid' doesn't sufficiently move away from the idea of two or more non-hybrid entities being mixed together, since 'the notion of hybridization does not resolve the problematic of a coded, discrete entity, because it is predicated on an assumption that there exist two distinct codes or separate entities which are combined' (Makoni, 2011, p. 683).

In the same vein, two of the chapters in the collection underline the inability of 'hybridity' to fully supplant the essentialist paradigm that sees language as separated into individual bounded systems, since 'it as a given that languages are discrete identifiable entities' (Saraceni, 2013, p. 192) and is an idea which is 'always looking backwards, always invoking precisely those essential categories that it aims to supersede' (Otsuji & Pennycook, 2013, p. 83). For this reason, Otsuji and Pennycook turn hybridity back to front:

> . . . it is not so much that languages . . . exist in isolation only to become hybrid when they come into contact under particular circumstances, but rather that their prior separation was always a strange artifact of particular ways of thinking. Hybridty, therefore, if we wish to use this term, needs to be seen as the unmarked starting point, the place of difference from which things emerge, rather than the endpoint towards which things converge. (p. 84)

Seen from this point of view, it can be said that the participants in the interactions in the Table 5.3 are *not* using two codes at all. 'English' and 'Malay', at least in this instance of communication (and many others!), cease to be separate languages altogether and are simply part of *one* shared set of linguistic resources, which also includes conventions of online discourse (with economical spellings, emoticons, etc.). In this sense, the way these groups of friends make use of their shared linguistic repertoire is not at all different from what other people do when they use only one named language ('Malay', 'English', 'Thai', etc.).

This is the kind of linguistic interactions that Otsuji and Pennycook describe as 'unremarkable' and 'unmarked', to highlight how they are eminently pervasive in situations of *metrolingualism*, a useful concept which, in an earlier paper, they define in the following way:

> Metrolingualism describes the ways in which people of different and mixed backgrounds use, play with and negotiate identities through language; it does not assume connections between language, culture, ethnicity, nationality or geography, but rather seeks to explore how such relations are produced, resisted, defied or rearranged; its focus is not on language systems but on languages as emergent from contexts of interaction. (Otsuji & Pennycook, 2010, p. 246)

The scenarios that Otsuji and Pennycook refer to are typical of urban settings – hence the prefix *metro*-– and are congruent with the notion of 'super-diversity' that Vertovec's uses in order to describe multi-layered and intersecting types of social diversities that exist especially in metropolitan areas such as London, where very diverse groups of migrants live. 'Super-diversity' goes beyond terms like 'multicultural', 'multiethnic' and 'multilingual', where the prefix *multi*- is insufficient to capture the interconnected nature of the many variables involved in this type of diversity, such as:

country of origin comprising a variety of possible subset traits such as ethnicity, language(s), religious tradition, regional and local identities, cultural values and practices

migration channel often related to highly gendered flows and specific social networks

legal status determining entitlement to rights

migrants' human capital particularly educational background

access to employment which may or may not be in immigrants' hands

locality related especially to material conditions, but also the nature and extent of other immigrant and ethnic minority presence

transnationalism emphasizing how migrants' lives are lived with significant reference to places and peoples elsewhere

the usually chequered responses by local authorities, services providers and local residents, which often tend to function by way of assumptions based on previous experiences with migrants and ethnic minorities. (Adapted from Vertovec, 2007, p. 1049, 2010, p. 87)

Blommaert (2010) borrows the term 'super-diversity' to talk about situations in urban neighbourhoods where waves of migration from different parts of the world result in 'extreme linguistic diversity' and 'complex multilingual repertoires in which often several (fragments of) 'migrant' languages and lingua francas are combined' (p. 7). Blommaert too, therefore, challenges the idea of languages as whole, self-sufficient systems. In its place, he introduces the concept of 'truncated repertoires' (pp. 103–106), which is based on the consideration that everybody only really knows a section of any given language, including the language that they consider 'native', and argues that in situations of super-diversity people operate linguistically by resorting to their various truncated repertoires according to the task at hand. Anecdotally, but efficiently, he describes his own experience of a user of truncated repertoires and notes how if his English were to be assessed in one of the widely available international exams, his score would vary significantly from 'very proficient user' to 'elementary' according to the competency that he might be tested on (e.g. academic writing vs. explaining a health problem to a doctor).

According to Blommaert and Rampton (2011, p. 3), '[i]f we are to grasp the insight into social transformation that communicative phenomena can offer us, it is essential to approach them with an adequate toolkit, recognizing that the traditional vocabulary of linguistic analysis is no longer sufficient'.

At this point, the question is: how can the World Englishes framework, with its emphasis on distinct (often nationally defined) varieties of English, accommodate such notions which destabilize the very concept of *a* language? How can the kind of linguistic diversity discussed in these pages be the starting point of analysis in a paradigm which privileges distinctions among Englishes and, at the same time, requires sufficient purity *within* them? Can World Englishes develop an adequate toolkit?

5.4.1   *World Englishes and super-diversity*

We have seen (Section 4.4.3) how the World Englishes framework has been criticized for privileging descriptions of a kind of language variation where departures from notions of 'standard English' are not such that varieties become excessively un-English. That is, for presupposing that Singapore English, Indian English, Nigerian English and so on need to display a certain amount of Singaporean, Indian and Nigerian 'flavour' while retaining a recognizably English character in their structure and vocabulary. One immediately obvious limitation with this analytical frame is that the scope of analysis is very restricted and too much language practice is simply left out of the equation.

However, the problem is not only one of reconciling the neatness of Englishes with the (super-)diversity of actual linguistic interactions. This stumbling block reveals a more profound issue, related to the geographical identification of varieties of English.

5.4.2   *Geography or language?*

The main frame of reference for the identification and naming of varieties of English in the World Englishes paradigm is a geographical one and, quite simply, corresponds to the political map of the world, with its ready-made names and subdivisions. So there is a Nigerian English because there is a country called Nigeria, Indian English because there is a country called India and so on.

The absolute faith in the political map of the world for the identification of varieties of English is problematic for two reasons. First, it presupposes that the distribution of languages and varieties follow national borders even though this, despite the existence of specific national language policies, is simply not true. People are mobile, and so are languages. In the case of world Englishes, it is patently even *less* the case. This goes back to the 'spot the difference' approach discussed earlier (Section 4.4). If, for example, one considers the names 'Singapore English' and 'Malaysian English', in order to justify the two different labels one would have to postulate the existence of two forms of English that are sufficiently homogeneous, one within Singapore and the other within Malaysia, as well as uniformly distinct from one another. But, quite clearly, that cannot be done, as no set of 'features' would have such neat distribution. What happens, therefore, is that certain individual items of lexis, grammar or pronunciation that are observable with an amount of regularity in the speech or writing of Singaporeans (or Malaysians) are arbitrarily elected as symbols of the nationally defined variety, no matter how small or insignificant they may be.

And no matter how little such 'features' actually stay enclosed within national borders. With reference to the pronunciation of Singapore English, for example, Deterding (2007, p. 13) observes:

> Perhaps the most salient segmental feature of Singapore pronunciation, the one that Singaporeans themselves are most likely to be aware of, is the tendency for [t] sometimes to be used instead of [θ], and [d] sometimes to be used in place of [ð] in words which start with 'th' . . . .

This may be a 'feature' of Singapore pronunciation but the shifts of [θ] towards [t] and, especially, of [ð] towards [d] are extremely common virtually everywhere, certainly well beyond the small island of Singapore. Indeed, often 'features' that are thought to identify this or that variety of English are not only found in many other parts of the world 'natively', so to speak, but are also adopted by people in different world regions as a result of global cultural flows. For example, what is popularly known as 'Australian questioning intonation', a tendency for intonation to rise towards the end of an utterance, has 'travelled' around the world, is used extensively especially by younger people and there's no certainty even about its actual 'origin' (despite the name). Similarly, many 'features' that are commonly thought of being distinctive of 'American English', often included in long lists defining differences between this variety of English and 'British English', are actually easily found nearly everywhere else in the world, including Britain. The power of American film industry, TV networks and popular music is far greater than imaginary language boundaries.

To be sure, however, linguistic 'features' may be oblivious to national borders but very strong significance can sometimes be attached to otherwise trivial aspects of how languages are spoken, if they are considered to be marks of national identity, just like any other otherwise similarly negligible traits:

> The very essence of a nation can come to be seen as residing within some superficially insignificant idiosyncrasy – the retention of a guttural fricative within the phonetic system, the ceremonial wearing of a kilt or serving of a dish that the neighbours find so repugnant as to make a joke of it. (Joseph, 2004, p. 106)

This takes us back to the link between language and nation (Section 2.3.1) and is related to the second reason why tracing varieties of Englishes along the contours of political maps is problematic. Considering each world English as the expression of a separate national culture operates within an essentialist frame which underpinned the rise of the nation-state ideology in eighteenth- and nineteenth-century Europe and inspired the discipline of linguistics that developed in the same period.

Very interestingly, Muysken points out how 'the fact that people are able to use several languages almost at the same time within the same conversation and even in the same sentence somehow runs counter to our basic (monolingual) view of what language and communication are all about'. Whose basic monolingual view? He is clearly – but implicitly! – referring to linguists operating within a European tradition, inspired by a two-century-old credo about the oneness of nation, state and language.

The construction of the nation-state idea was based on the proposition – rooted in ideas about language and nation that can be traced all the way back to the Bible – that humanity was divided into separate but homogeneous groups, or nations, each one of which inhabited their own territory, to which they were naturally bound. Language was the principal defining factor for the identification of such nations. So, there was a strong and unique bond between *one* nation, *one* territory and *one* language (Figure 5.2), this tripartite relationship being further reinforced by associations to religion and ethnicity.

The combined forces of political and intellectual efforts of the time were directed at demonstrating how nations represented natural and primordial ways in which human beings were grouped and the idea of separate national languages played a very instrumental role in that argument. The third of Herder's 'natural laws' in his *Treatise on the Origin of Language* (1772) stated:

> Just as the whole human species could not possibly remain a single herd, likewise it could not retain a single language either. So there arises a formation of different national languages. (Herder, 1772/2002, p. 147)

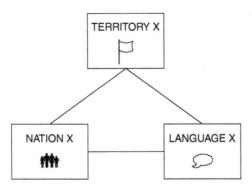

FIGURE 5.2 *The connection between territory, nation and language.*

Each national language therefore had to be externally distinct from other national languages and internally uniform. This also meant that belonging to a nation entailed speaking the language that defined that very nation. Language and nation were inseparable and between the two there existed a one-to-one relationship. This is the root of the 'strange artifact' that Otsuji and Pennycook refer to (page 123) which has since then imposed monolingualism as the rule in Western thinking about language.

But the socio-cultural and political milieu that produced the philosophy which held that there was a natural link binding territory, nation and language in Europe was the same one that, elsewhere, produced, financially supported and glorified global imperial forces which *detached* people from territories and brought them together with other people of different languages, religions and ethnicities, all within the same territories. These colonies, arbitrarily named 'Nigeria', 'Sierra Leone' and so on, were delimited by borders that were created by European imperialists who drew lines on a map with complete disregard to local demography. The countries that emerged out of colonization were the direct descendants of those territories. So, even though modern political maps of South America, Africa and Asia look graphically similar to the political map of Europe, the entities that their coloured areas refer to are socially, culturally and linguistically very different.

It is for this reason that the identification of varieties of English on the basis of ready-made classifications seductively offered by political maps constitutes a paradox, as it embraces a philosophy of language (and of humanity in general) that was produced by and for European imperialism, thereby seriously undermining the anti-imperialistic ethos of the World Englishes philosophy.

So, I would argue that in order for the anti-imperialist stance in World Englishes philosophy to continue to hold true it needs to come to terms with this conundrum. The complexity of super-diversity, metrolingualism and translanguaging needs to be tackled head on. Not only because these are very real phenomena in an era of globalization, but also, and even more importantly, because they have characterized language practice *everywhere* and *in all historical eras*. If it doesn't lose sight of the fact that monolingualism and language purism are political products of European nationalism and are ideologically very close to concepts of racial purity (with all the consequences that it entails), a philosophy of language that is truly alternative needs to decidedly look elsewhere and reject, rather than be seduced by, any claims of 'universal truth' that might still stem from those Eurocentric doctrines it wishes to oppose. A paradigm can be shifted only if all its principles are unhinged first.

An *anti*-colonial stance needs to be able to look beyond the imperial enterprise on either of its sides, that is, before and after. On the one hand, it needs to deal with forms of hybridity, translanguaging, metrolingualism and truncated repertoires resulting from global cultural flows, mobility and super-diversity in the twenty-first century. On the other hand, crucially, it needs to consider the *pre*colonial condition as the site where borderless-ness takes centre stage so that a radical re-conceptualization of language can be made and a new blueprint for analysis drawn.

Canagarajah (2013) remarks how what he calls 'translingual practices' have always been pervasive, especially in non-Western regions of the world in precolonial times, and that the force of colonization has both physically destroyed published records of such practices and reduced its vibrancy through the imposition of Western monolingual language ideologies (p. 36). According to him, it is therefore wrong to consider translingual practices exceptional or a product of contemporary instances of mobility, migration or technological advancements: 'Postmodern social conditions and discourses didn't *create* translingual practices. They have only created more visibility for them' (p. 37).

With specific reference to precolonial Africa, Makoni (2011) points out how '[t]he idea of language as understood in western scholarship . . . is . . . a 'myth' . . . part of a process of invention, a process set in motion in colonial Africa' (p. 681), a concept which he then elaborates:

The process of invention has been at two different levels. First, the speech forms used for communication acquired a name. . . . Second, an ethnic identity based on language was then introduced. For example, in Southern Africa, speech forms used for communication in the area currently known as Kwa-Zulu Natal became Zulu; the speakers were assigned an ethnicity and were then referred to as Zulus. Yet prior to this the speech forms used for communication were simply referred to as *isintu* (human speak) and speakers were referred to as 'usuthu'. (Makoni, 2011, p. 681)

In fact, language was borderless for a very long time in the West too. Adams (2003), for example, has shown how ancient Latin was routinely mixed with many other languages throughout the Roman empire and what he calls' 'intra-sentential switches' were pervasive even in the language of such an orator as Cicero (p. 24). Indeed, the monolingual ideology is relative recent in Europe (see also Section 2.3.1):

> The political history of the 19th and 20th centuries and the ideology of 'one state – one nation – one language' have given rise to the idea that monolingualism has always been the default or normal case in Europe and more or less a precondition for political loyalty. . . .

> Such a close connection between language on the one hand, and political loyalty and personal identity on the other did not become evident before the end of the 18th century. (Braunmüller & Ferraresi, 2003, p. 1)

Prior to that period, monolingualism 'would have been the non-normal case in the upper layers of European societies' (p. 2), and in the Middle Ages, 'the boundaries were even more fluid' (p. 2).

Of course, multilingualism and language mixing has been common in Britain, too. As Schendl and Wright (2011, p. 18) point out, '[t]hroughout its attested history and irrespective of its political structure, Britain has been a multilingual country'. In the same volume, for example, L. Wright (2011) discusses how medieval business writing in Britain systematically involved the simultaneous use of Medieval Latin, Anglo-Norman and Middle English. As we saw in Section 2.2.4, language hybridity is shown on the *Franks Casket*, one of the earliest records of written 'Old English', indicating, once again, that mixing, hybridity, translanguaging are far more common and normal than is recognized in dominant discourses still inspired by nineteenth-century European ideologies.

To be sure, the fundamentally borderless nature of language has been recognized in sociolinguistics for some time now. According to Lamb (2004, p. 413), '[t]here is no generally applicable way to make the distinction between one language and another' and '[l]anguages are neither discrete objects nor are they uniform across speakers'. In a similar vein, Hudson (1996, p. 39) remarks that 'there is no way of delimiting varieties, and we must therefore conclude that varieties do not exist' and so 'the search for language boundaries is a waste of time' (p. 36).

5.4.3   *ELF across borders*

A similar evolution in the conceptualization of language has occurred in the field of ELF. In particular, in a relatively short period of time, there has been a definite shift of focus in the aims of ELF research, from attention being paid almost exclusively to the identification of salient linguistic features in ELF interactions to a growing interest in the ways in which ELF speakers draw from multiple semiotic resources in achieving mutual understanding. As Cogo and Dewey (2012, pp. 2–3) remark:

> As ELF has continued to develop as a distinctive field, however, the trend more recently has been for researchers to shift the focus away from identifying the features of ELF talk themselves towards an interest in the underlying processes that give rise to the emerging forms. . . . This has largely come about with the greater realization that ELF communication is by nature especially fluid, and that speakers' use of linguistic forms especially variable [*sic*].

This evolution began to take shape towards the end of the first decade of the century, when ELF research received a certain amount of critical attention from other sociolinguists sharing the same interests. Canagarajah (2007), for example, felt that the nature of lingua franca communication was too fluid and diverse to be captured in systematic descriptions:

> Because of the diversity at the heart of this communicative medium, LFE [Lingua Franca English] is intersubjectively constructed in each specific context of interaction. The form of this English is negotiated by each set of speakers for their purposes. The speakers are able to monitor each other's language proficiency to determine mutually the appropriate grammar, phonology, lexical range, and pragmatic conventions that would ensure intelligibility. Therefore, it is difficult to describe this language a priori. (2007, p. 925)

Together with doubts over the possibility of describing and codifying something as potentially vast and changeable as ELF, the point was made that '[i]t is perhaps helpful to see lingua franca more as a functional term rather than a linguistic one' (Kirkpatrick, 2008a, p. 28; see also Saraceni, 2008b) or even as 'an abstraction, a concept [rather than] a language (or variety) per se' (Berns, 2009, p. 196). In the meantime, ELF researchers began to acknowledge that surface-level features weren't as interesting as originally thought, after all, and that 'it is an understanding of the more general communicative processes that is the main objective of documenting and observing how ELF speakers interact' (Seidlhofer, 2009b, p. 240; see also Cogo & Dewey, 2012, p. 167).

The fluidity of ELF is becoming increasingly prominent in the relevant literature: 'research findings to date have shown that ELF interaction is characterized by an inherent fluidity of forms' (Cogo & Dewey, 2012, p. 77). So is hybridity: 'ELF is . . . marked by a degree of hybridity not found in other kinds of language use, as speakers from diverse languages introduce a range of non-English forms into their ELF use' (Jenkins, 2013, p. 31). Ultimately, then

> What we are looking at in ELF, then, is an entirely new, communication-focused way of approaching the notion of 'language' that is far more relevant to twenty-first century uses of English (and probably other global languages) than traditional bounded-variety approaches, and one that has far more in common with post-modern approaches to language. (2013, p. 37)

5.5   Conclusion: From World Englishes to Language Worlds

So, where does this leave World Englishes? One area towards which the field has recently enlarged its scope of research is that of urban linguistic landscapes exhibiting forms of language hybridization directly associated to globalization phenomena (see, among many others, Higgins, 2009; Rubdy, 2013). Significantly, an entire issue of the *World Englishes* journal was dedicated in 2012 to this theme, precisely on the basis of the consideration that, as Bolton (2012) put it in the introductory article, 'the scope of WE is obviously not simply related to the analysis of particular 'varieties of English', but much more besides' (p. 30).

The 'much more besides' is where new horizons and challenges lie. The 'intriguing mix of languages, scripts and modalities' (Rubdy, 2013, p. 43) that can be observed in urban linguistic landscapes is a very tangible evidence of the volatility of language borders and of how people manipulate them creatively. Further, it is also something that forces us to reconsider the very concept of 'a language'.

According to Pennycook (2007b, p. 95), 'languages exist only to the extent that speakers perceive them to do so'. As I remarked elsewhere, however, this doesn't reject the existence of languages but merely relocates it 'from the plane of objective, primordial reality to that of the sociopolitical persuasion, both collective and individual' (Saraceni, 2013, p. 193). Our awareness of the constructedness of discrete languages and varieties doesn't make their significance go away. As Joseph (2006, p. 27) notes, '[s]o long as people believe that their way of speaking constitutes a language in its own right, there is a real sense in which it is a real language'. Indeed, 'the factuality of named languages continues to be taken for granted in a great deal of contemporary institutional policy and practice' (Blommaert & Rampton, 2011, p. 4).

Ultimately, '[i]t is not because Languages "do not exist" that the belief in their existence cannot have powerful effects' (Blommaert, 2013, pp. 4–5). Such effects can be very visible and tangible. Language, for example, is often at the centre of social unrest, sometimes in tragic circumstances. For example, much of the discourse over the 2014 conflict in Ukraine between pro-Russian and pro-West Ukrainians revolves around issues of language and how they relate to identity and national allegiance. So, although Russian and Ukrainian are similar, have co-existed for a long time and indeed represent a good case study of how it is impossible to draw borders between languages, it is their distinction that is emphasized as part of the rhetoric in the conflict. Those in the pro-Russian faction identify themselves by being Russian speakers and, vice versa, those who favour complete independence from Russia identify themselves as Ukrainian speakers. Quite clearly, sociolinguistic reflections on the absence of linguistic borders or the non-existence of languages aren't likely to be very relevant in this context.

Even if the example of the Ukraine conflict may seem to be a rather extreme one, it serves to make the point that after essentialist conceptualizations of language(s) have been challenged, destabilized or even discarded as a 'strange artifact', a shift of orientation becomes necessary in World Englishes research, as Yano (2009, p. 212) contends, 'from the geography-based model to the person-based model of English speakers'. Blommaert and Rampton (2011) explain this particularly well:

> research . . . has to address the ways in which people take on different linguistic forms as they align and disaffiliate with different groups at different moments and stages. It has to investigate how they (try to) opt in and opt out, how they perform or play with linguistic signs of group belonging, and how they develop particular trajectories of group identification throughout their lives. (Blommaert & Rampton, 2011, p. 5)

A person-based model adopts the 'practice' view of language and re-orients research aims from questions that ask 'what does this variety of English look like?' to questions that ask 'what do people *do* when they use language resources that they identify as "English"?' 'how do they position themselves towards it?' 'what does it mean to them?' In this context, Bolton (2013)'s idea of *language worlds* encapsulates the shift from system to practice very effectively. The term refers to the perceptions that each individual has of the set of languages and linguistic resources that she or he uses and is surrounded by, and has the capacity to highlight the primacy of language as integral to people's lived experience, rather than a detached system of words and sounds.

This becomes even more relevant when English is discussed more overtly in conjunction with issues such as linguistic and language rights, addressed in Part Three of this book.

Key reading

- A key publication that has made a significant contribution in sociolinguistics is:
  Blommaert, J. (2010). *A Sociolinguistics of Globalization*. Cambridge: Cambridge University Press.

- Alastair Pennycook has written extensively about the global reach of English and the impact that it has on local practice. This volume contains a comprehensive overview:
  Pennycook, A. (2010). *Laguage as a Local Practice*. London: Routledge.

- The notion of 'language across borders' has been discussed in a number of recent publications. Two of which are:
  Canagarajah, S. (2013). *Translingual Practice: Global Englishes and Cosmopolitan Relations*. London: Routledge.
  Rubdy, R. & Alsagoff, L. (Eds) (2013). *The Global–Local Interface and Hybridity: Exploring Language and Identity*. Bristol: Multilingual Matters.

PART THREE

Ideology

6

Linguistic imperialism and resistance

. . . everybody wants to be certain countries, like everybody wants to be the U.S.A. and Britain and Canada and Australia . . . Nobody wants to be rags of countries like Congo, like Somalia, like Iraq, like Sudan, like Haiti, like Sri Lanka, and not even this one we live in—who wants to be a terrible place of hunger and things falling apart?
NOVIOLET BULAWAYO

Keywords

appropriation • language ownership • linguistic imperialism • linguistic determinism • linguistic relativity

6.1 Introduction

The news agency *Reuters* recently reported a piece of news (largely ignored by British media but published by *Al Jazeera*) with the following headline:

Gambia to stop using 'colonial relic' English – president. (Reuters, 12 March 2014)

The article makes it very clear, right from the headline, that the decision to 'drop' English was made by the president of Gambia, Yahya Jammeh, who is reported to have made the following statements:

We no longer believe that for you to be a government you should speak a foreign language. We are going to speak our own language.

The British did not care about education, that means they were not practising good governance. All they did was loot and loot and loot.

These statements are embedded in a text which invites readers to interpret Jammeh's behaviour as illogical and driven by anti-Western sentiments. First of all, the president is said to have announced the decision to abandon English as the official language of the country 'without indicating which language the tiny West African country would use in its place'. The preposition *without* refers to the fact that Jammeh failed to provide a vital piece of information, and begins to cast doubts over the soundness of this decision. This seems to be confirmed in the next sentence, where readers are informed that Gambians speak 'several African languages', hinting at the fact that selecting one of them as the national language would be very difficult. The description of Gambia as 'tiny' also adds to the feeling that abandoning English doesn't seem to be a particularly wise move. The credibility of Jammeh's plan is further undermined by the president's failure to indicate 'a precise time frame for the dropping of English', which casts doubt over the credibility of the plan. Moreover, the representation or this decision as unreasonable is reinforced when it is contrasted with the fact that 'English is the main language of education'.

Crucially, the article also contains information that is completely unrelated to the use (or not) of English as the official language of Gambia. Readers are reminded that the president 'seized power in a 1994 coup', 'drew international criticism after he executed a number of prisoners in 2012' and 'accused the United States and Britain of fomenting coup attempts and supporting the opposition'. So, the decision to drop English manifestly comes from a man who had made himself known for all the wrong reasons. I should clarify that the point of my comments of course is not to defend the Gambian president, but to re-iterate, and begin to examine more in depth, the political and ideological significance of language, and of English in particular.

So, the article expresses two positions: that of the president, who sees English a relic of imperialism, and that of Reuters journalists, who report Jammeh's decision within a broader representation of him as a despotic dictator animated by anti-Western sentiments. In this chapter, I aim to do two things: (1) explore the historical and ideological motivations behind these positions and (2) discuss the position of World Englishes within this scenario.

Before doing so, it is important to re-iterate the importance to avoid the temptation to treat the 'English language' as if it were an independent entity, capable of performing its own actions or even making its own decisions. Whatever we understand, linguistically and philosophically, by the term 'English language', we mustn't lose sight of the fact that agency always remains firmly and exclusively a prerogative of people, not of the languages they speak. Accordingly, it is important to be suspicious of accounts which consistently put language as an 'actor' in events being narrated.

This is the case of Crystal's *English as a Global Language* (2003), a book for which he has been criticized for excessively sanitizing the spread of English, for example, through statements suggesting that 'the English language has repeatedly found itself "in the right place at the right time"' (pp. 77–78). Significantly, the scare quotes around the phrase *in the right place at the right time* were added in the second edition of the book as a way of attending to the criticism that Phillipson (1999) made in a review of the book. In it, Phillipson contended that this particular statement 'trivializes the issue and is in fact in conflict with the analytical underpinning he [Crystal] begins the book with, where he admits that what is decisive for the expansion of a language is power of various kinds' (p. 273). Crystal (2000), who offered a vigorous retort in a subsequent issue of the same journal (*Applied Linguistics*), re-iterated his explanation of his use of the phrase in a footnote of the book:

> As this phrase . . . apparently has a jingoistic ring to some people, it is perhaps necessary to draw attention to its ironic tone. In using it, I intended to suggest, with a Welsh tongue in cheek, that English has been fortunate indeed to do so well – just as someone turning up at a bar 'at the right time' might end up being given a free drink from the person buying a round. (Crystal, 2003, p. 78, footnote 10)

The crucial point, however, is not so much whether the phrase was intended ironically. What trivializes the issue is not so much the 'triumphalist' (Phillipson, 1999, p. 268) tone that the word *right* is assumed to be indicative of in Crystal's story of English as a global language. What trivializes the issue is the removal of human agency. The perpetual portrayal of the English language as the *doer* of actions lessens (or eliminates) people's responsibility for the events narrated. If English is metaphorically compared to someone who turns up at a bar, there is no need to mention the fact that somebody *took* it there. This chapter, therefore, also discusses the ideological implications of the fact that English did *not* just turn up at a bar ready to buy a round of drinks for everybody.

6.2   An unequal world

That we live in a profoundly unequal world is a well-rehearsed point. It is also a point that needs to be made with as much clarity as possible, since many of the tensions and conflicts that afflict the world originate from that same source: inequality. As Callinicos (2009, p. 8) says, 'the world in which we live is characterized by enormously unequal distributions of economic power that drastically limit the life chances and well-being of the large majority of the world's population'. To have a sense of this imbalance, one can consider that the 32 million millionaires (in US dollars) in the world, that is 0.45 per cent of the world population, own 41 per cent of the planet's wealth and the vast majority of them (78%) are located in North America and Europe; by contrast, '[t]wo-thirds of adults in the world have wealth below USD 10,000 and together account for merely 3% of global wealth' (Credit Suisse, 2013, p. 21) – more than 90 per cent of these are in India and Africa. While a thorough discussion of this issue is obviously well outside the scope of this book, I will however attempt to address it from a specific point of view that takes the English language as the starting point.

That the English language, whatever we understand by the term, is deeply connected with issues far larger than grammar and vocabulary is abundantly clear. I recently bought, for one pound in a London second-hand bookshop, *A History of the English-Speaking Peoples since 1900*, a book by the well-known British historian Andrew Roberts. The book has nothing to do with English, not in a linguistic sense (the word 'language' isn't even included in the index), but it has very much to do with a particular ideological representation of the world. Borrowing its title from Winston Churchill's four-volume work on the history of Britain and its former empire, Roberts's tome is a 700-page eulogy of (his view of) Britain and the United States. It exalts their superior civilizations and narrates how they heroically withstood and defeated four successive 'assaults' to their dominant position in the world in the twentieth century and the beginning of the twenty first: 'Wilhelmine Prussian militarism, then the Nazi-led Axis, then global Marxism-Leninism, and presently . . . Islamic fundamentalism' (p. 2). In all seriousness, without a trace of irony, Roberts declares that, having defeated these evil forces, 'English-speaking peoples . . . remain the last, best home for Mankind' (p. 2).

A book like this represents an extreme example of revisionism, but the point that I'd like to stress here is that Roberts, like Churchill before him, has chosen language as the primary trait that, in his mind, binds, almost spiritually, a particular group of 'earthlings', as he puts it. We saw, in the previous chapters, how language was ideologically linked to the nation-state as a political entity in nineteenth-century Europe. But Roberts's depiction goes one step further: the English language represents the dominance of Britain and the United States in the world. But *History of the English-Speaking Peoples* can also be read more critically and, in many ways, it can be seen as a book entirely dedicated to inequality and how the English language is deeply rooted in it. Indeed, stripped of all its fiercely romantic and visionary (re-)reading of twentieth-century history that this book puts forward, the idea of the dominance of the 'English-speaking peoples' can be rendered numerically and, specifically, with numbers related to the distribution of wealth in the world. Using the data made available by *Credit Suisse*, it is possible to quantify the Inner Circle and the Outer Circle in terms of their respective shares of the planet's wealth. The differences couldn't be more marked. If we consider wealth and population figures, the two Circles are perfectly specular. While the Inner Circle has more than 30 per cent of the planet's wealth and only 6 per cent of its population, the Outer Circle has exactly the opposite: 6 per cent of the word's wealth and 30 per cent of the world's population (see Figure 6.1).

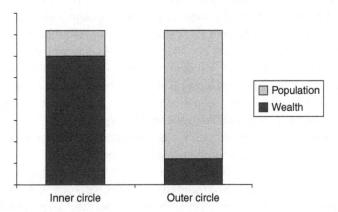

FIGURE 6.1 *The distribution of wealth between the Inner Circle and the Outer Circle.*

These are staggering statistics. The question is: what role (if any) does the English language play in this scenario? If one were to take Roberts's book title literally, then there would only be one possible conclusion: the English language is the *primary* cause of inequality. Indeed, if one were to take the notions of Inner Circle and Outer Circle equally literally, the conclusion wouldn't be too different. Is it a coincidence that the 'cultural base' of English is so much wealthier than the world regions where English co-exists side by side with other languages? Again, this question potentially suggests a close correlation between the English language and wealth. This is a point that is often made in Malaysia, for example, in debates over the status that is granted to English. Despite the fact that Malaysia experienced rapid growth in its economy since it gained independence from Britain in 1957, it compares rather unfavourably to neighbouring Singapore, one of the four so-called Asian Tigers and one of the richest countries in the world, where the GDP per capita is much higher than that of Malaysia. For this reason, differences in the economies of the two countries are often attributed to the different language policies adopted after independence: while Singapore has always promoted English as one of the official languages and, especially, as the medium of instruction at all levels of education, Malaysia has taken a much more ambivalent approach towards English, whose status has fluctuated over the years, with an overall downward trend.

The attribution of greater wealth to higher levels of proficiency in English is rather common. The private company *EF* (which makes its acronym stand for 'English First' as well as 'Education First'), for example, claims that '[o]ver the past six years, we have found strong and consistent correlations between English proficiency and a number of social and economic indicators' (EF, 2013, p. 34). Such indicators include volume of exports, level of income, ability to do business and even better quality of life (pp. 34–9). These correlations are described in the third global survey of English-language skills conducted in 2013 by *EF*, called the *English Proficiency Index* (available at www.ef.com/epi). In the report, nearly every country in the world is ranked on the basis of the level of proficiency in English observed in it. As *EF* is in the business of English language teaching, the report is obviously biased and the methodology for its data collection flawed (see a comment on the 'Johnson' blog on the *Economist* website, www.economist.com/blogs/johnson/2012/10/language-skills). However, with all its shortcomings, the report contributes to reinforcing the simple idea that more English equates to more money.

Once again, given the numbers, it's difficult to argue against such an equation. However, rather than arguing against them, it's probably more useful to interrogate those statistics and try to understand how they have come about.

6.2.1   *Where do the numbers come from?*

6.2.1.1   Linguistic relativity?

The first point I wish to address is Roberts's suggestion that the English language is somehow naturally, or even super-naturally, connected to the unrivalled 'might, wealth or prestige' of the English-speaking peoples (p. 647). While the British historian's take on world affairs is evidently skewed and often racist, it is nonetheless possible to see links between his extreme views and the theory of *linguistic relativity*, also known as the Sapir-Whorf hypothesis, from the names of the main proponents of the theory: Edward Sapir and Benjamin Lee Whorf.

The basic principle of linguistic relativity is that people's cognition of the world depends on the language they speak. This notion is rooted in Wilhelm von Humboldt's ideas about language:

there resides in every language a characteristic world-view. As the individual sound stands between man and the object, so the entire language steps in between him and the nature that operates, both inwardly and outwardly, upon him. He surrounds himself with a world of sounds, so as to take up and process within himself the world of objects. These expressions in no way outstrip the measure of the simple truth. Man lives primarily with objects, indeed, since feeling and acting in him depend on his presentations, he actually does so exclusively, as language presents them to him. By the same act whereby he spins language out of himself, he spins himself into it, and every language draws about the people that possesses it a circle whence it is possible to exit only by stepping over at once into the circle of another one. To learn a foreign language should therefore be to acquire a new standpoint in the world-view hitherto possessed, and in fact to a certain extent is so, since every language contains the whole conceptual fabric and mode of presentation of a portion of mankind. (von Humboldt, 1836/1999, p. 60)

The connection between human beings and 'the world of objects' surrounding them is central in linguistic relativity. The following extract is one of Sapir's most frequently cited passages because it illustrates the principle very clearly:

Human beings do not live in the objective world alone, nor alone in the world of social activity as ordinarily understood, but are very much at the mercy of a particular language which has become the medium of expression for their society. It is quite an illusion to imagine that one adjusts to reality essentially without the use of language, and that language is merely an incidental means of solving specific problems of communication or reflection. The fact of the matter is that the 'real world' is to a large extent unconsciously built up on the language habits of the group. No two languages are ever sufficiently similar to be considered as representing the same social reality. The worlds in which different societies live are different worlds, not merely the same world with different labels attached . . . . We see and hear and otherwise experience very largely as we do because the language habits of our community predispose certain choices of interpretation. (Sapir, 1929, pp. 209–210)

In the words of Benjamin Lee Whorf, who was Sapir's student, the principle can be encapsulated thus:

The point of view of linguistic relativity changes Mr. Everyman's dictum: Instead of saying, 'Sentences are unlike because they tell about unlike facts', he now reasons: 'Facts are unlike to speakers whose language background provides for unlike formulation of them'. (Whorf, 1941/1956, p. 235)

If one agrees that the way we experience the world depends to a large extent on the language we speak, one might be tempted to jump to the conclusion that the 'English-speaking peoples' primacy' derives from the fact that their language somehow affords them an understanding of the world that is more profound, sophisticated and precise than that of speakers of all other languages and this, in turn, gives them an unbridgeable advantage over their 'competitors'. However, intriguing as it may be, such a hypothesis can be easily dismissed.

What Roberts really refers to by 'peoples' is the political, commercial and military apparatuses of Britain and the United States, not groups of human beings. If the word did refer to actual human beings who speak English, the entire theory would collapse instantly. People who speak English as their primary or only language, obviously, occupy a very broad spectrum in terms of social class, education, income, ethnicity, cultural and religious affiliations – they're not just white, Anglo-Saxon, Protestant millionaires. So, the language element, per se, needs to be repositioned in our interrogations that seek to explain the statistics seen earlier.

6.3   Language and empire

It was not their being 'English-speaking' that granted Britain and the United States a dominant position in the world. It was, and still is, imperialism.

Generally speaking, the word 'imperialism' doesn't tend to conjure up anything particularly positive: 'there is an element of the unethical and morally reprehensible attached to the term' (Phillipson, 1992, p. 46). Querying the enTenTen corpus reveals that *imperialism* is used in the same lexical environment as words such as *fascism, militarism, dictatorship, oppression, domination, tyranny, racism,* as well as less obviously negative words like *colonialism, capitalism* and *nationalism.* This seems to confirm that in the latter part of the twentieth century 'imperialism' 'has gradually acquired, and is now unlikely to lose, a pejorative colouring' (Hobsbawm, 1987, p. 60). However, while imperialism is 'commonly something to be disapproved of, and therefore done by others' (p. 60), 'empire' doesn't have the same negative connotation. Performing the same query on the word *empire* yields very different results. The first ten words that share the same lexical environment are *civilization, kingdom, ruler, regime, army, nation, capitalism, monarchy, dynasty, democracy.* With the sole exception, perhaps, of *regime,* none of these words are particularly negative, with *civilization* and *democracy* standing out as decidedly positive. This seems to be rooted in perceptions of the empire that were typical in the nineteenth and early twentieth century, when one of the leitmotifs in the discourse that supported British imperialism was that it fulfilled a civilizing mission and exported democracy and other British values to other parts of the world.

Indeed, a hundred years ago, 'plenty of politicians were proud to call themselves imperialists' (Hobsbawm, 1987, p. 60). This was part of a larger discourse. In the preface of a book entitled *Our Empire Story*, expressly written for 'boys and girls' in the beginning of the twentieth century, Henrietta Elizabeth Marshall (1908) explained to her young readers the purpose of her book:

> . . . although we are proud of our Empire, it may be that some of us know little of its history. We only know it as it now is, and we forget perhaps that there was a time when it did not exist. We forget that it has grown to be great out of very small beginnings. We forget that it did not grow great all at once, but that with pluck and patience our fellow-countrymen built it up by little and by little, each leaving behind him a vaster inheritance than he found. So, 'lest we forget', in this book I have told a few of the most exciting and interesting stories about the building up of this our great heritage and possession. (p. vii)

Although actual 'pride' is perhaps no longer such a common sentiment that is expressed for the empire, views continue to be mixed, especially in Britain. Even if one disregards such extreme opinions as Roberts's, expressed in a kind of rhetoric that often makes it indistinguishable from (self-)parody, it is still common to read that it is difficult to judge the overall enterprise of the British empire with the necessary detachment:

> It is not easy to make a definitive judgment. 'Balance-sheets of empire', whether it was worthwhile, a good thing or a bad thing, have a long future in front of them. Subjective judgments are bound to prevail. Evidence can as easily be found for useful benefits and altruistic efforts as a for brutality and exploitation and sheer indifference. All these ambiguities have to be taken seriously into account. Like most things in life, 'the empire' was neither black nor white, but a mixture, a not altogether hopeless shade of grey perhaps. (Hyam, 2010, p. 14)

Of course, part of the complexity lies in the vastness of what we rather simplistically render into a small noun phrase: 'British empire', as if it was an event that just took place. The vastness I'm referring to isn't so much geographical, but social, political and cultural. The communities and individuals that, in the course of three hundred years, were involved in, and affected by, the British empire were innumerable and, of course, some evidence, somewhere, can be found for 'useful benefits and altruistic efforts'. But to take this as an argument for the impossibility to make 'definitive judgments' is rather disingenuous. Unless, of course, one is to assess how worthwhile the empire was exclusively from a narrowly utilitarian British point of view. Similarly, the use of a trite and largely meaningless expression such as 'most things in life' in order to justify assessments of the empire in 'shades of grey' rather than by bolder colours can be seen as a quick escape route out of possible ideological entanglements presumably deemed uncomfortable. This is a stance that, therefore, I wish to avoid.

From a less parochial standpoint, definitive judgments *can* be made and *have* been made for a long time. At the beginning of the twentieth century, John Atkinson Hobson (1902) made his position very clear in the preface of his seminal study of imperialism:

> Those readers who hold it that a well-balanced judgment consists in always finding as much in favour of any political course as against it will be discontented with the treatment given here. For the study is distinctively one of social pathology, and no endeavour is made to disguise the malignity of the disease. (p. vi)

A few pages later, he describes the 'spirit of Imperialism' with words that are at one time unequivocally evaluative and uncomfortably prophetic:

> Earth hunger and the scramble for markets are responsible for the openly avowed repudiation of treaty obligations which Germany, Russia, and England have not scrupled to defend. The sliding scale of diplomatic language, hinterland, sphere of interest, sphere of influence, paramountcy, suzerainty, protectorate, veiled or open, leading up to acts of forcible seizure or annexation which sometimes continue to be hidden under 'lease', 'rectification of frontier', 'concession', and the like, is the invention and expression of this cynical spirit of Imperialism. (p. 11)

Closer to our time, Philippa Levine (2013, p. xi) says,

> the British Empire was not a benign and kindly force when compared to its rivals, but a powerhouse always capable of attempting to impose its will through violence and coercion; . . . [it] was shaped by a deliberate set of policies and not acquired accidentally. . . .

Unbiased and non-sentimental accounts of the empire have also been expressed by critics holding more conservative political views. For example, Niall Ferguson (2003), who certainly couldn't be called an 'anti-imperialist' and for whom the British empire was 'an agency for imposing free markets, the rule of law, investor protection and relatively uncorrupt government on roughly a quarter of the globe' (p. xxi), strips his description of the early stages of the empire of every sliver of romanticism that anyone may imagine to attach to it, and talks about it in terms of organized crime carried out by buccaneers and pirates with the support of the British government:

> In December 1663 a Welshman called Henry Morgan sailed five hundred miles across the Caribbean to mount a spectacular raid on a Spanish outpost called Gran Grenada, ... The aim of the expedition was simple: to find and steal Spanish gold – or any other movable property. . . . It was the beginning of one of the seventeenth century's most extraordinary smash-and-grab sprees.

> It should never be forgotten that this is how the British Empire began: in a maelstrom of seaborne violence and theft. It was not conceived by self-conscious imperialists, aiming to establish English rule over foreign lands, or colonists hoping to build a new life overseas. Morgan and his 'buccaneers' were thieves, trying to steal the proceeds of someone else's Empire.

> The buccaneers. . . were engaged in organized crime. . . . The English government not only winked at Morgan's activity; it positively encouraged him. Viewed from London, buccaneering was a low-budget way of waging war against England's principal European foe: Spain. In effect, the Crown licensed the pirates as 'privateers', legalizing their operations in return for a share of the proceeds. Morgan's career was a classic example of the way the British Empire started out, using enterprising freelances as much as official forces. (Ferguson, 2003, pp. 1–2)

It shouldn't be forgotten that this is how the British empire began and neither should it be forgotten that this is how the English language began to be brought around the world. Indeed, the English language is the first item that Ferguson lists when he says that '[w]hen the British governed a country – even when they only influenced its government by flexing their military and financial muscles – there were certain distinctive features of their own society that they tended to disseminate' (p. xxii). This is a point that is inescapably central to any discussion about the presence, status, forms and functions of English in the world.

6.3.1   *American imperialism*

The British empire lasted until around the mid-twentieth century. At that point, English was already a very large international language. Many of the former British colonies adopted it as an official language. In this sense, the status of English in the world was very similar to that of French. The decades that followed, however, saw the two languages on opposite trends: while the importance and the diffusion of English in the world grew, that of French declined. Given that the international expansion of both languages was largely a consequence of imperialism, and that the two empires were of similar sizes and ended during the same period (the decades following the Second World War), it would be reasonable to assume that English and French would continue to share the same fate. The reason why this hasn't happened is that by the time the British empire crumbled, the United States had risen to be a world super-power (see also Section 3.2.1).

So, while British imperialism brought English around the world, American imperialism not only ensured that the language didn't decline, but also boosted its importance, especially as the language of international trade, technology and popular culture (for extensive and detailed statistics concerning English in the world, see Graddol, 1997, 2006, 2010).

6.3.1.1   Imperialism and coffee

So far I've been using the word 'imperialism' in the sense which corresponds to Meinig's (1986, p. xviii) definition: 'the aggressive encroachment of one people upon the territory of another, resulting in the subjugation of the latter people to alien rule'. This meaning is related to the kind of empire building based on the annexation of territories for the purpose of exploitation and/or settlement (see Section 3.2.2).

The United States have also been actively involved in this kind of imperialism. As Golub (2010) explains:

> American territorial and economic expansion over the course of the nineteenth century was an integral and dynamic component of the general movement of western imperial expansion that created the historical structures and hierarchies that have shaped the modern world. (p. 20)

> . . . the US armed forces were involved in overseas imperial operations in one part or another of the world throughout the nineteenth century. (p. 41)

> Overseas territorial empire would not only secure an open door for American commerce in Asia . . . but also establish the United States as a 'Great Power' and allow it to compete in the partition of the world on at least an equal footing with the European imperial states. (p. 46)

However, when we now talk about 'American imperialism', we generally tend to refer to another sense of the word, which has to do not so much with the territorial expansion of a nation-state, typical of European empire building from the sixteenth to the early twentieth century, but with other forms of expansion and exploitation (see, among others, Hardt & Negri, 2000; Hall,

2003; N. Smith, 2003; Panitch & Gindin, 2004; Bowden, 2009; Callinicos, 2009; Golub, 2010).

One of them is the expansion of large US-based corporations which grow well outside, and mostly independently of, national borders. An example would be a company which buys coffee beans very cheaply from, say, Indonesian farmers and then sells them back, at a significantly greater price, to middle-class Indonesians, in the form of 'latte' or 'cappuccino', in coffee-shops that it owns together with thousands of identical shops scattered all over the world. This global presence makes it very difficult for local independent coffee shops to survive and many of them are simply pushed out of business by the unbearable pressure of unequal competition. Additionally, these multinational companies also contribute to the worldwide increase in consumption of, and demand for, coffee, which in turn requires larger plantations and causes deforestation (to make space for them), and even lower, and hence more exploitative, production costs. Therefore,

> The activities of corporations are no longer defined by the imposition of abstract command and the organization of simple theft and unequal exchange. Rather, they directly structure and articulate territories and populations. They tend to make nation-states merely instruments to record the flows of the commodities, monies, and populations that they set in motion. The transnational corporations directly distribute labor power over various markets, functionally allocate resources, and organize hierarchically the various sectors of world production. (Hardt & Negri, 2000, pp. 31–32)

6.4   Linguistic imperialism

This is the frame of reference for the theory of *linguistic imperialism*, which sees a direct and two-way link between the expansion of the English language and imperialism, in both senses of the word seen earlier. Robert Phillipson (1992), the main proponent of the theory, defines linguistic imperialism thus:

> *the dominance of English. . . asserted and maintained by the establishment and continuous reconstitution of structural and cultural inequalities between English and other languages*. Here *structural* refers broadly to material properties. . . and *cultural* to immaterial or ideological properties. . . . English linguistic imperialism is one example of *linguicism*, which is defined as 'ideologies, structures, and practices which are used to legitimate, effectuate, and reproduce an unequal division of power and resources (both material and immaterial) between groups which are defined on the basis of language'. . . . (1992, p. 47)

Within this frame of analysis, the international role of English is inextricable from imperialism. On the one hand, forms of Anglo-American imperialism perpetuate a situation in which English is imposed as a dominant language around the world, at the expense of local languages which become marginalized or even eventually extinct. On the other hand, the English language is itself 'the key medium for the process of "Americanization" or "Westernization"' (1992, p. 59), thereby creating a diabolical combination of forces that serve the interests of those who are in the driving seat of global economic forces. English, within this frame of analysis, plays a pivotal role in contemporary world order.

6.4.1   Macaulay's 'minute'

One of the documents that have most frequently been cited as evidence of the importance of the strategic dissemination of the English language and the more general imperial philosophy of the superiority of British and European civilizations is a letter dated 2 February 1835 in which historian and politician Thomas Macaulay, who served as chairman of the Governor-General's Committee on Public Instruction, recommended that the English language was far more useful than Sanskrit or Arabic to form 'a class of persons Indian in blood and colour, but English in tastes, in opinions, in morals and in intellect' and that it should therefore be taught in India:

> We have a fund to be employed as Government shall direct for the intellectual improvement of the people of this country. The simple question is, what is the most useful way of employing it?
>
> All parties seem to be agreed on one point, that the dialects commonly spoken among the natives of this part of India contain neither literary nor scientific information, and are moreover so poor and rude that, until they are enriched from some other quarter, it will not be easy to translate any valuable work into them. It seems to be admitted on all sides, that the intellectual improvement of those classes of the people who have the means of pursuing higher studies can at present be affected only by means of some language not vernacular amongst them.
>
> What then shall that language be?. . .
>
> I have no knowledge of either Sanskrit or Arabic. But I have done what I could to form a correct estimate of their value. . . . I am quite ready to take the oriental learning at the valuation of the orientalists themselves. I have never found one among them who could deny that a single shelf of a good European library was worth the whole native literature of India and Arabia
> . . . .

. . . It is, I believe, no exaggeration to say that all the historical information which has been collected from all the books written in the Sanskrit language is less valuable than what may be found in the most paltry abridgments used at preparatory schools in England. . . .

How then stands the case? We have to educate a people who cannot at present be educated by means of their mother-tongue. We must teach them some foreign language. The claims of our own language it is hardly necessary to recapitulate. It stands pre-eminent even among the languages of the West. . . . It may safely be said that the literature now extant in that language is of greater value than all the literature which three hundred years ago was extant in all the languages of the world together. . . . Whether we look at the intrinsic value of our literature, or at the particular situation of this country, we shall see the strongest reason to think that, of all foreign tongues, the English tongue is that which would be the most useful to our native subjects.

. . .

. . . I think it clear . . . that we are free to employ our funds as we choose, that we ought to employ them in teaching what is best worth knowing, that English is better worth knowing than Sanskrit or Arabic, that the natives are desirous to be taught English, and are not desirous to be taught Sanskrit or Arabic, that neither as the languages of law nor as the languages of religion have the Sanskrit and Arabic any peculiar claim to our encouragement, that it is possible to make natives of this country thoroughly good English scholars, and that to this end our efforts ought to be directed.

. . . I feel . . . that it is impossible for us, with our limited means, to attempt to educate the body of the people. We must at present do our best to form a class who may be interpreters between us and the millions whom we govern, – a class of persons Indian in blood and colour, but English in tastes, in opinions, in morals and in intellect. To that class we may leave it to refine the vernacular dialects of the country, to enrich those dialects with terms of science borrowed from the Western nomenclature, and to render them by degrees fit vehicles for conveying knowledge to the great mass of the population. (Macaulay, 1835/1967)

One aspect in Macaulay's 'Minute' that is particularly striking is the absolute conviction with which he described the superiority of the English language, literature and culture over Indian ones. As mentioned earlier, this has always been a fundamental trait in the discourses explaining, justifying and supporting all imperialist activities, and was particularly prominent in British imperialism. Imperialism is often lined with a discursively constructed overlay of morally acceptable activities. As Hardt and Negri (2000) note, 'Empire is formed not on the basis of force itself but on the basis of the capacity to present force as being in the service of right and peace' (p. 15). Bringing higher forms of civilizations to other people is an over-arching mission which fulfils this necessity. By demonstrating that it elevated the 'natives' from their primitive state of barbarism by granting them access to superior forms of religion, law, language and literature, the empire could be seen to carry out its grand mission. Of course, the persuasive power of this idea depended heavily on the re-iteration of the fact that local religions, laws, languages and literatures were virtually worthless. Macaulay's assertions in this sense sound hyperbolic to contemporary ears but were perfectly in line with a very precise system of thought in his time.

Embedded in this rhetoric, the promotion of English was very clearly part of a larger imperialistic strategy. In his articulation of 'linguistic imperialism', Phillipson has repeatedly referred to the 'Minute' as eminently symbolic of the role that the English language has played both within British imperialism and within contemporary forms American imperialism. He sees substantial continuity in the ways in which imperialism, old and new, has both capitalized on English and imposed it as global linguistic capital (2012a, b), and Macaulay's document illustrates how the goals of the active diffusion of English have always been commercial and political.

This is a thesis that Phillipson has re-iterated through the years, with increasing emphasis on how the diffusion of English runs parallel to, and is entrenched in, the affirmation of a neoliberal agenda dictated by American neoimperialism:

We are experiencing massive changes in the world's economy, ecology, and communications. There is increasing inequality in our societies, and the military budget of the United States has doubled under President George Bush. In tandem with these momentous changes, the use of English is increasing. There is therefore a real challenge to explore how and why language use is changing, and how this relates to economic and political factors. (Phillipson, 2008b, p. 2)

The main outcome of that exploration is, for Phillipson, the recognition that '[l]inguistic neoimperialism dovetails with political and military subordination' (2008b, p. 24) and that 'global English [is] the capitalist neoimperial language that serves the interests of the corporate world and the governments that it influences so as to consolidate state and empire worldwide' (p. 33). With reference to the ways in which the world of global corporations evolved in recent decades, Hall (2003, p. 84) notes:

This New World elite of high finance helped transmute the old imperialisms of Europe towards the kind of supranational agencies that have risen above the sovereign control of all the world's nation-states save one. Most often the border-piercing language of these global corporate entities is English, the familial tongue of the 'cousins' continuity between the British and the American empires.

In this scenario, Phillipson sees English Language Teaching (ELT) as playing a central role in ensuring that English remains the world's dominant language, thereby serving imperialistic interests: 'the role played by ELT is integral to the functioning of the contemporary world order' (1992, p. 318).

During the course of the last three decades, and especially after the publication of *Linguistic Imperialism*, Phillipson's work has been extremely influential and the impressive volume of energetic debate that it has generated has undoubtedly stimulated profound reflection and encouraged the development of new ideas and beliefs about English, and the teaching of it, in the world. Some of the big questions raised are listed in an article published in the *World Englishes* journal in 2008:

- Is the expansion and/or learning of English in any given context additive or subtractive?

- Is linguistic capital dispossession of national languages taking place?

- Is there a strengthening or a weakening of a balanced local language ecology?

- Where are our political and corporate leaders taking us in language policy?

- How can academics in English Studies contribute to public awareness and political change?

- If dominant norms are global, is English serving local needs or merely subordinating its users to the American empire project? (Phillipson, 2008a, p. 265)

With particular reference to the linguistic situation of the European Union, where English is increasing its dominant position as *the* lingua franca despite the presence of official policies which expressly promote multilingualism, in this paper Phillipson wonders whether English shouldn't be more aptly named *lingua frankensteinia*, to reflect the monstrous purposes that the language has too often, and for too long, been promoted and taught worldwide. The editors of the journal invited a few scholars to write short comments on Phillipson's paper. In many ways, the seven responses to Phillipson's article published in the same issue represent the range of reactions that Phillipson's work and the theory of linguistic imperialism in general have attracted over the years. The following section provides an overview.

6.5   Responses to linguistic imperialism

It is quite clear that 'linguistic imperialism' has provoked strong feelings and, accordingly, responses to it have tended to be expressed rather animatedly. In an interview that Ana Wu conducted with him in the 'Non-Native English Speakers in TESOL of the Month' blog, Phillipson recounted: 'Tove [Skutnabb-Kangas] told me, as soon as *Linguistic Imperialism* was published, that I would need to develop a thick skin. I felt the need to spend quite a bit of time responding to critiques of my work that I thought were invalid, in several journals' (Wu, 2009).

In the following subsections, I have attempted to categorize the responses to 'linguistic imperialism' into three main types. Of course, the headings that I've chosen suffer from all the inevitable flaws that any classification like this entails. Like all categorizations, mine is an a posteriori attempt to identify patterns, rather than to pigeonhole ideas or the people who put them forward:

Agency: Phillipson makes numerous references to various people – politicians, language educators, academics and so on – in the Inner Circle who are the perpetrators of the continued dominance of English in the world, with all the consequences that this produces. But what about those in the so-called 'Periphery'? Are they irremediably the victims of somebody else's plans? Aren't they able to make their own informed decisions concerning which language(s) they choose to use and/or learn?

Linguistic determinism: Some scholars have objected that 'linguistic imperialism' seems to be based on a rather strong version of linguistic relativity, also referred to as *linguistic determinism*, in its suggesting that particular cultural/ideological values are 'hard-coded' in the linguistic forms of English (i.e. its vocabulary, grammar and syntax). Thus, while a number of scholars may share many of Phillipson's critiques of (neo-)imperialism, they feel that the problem doesn't necessarily lie specifically with the language itself, but with large socio-economic factors related, for example, to the unequal distribution of wealth.

Appropriation: This, in a way, is the most classic 'World Englishes' response and points out that English doesn't have to be accepted 'as is', a-critically and tout court. Wherever English has been transplanted, it hasn't been adopted as an unchanging monolith but has been moulded so as to fit the different socio-cultural milieus in which it has set new roots. That's how English has become English*es*. By transforming the language and bending its rules to make it suit their own experiences, Nigerian, Indian, Singaporean and so on speakers have been able to take possession of it, thereby enacting forms of linguistic *anti*-imperialism.

6.5.1   The 'agency' response

As it's considered to be part of a precise strategy to impose a world order policed and dominated by the United States, the promotion and diffusion of English everywhere is fundamentally a one-way process in the 'linguistic imperialism' frame. But this also means that those at the receiving end of this strategy are automatically depicted as passive victims who have English 'pushed down their throats'. This view has raised several objections by scholars who have asserted people's capacity to make independent choices. In one of the comments in the afore-mentioned issue of *World Englishes*, Fatima Esseili (2008) noted:

> While it is true that the actions of language agencies and the speeches of politicians provide evidence of the underlying agendas of some countries, like the USA, this is not proof that people and nations are unaware of such agendas, or that the choices they are making are uninformed, rather than driven by practicality and economics in the first place. (p. 274)

I made a similar remark in my own response, when I lamented that the 'linguistic imperialism' framework (which I inappropriately and far too cursorily dubbed as a 'conspiracy theory') didn't envisage the possibility of 'conscious, intelligent, and informed agency on the part of the stakeholders' (Saraceni, 2008a, p. 280). But this kind of objection comes from a long way. One of the first and best-known contributions to this very argument was made by Joseph Bisong (1995) in an article in which he engaged with many of the issues raised in Phillipson's *Linguistic Imperialism*. The main point he made was that 'Nigerians are sophisticated enough to know what is in their interest, and that their interest includes the ability to operate with two or more linguistic codes in a multilingual situation' (Bisong, 1995, p. 131).

Phillipson (1996) responded to Bisong's critique in an article published in the same journal, where he maintained that while he didn't intend to judge the choices that parents make when they decide to send their children to English-medium schools 'for pragmatic reasons', this did 'not alter the fact that the school system may be run on less than optimal lines, and definitely serves particular interests' and contended that '[c]hoice of school is in part a practical matter, and in part a question of how enlightened the education system is, and whether parents are aware of options and possible outcomes' (1996, p. 165).

Essentially, Phillipson's argument is that '[i]ndividual agency and decision-making reflect a range of societal forces and ideologies' (2008b, p. 34) and it is illusory to believe that they are entirely free and independent. As he pointed out in directly addressing my own comment, what one might too superficially identify as personal choice is often constrained by larger mechanisms such as 'social stratification, language policies in education, the media, commerce, etc. that privilege one language above others' (Phillipson, 2009, p. 193). This is certainly a valid point, which, in hindsight, I take on board. The point, however, remains a contentious and not easily solvable one: is it really impossible for people around the world to make choices that are both fully informed *and* independent of a world order in which English is, at least at the moment, the undisputed dominant language? In actual fact, this is probably the wrong question to ask. Or, rather, it's a question whose answer can only be *no*: people do choose English *because* it's the dominant language, no matter how freely they make the choice. A better question is: are people empowered or disempowered when they choose English?

Of course, there is no easy answer to this question and certainly not one that can apply universally. For a start, 'English' can't be viewed only as 'good' or 'bad'. As Parakrama (2012) notes,

> It is presumed, both naively and disingenuously, that English is not a weapon of oppression . . . but rather it is a neutral and transparent medium, which is equally accessible and benevolent to all. Diametrically opposed to this view are those who see English only as an oppressive class-sword, utterly oblivious to the opportunities for upward mobility and a slice of the pie that the language provides. . . . (p. 120)

In the same way as 'English' is not one thing, so there is no such person as the prototypical 'speaker of English'. Many variables are involved, concerning both global cultural, economic and demographic flows and the local circumstances in which each individual operates. Ultimately, therefore, each individual has their own story where English plays a different role. In their detailed assessment of 'global English' as capital in the neoliberalist world order, Park and Wee (2012) say that

> The problem is that the image of the entrepreneurial self leads us to believe that if one has access to English, that will serve as linguistic capital with maximal convertibility, allowing us to reach diverse audiences, fully develop our untapped potential, and become a well-adapted person in the neoliberal market – when this is patently not true. (Park & Wee, 2012, p. 161)

I fully agree with Park and Wee. The image of 'entrepreneurial self' is constructed within, and actively encouraged in, neoliberalism. It is indicative, for example, that, in a context where everything is commodified, knowledge is turned into an item for sale too, capitalized in the education system into something that can be directly converted into 'employability'. Within this scenario, universities have embraced a marketing model and are transforming themselves into knowledge service providers whose customers are turned into infinite replicas of employable entrepreneurial selves ready to enter the 'labour market'. In many parts of the world, 'English' – or the images that are constructed of it – is a core component of this knowledge-as-commodity (P. K. W. Tan & Rubdy, 2008; Chowdhury & Phan Le Ha, 2014), as it is packaged and sold to young people aspiring to benefit from all the advantages advertised on the box.

However, I believe a central point here is the difference between access to English as a linguistic code and access to *discourses* that are often realized *through* English. That access to English brings material advantages in certain contexts and for certain people is undeniable. The reasons and the consequences of this can be discussed politically, sociologically, historically at length, but the crude fact is unquestionable and there's therefore a risk that such discussions hit a dead-end where hypothetical 'solutions' sit awkwardly in the company of semi-apocalyptic scenarios where English is the only language left in the world. As Mufwene (2010, p. 927) notes, '[m]any people who are struggling to improve their living conditions in the current ever-changing socio-economic ecologies are not concerned with maintaining languages and heritages, which are more properly archived in libraries and museums'. But if we shift the discussion to the plane of discourses, then *access* acquires a fundamentally different value. The next section explores this more in detail.

6.5.2   *The 'linguistic determinism' response*

One of the principles in 'linguistic imperialism' is that between 'language' and 'culture' there is an inextricable link and each language expresses its own culture. In the words of Franz Fanon (1952/1967): 'To speak means to be in a position to use a certain syntax, to grasp the morphology of this or that language, but it means above all to assume a culture' (pp. 17–18). This is a central idea underpinning the concern that the minds of those who learn to speak English are inevitably 'colonized' by the ideologies engrained in the language:

One does not learn a language solely as a system of lexical usage, grammar, and pronunciation utilized to express meaning, but also as a vehicle for the conveying of ideologies which seek to define the individual, the world, and the social realities which frame human experience. In the process of learning a language, one is ontologically colonized by the ideologies which flourish in the acquired tongue. (Modiano, 2001, p. 161)

These ideologies are 'interwoven into the use of language' and 'come to inhabit the minds of the learners of English, like soldiers hiding in a Trojan horse', as 'an ontological imperialism is given new territory to conquer' (p. 164). The idea that people see and understand the world through the lens of the language they speak echoes the concept of linguistic relativity seen earlier (Section 6.2.1). Wierzbicka (2006, 2010) has applied Humboldt's linguistic principles in order to uncover the 'hidden cultural legacy of English', focussing particularly on specific keywords which 'define the conceptual world inhabited by speakers of what [she] call[s] "Anglo English"' (Wierzbicka, 2010, p. 3).

Arguing that Humboldt's ideas about language are still perfectly valid, Wierzbicka rejects the possibility that English may be a 'neutral' language, but argues that it is, like all other languages, inexorably bound to the culture it expresses and represents. Accordingly:

> With the ever-increasing dominance of English in the contemporary world (cf., e.g. Graddol 2006), there is a growing urgency to the question of whether an irreconcilable conflict exists between the view that English is shared by people from many different cultural traditions and the notion that English itself – like any other language – has certain cultural assumptions and values embedded in it. (Wierzbicka, 2010, pp. 4–5)

From the point of view of 'linguistic imperialism', the fact that English is shared by people from many different cultural traditions doesn't help solve the problem that the language actually imposes a particular worldview. On the contrary, this is seen as *the* problem:

> This is the Anglo-American civilising mission of the 20th century, to ensure that all citizens of the world . . . are not confined to English for merely instrumental purposes. Its users will also adopt worldviews that will make them understand that the West, out of sheer benevolence, has taken upon itself the right to decide how world affairs should be run. (Phillipson, 2008b, pp. 14–15)

This is why, according to Phillipson, the discourse of 'those who celebrate the dissemination of English worldwide . . . serves both to constitute and confirm English dominance and American empire, and the interlocking structures and ideologies that underpin "global" English and corporate interests' (p. 4), and so '[t]he scholarly cheer-leaders of global English are complicit in legitimating this dominance' (p. 8). Indeed, one definition of 'linguistic imperialism' cited in Phillipson's book explicitly establishes a link between language and the effects it has on the minds of its speakers:

> The phenomenon in which the minds and lives of the speakers of a language are dominated by another language to the point where they believe that they can and should use only that foreign language when it comes to translations dealing with the more advanced aspects of life such as education, philosophy, literature, governments, the administration of justice, etc. . . . Linguistic imperialism has a subtle way of warping the minds, attitudes, and aspirations of even the noblest in a society and of preventing him from appreciating and realizing the full potentialities of indigenous languages. (Ansre, 1979, pp. 12–13, cited in Phillipson, 1992, p. 56)

But all of this, of course, relies on blind faith in the axiom that the linguistic forms of a language constitute an ideological straitjacket that constricts the speaker within the language's own culture. It also relies on absolute trust in the capacity of an assortment of politicians and commentators (like Macaulay earlier) to display deep and sophisticated understanding of language. In an editorial in the *Guardian* on 29 June 1986, for example, the conservative politician Kenneth Baker, who at the time was Secretary of State for Education and Science, said:

> If our partners, wherever they may live, are obliged to speak English as their second language, as most have been brought up to do, are we not more likely to compete effectively by communicating on unequal terms: terms in which the inequality counts in our favour? . . .
>
> This is not a question of arrogance, simply of commercial prudence. Like North Sea Oil, the universality of English is a gift of history which it is in no way improper to exploit.

This is one of the many voices that Phillipson has quoted over the years in order to demonstrate that the diffusion and promotion of English worldwide is part of a precise strategy. Another one is that of David Rothkopf, the former Deputy Undersecretary of the Commerce Department under the Clinton Administration, who, in an article entitled 'In praise of cultural imperialism?' made references to the English language as part of his view of US-led world order:

> It is in the general interest of the United States to encourage the development of a world in which the fault lines separating nations are bridged by shared

interests. And it is in the economic and political interests of the United States to ensure that if the world is moving toward a common language, it be English; that if the world is moving toward common telecommunications, safety, and quality standards, they be American; that if the world is becoming linked by television, radio, and music, the programming be American; and that if common values are being developed, they be values with which Americans are comfortable.

These are not simply idle aspirations. English is linking the world. (Rothkopf, 1997, p. 45)

These, and many other similar citations, constitute compelling evidence that some people, among whom we certainly find politicians, journalists, educationalists and so on, firmly believe that if the world speaks English, this will serve the interests of America and/or Britain. But do we, in sociolinguistics, have to accept this view completely a-critically? Do we not have anything else to contribute to the debate apart from a meticulous identification of the voices of those who say they wish to rule the world via the precious help of the English language? Do we succumb to the metaphor of ENGLISH IS A KILLER?

Not everybody agrees. In another of the comments to the aforementioned article by Phillipson in *World Englishes* Bolton (2008) remarked that he did not 'see English *per se* as the major cause of such concerns' (p. 270), which encapsulates the type of response that I've put under the heading 'linguistic determinism', to denote disagreement with the suggestion that language per se determines particular worldviews. This is explained by Pennycook in the concluding chapter of a recent volume (Rapatahana & Bunce, 2012) whose title suggests the metaphor ENGLISH IS HYDRA (a many-headed monster from ancient Greek mythology):

The point that we need to try to get at is this: it is not English – if by that, we mean a certain grammar and lexicon – that is the problem. It is the discourses of English that are the problem, it is the way that an idea of English is caught up in all that we do so badly in the name of education, all the exacerbations of inequality that go under the label of globalization, all the linguistic calumnies that denigrate other ways of speaking, all the shamefully racist institutional interactions that occur in schools, hospitals, law courts, police stations, social security offices and unemployment centres. (Pennycook, 2012, p. 26)

Here Pennycook is referring to what he previously described as 'the power and the fixity of the discourses of colonialism as they adhere to English' (1998, p. 214). The idea of discourses that 'adhere to English' is very different from the nuts and bolts, the internal workings, of the language. Discourse does not equate to *code*. Once again, this is the distinction that runs through this entire book, namely that between language as system and language as practice. Once this distinction is accepted, possibilities begin to appear for people to articulate alternative discourses while still operating within the same conventions of what we call 'English'. The best demonstration that this is entirely possible is represented by the fact that most of the anti-imperialist discourse within the 'linguistic imperialism' frame is 'in English'. One of the most powerful calls for cultural and linguistic decolonization, entitled *Decolonising the Mind*, in which Kenyan writer Ngũgĩ wa Thiong'o (1986) denounced the negative effects of the dominance of English on African languages, was written 'in English'. Doesn't this show that discourses and counterdiscourses can be enacted regardless of the actual *code(s)* in which they are linguistically realized?

Whoever plots to rule the world by ensuring that the world speaks English may have to re-think the plan. One of Edwin Thumboo's best-known poems, *May 1954*, tells the 'white man' to depart from the shores of Malaya in the white man's own language and warns him: 'we know your language', to make him aware that he can no longer hide his voice, intentions and actions in the 'safety' of a language that is no longer his own private property. Similarly, 'while it is centrally through English that Indigenous people in Australia are racially defined, it is English that they need to know in order to understand those definitions, and to oppose them' (Pennycook, 1998, p. 216). In general, it is English that we all need to know in order to have access to the discourses produced in the (re-)configuration and (re-)assertion of power balances in the world. The idea that when people learn a language they also automatically embrace the 'culture' that supposedly comes with it is underpinned by an idea of language as a fixed system which 'naturally' belongs to a specific 'people' and is expression of their specific culture. From this point of view, English is Hydra. But if we 'address issues arising from the real world of socioeconomic inequality more globally and not just from the point of view of languages as maps of world views and illustrations of mental/cognitive variation' (Mufwene, 2010, p. 927), and we 'reconsider what we mean by the Hydra or by language, things might start to look a bit different' (Pennycook, 2012, p. 261).

One of the ways in which the notion of English has been re-conceptualized concerns its 'ownership', and this represents to the third type of response to 'linguistic imperialism', examined in the next section.

6.5.3   The 'appropriation' response

In another one of the comments to Phillipson (2008a), Bhatia (2008) responded to the suggestion that English is a *lingua frankensteinia* by invoking a classic

World Englishes position: 'The fusion of the so-called Standard English and Indian cultures produces a distinct variety of English which reflects the identities and thought processes of Indians across the globe' (p. 268). Such a localized variety can then be seen as evidence of the fact that Indian users of English have in some way claimed 'ownership' of the language, echoing the declarations of linguistic independence made by postcolonial writers (Section 3.4.2).

Indeed, there is apparent subversive potential in the idea of claiming ownership of a language perceived to be somebody else's imposition dictated by global market forces that are in turn determined by unequal power balances in the world. When Thumboo's 'we know your language' becomes 'we *own* your language', it's not just a matter of understanding somebody else's discourses, or having enhanced opportunities in the job market, but one of being able to (re-)construct alternative discourses. As we saw in Section 3.4.2, Salman Rushdie (1982) used the metaphorical image of 'carving out large territories within the language for themselves', which he saw as the precondition whereby de-colonized communities could effectively 'write back', that is, articulate counterdiscourses of the former colonial world by 'forging English into new shapes'. This is an idea that originates from early debates on postcolonial writing and continues to be expressed in virtually the same terms by contemporary writers, such as Chimamanda Ngozi Adichie and NoViolet Bulawayo, who expressly state that they have claimed 'ownership' of English:

> English is mine. Sometimes we talk about English in Africa as if Africans have no agency, as if there is not a distinct form of English spoken in Anglophone African countries. I was educated in it; I spoke it at the same time as I spoke Igbo. My English-speaking is rooted in a Nigerian experience and not in a British or American or Australian one. I have taken ownership of English. (Azodo, 2008)

Canagarajah (1999) has taken that very concept and applied it in the context of English language teaching/learning expressly as a way in which students enact forms of resistance to linguistic imperialism. In his study, Canagarajah was able to ascertain that learners were actors of 'discursive appropriation' of the language by operating modifications 'at the level of textual structure, communicative conventions, idea development, tone, . . . style [and] also grammar' (p. 175). To be sure, this doesn't simply involve taking the frame of 'appropriation' from postcolonial writing and applying it to language pedagogy, but represents a step forward from suggestions that 'turning English into a tool for one's own use is simply a matter of writing about the local context and sprinkling a few local words here and there' (Pennycook, 1998, p. 193). It is, instead, a way of claiming possession of the language but also, and possibly even more importantly, a way of redefining the concept of 'standard' more dynamically and locally situated, namely as a pragmatic system 'developed in the process of linguistic interaction by each speech community to conduct effective communication' (Canagarajah, 1999, p. 181).

The metaphor LANGUAGE IS PROPERTY, therefore, can be a powerful one. Going back to Macaulay's 'Minute' for a moment, another aspect that must be noted is the fact that according to his recommendations it was only a small proportion of the Indian population that needed to be taught English. The seemingly altruistic motive behind the choice of English as 'the most useful to our native subjects' is openly contradicted later in the 'Minute' when it becomes clear that the intention was to 'form a class who may be interpreters between us and the millions whom we govern'. English, therefore, was to become the language of a privileged Anglophone and Anglophile elite that would intercede between British officials and the rest of the Indian population. This point is particularly important given the misinterpretation that has sometimes been made of the 'Minute' as advocating the wholesale replacement of Indian languages with English. As Brutt-Griffler (2002) explains:

> Macaulay had no intention of 'Anglicizing' all of India, as is generally supposed. . . .
>
> . . . Most important to the adoption of Macaulay's policy, the British Parliament in 1833 issued a directive to the government of India that Indians were to be employed in ever growing numbers in the administration of the colony, a policy actuated not by ideological motives but for reasons of economy in the cost of governance. (Mayhew, 1926, p. 19)
>
> As a British administrator in India remarked, 'to give the natives a complete English education was the surest way of putting them in real and practical possession of the privilege of eligibility to all offices in their own country' (Cameron, 1853, p. 63), so long as that country was to fall under British rule. (2002, pp. 41–42)

The word *possession* is significant here. It would have been against Britain's interests to grant this privilege to all Indians. English was meant to be an elite language. To some extent, this is still the case in the Outer Circle, where English tends to be used more commonly by the urban middle-class, while its use in other sectors of the population is generally less frequent or even completely absent. So, the postcolonial claim of language ownership acquires even more value, in this sense.

6.5.3.1 Who owns what?

But the LANGUAGE IS PROPERTY metaphor can be a slippery one, too. Ngũgĩ wa Thiong'o, for example, completely rejects the notion that English can be 'owned' by Africans. In a recent interview on the BBC, he argued that claiming 'ownership' of English was part of what he called the 'metaphysical empire', whereby local African languages continue to be marginalized at the expense of English:

> English is not an African language. Full stop. . . . We have genuine African languages. . . . [Writers who claim ownership of English] are a product of the metaphysical empire, which is when people now begin to claim 'this place is really mine' . . . But when we use English we're contributing to the expansion and deepening of the English language, not Yoruba, or Gĩkũyũ, or Kiswahili. (Ngũgĩ wa Thiong'o, 2013)

But, even apart from this argument, the idea of property presupposes the existence of a material object that can be possessed. That language can be an object is something that has been repeatedly challenged in this book. If language is social practice, 'ownership' and 'property' can't easily be seen as valid notions.

Perhaps not coincidentally, the concept of 'language ownership' doesn't seem to resonate as a particularly intuitive one whenever I discuss it with my students, who often demand further explanation before they are willing to engage with it. Even then, they tend to be reluctant to accept the metaphor. I feel, in those occasions, that I might be forcing a concept onto them. I would *like* them to say something that conforms with my ideological convictions without however fully considering that the ideas I have in mind, and their metaphorical representations, may be totally alien to my students. In a sense, in trying to project onto them a metaphorical notion of 'ownership' that is actually more mine than theirs, I take possession of it, which is doubly paradoxical, since not only do they not feel a sense of ownership of English, but also they don't even entertain the idea that one can in fact 'own' a language.

Therefore, the property metaphor rests on rather fragile ground. Creative writers are, after all, a very restricted and special type of language users. My students are much more ordinary. So were those in Canagarajah's study. There, however, as well as in other studies (e.g. Norton, 1997; Higgins, 2003; Bokhorst-Heng et al., 2010), 'appropriation' and 'ownership' are not openly declared by participants but inferred by researchers on the basis of the ways in which language users 'project themselves as legitimate speakers with authority over the language' (Higgins, 2003, p. 615). Again, it can be said that, in a way, the property metaphor is (at least partly) (re-)possessed by researchers.

The process of (re-)possession is more complete when language users' feelings are entirely divorced from the equation and replaced by statistics regarding the number of 'native' and 'non-native' speakers in the world. In one of the most frequently cited passages in the relevant literature, Widdowson (1994) famously declared:

> How English develops in the world is no business whatever of native speakers in England, or the United States, or anywhere else. They have no say in the matter, no right to intervene or pass judgement. They are irrelevant. . . . [English] is not a possession which they lease out to others, while still retaining the freehold. Other people actually own it. (p. 385)

Similarly, Brumfit (2001):

> the English language no longer belongs numerically to speakers of English as a mother tongue, or first language. The ownership (by which I mean the power to adapt and change) of any language in effect rests with the people who use it. . . . Statistically, native speakers are in a minority for language use, and thus in practice for language change, for language maintenance, and for the ideologies and beliefs associated with the language. (p. 116)

Essentially, what Widdowson and Brumfit contend is that since 'non-native' speakers constitute the majority of English language users in the world, they also have 'ownership' of the language, due to the sheer power of the numbers (billions?) among their ranks. But this is not a battle between armies equipped with equal weapons. As I will discuss more in detail in the next chapter, in the discourses that adhere to the English language – and, especially, to English language teaching – the concept of 'native' speaker has nothing to do with a particular mode of language acquisition but is an ideological construct defined according to geography *and* ethnicity. Those defined and recognized as 'native' speakers are 'white' (another construct!) people from Inner Circle countries. Therefore, considering everything that has been discussed in this chapter, starting from the extremely unequal (and increasingly so) distribution of wealth in the world, it is clear how a numerical majority certainly doesn't automatically constitute a *powerful* majority.

Additionally, *power* to adapt and change the language is one thing, but the *feeling* of 'ownership' is quite something else. As I, rather polemically, commented elsewhere:

> . . . it is up to the individual speaker to feel, or not, a sense of ownership towards [English]. . . . Regarding a language as one's own, or deliberately refusing to do so, depends on factors that have nothing to do with someone else's vague awareness that one belongs to an imagined community of billions of other speakers of the same language. If those who consider themselves 'native speakers' are not the custodians of English, neither

should they be the ones who decide and declare who owns it and who does not. Otherwise, there would be very little substantial difference between leasing it out and giving it away for free, as the agency of the act would remain firmly in the donors' hands, no matter how magnanimous the act may be.

The ownership and the appropriation of English, as well as the right to subvert its rules, have very little to do with what linguists have to say about them. They reside intimately within the conscience, individual and/or collective, of speakers of English. Those who do feel a sense of ownership towards the language do not require authorisation from professional linguists, whose seals of approval are of little consequence. (Saraceni, 2010, pp. 14–15)

6.5.3.2   Open-source English

But perhaps we should do away completely with the ideas of 'ownership' and 'property'. Perhaps my students are right in rejecting these metaphors, in the same way as many of us in sociolinguistics are uncomfortable with the LANGUAGE IS COMMODITY metaphor. There is a useful parallel that can be drawn here between language and the development and use of software. Software can be either proprietary or 'open source'. In the case of proprietary software, private companies (often large corporations) develop programmes that help carry out certain tasks – for example, write a book, compose music, edit digital images and so on – and sell them to customers, who are obliged to agree to the terms stipulated in the license that these products come with. Essentially, the license says that the *code* of these pieces of software, that is, the actual sets of instructions that make programmes do what they do, is strictly the private property of the companies that develop them and the customer is not allowed to access, modify or redistribute it.

Open-source software is diametrically opposite. It still helps people carry out tasks, but programmes are developed collaboratively by groups of enthusiasts and made publicly available for anyone to use freely. Not only, but everyone is also encouraged to modify the code, if they're able to do so, in order to make a particular piece of software more robust or simply to customize it and make it suit their needs better. In this way, software is not 'owned' by any one person or company. Open-source software developers don't abide to copyright, but to *copyleft*, which guarantees that the ability to modify and/or freely redistribute a piece of software remains intact as the programme is further developed and shared by more and more people.

Could English, and indeed language in general, not be thought of as a non-proprietary collaborative effort, where 'ownership' and copyright have no place, which people make use of as they see fit as part of what they do? Isn't this a healthier and more democratic way of thinking of language than seeing it necessarily as a thing that somebody must own? Isn't the use of language displayed in Table 5.3 not evidence of this conception of language?

6.6   Conclusion

In this chapter, I've illustrated the theory of 'linguistic imperialism' and the responses that it has attracted over the years. The classic World Englishes response, which emphasizes the different varieties of English and the consequent local 'appropriation' of the language, helps envisage a scenario where the world is not dominated by ideologies embedded within the English language. However, the notion of 'language ownership' is not a straightforward one, as it often doesn't take into sufficient account, or attempts to (over-) interpret, the feelings of language users. The main problem seems to be not so much with the language per se, but with the discourses that adhere to it and that language users and learners seem to be influenced by. In a rather pessimistic note, Parakrama (2012) laments that learners in Sri Lanka still display a colonial mentality with regard to English:

> learners of English are actually hoping to become better human beings through English, and, as a corollary, people whose English is manifestly impeccable, in their eyes, are 'decent', 'punctual', team players, etc. Note, also, that the neo-colonial value system, which re-invests English in its colonial garb as the purview and prerogative of (white) English men and women, is also thriving here. . . . The values espoused by these students are reminiscent of a by-gone era. . . .

> It took us 40-odd years to uncouple the English language from England and the old colonial bandwagon, but the jolly old umbilical cord is still in place, it seems. (p. 122)

If the umbilical cord is still in place, it means that there is still work to do. So, where does this leave us? Without wanting to be too 'interventionist', taking into account the centrality of the *users* of English and of their agency, the obvious next step is to consider all the issues discussed so far in this book within the context of education, which, after all, has always been one of the main frames of reference in the field of World Englishes. In the final part of this book, therefore, I will address questions that are specifically related to the teaching and learning of English. Can education finally help permanently uncouple the English language from England in the minds of those who learn and use this language as part of their social practice? Can it foster the concept of 'open-source' English?

Key reading

- The authentic 'milestone' with regard to linguistic imperialism is the book which bears its name:
  Phillipson, R. (1992). *Linguistic Imperialism.* Oxford: Oxford University Press.

- Since then, Phillipson has continued to write about the topic. A useful compendium is: Phillipson, R. (2009). *Linguistic Imperialism Continued.* Hyderabad: Orient Blackswan.

- A very good recent edited volume is:
  Rapatahana, V. & Bunce, P. (Eds) (2012). *English Language as Hydra: Its Impacts on Non-English Language Cultures.* Bristol: Multilingual Matters.

PART FOUR

Pedagogy

7

Teaching World Englishes

I've learned that people will forget what you said, people will forget what you did, but people will never forget how you made them feel.

MAYA ANGELOU (1928–2014)

Keywords

de-anglicization of English • language and culture • models of English • native speaker • non-native speaker • paradigm shift

7.1 Introduction

Language education has always been a primary concern in World Englishes. The early debates outlined in Chapter 4 were all about the teaching and learning of English. Since the early days of World Englishes, pedagogy has continued to be one of the main preoccupations in the field, where a plethora of publications have been dedicated to this subject. Recent edited volumes include Gagliardi and Maley (2010), Alsagoff et al. (2012), Kirkpatrick and Sussex (2012a), Matsuda (2012), Zacharias and Manara (2013), Mahboob and Barratt (2014) and Marlina and Giri (2014).

In general, particular attention has been paid on three main questions/challenges:

1 *which* model(s) of English should be taught?

2 *who* should be teaching English?

3 *what* is the role of culture in ELT and how can we avoid the dangers of cultural and linguistic?

All three questions originate from the new ideas that were introduced with the development of the World Englishes paradigm in the early 1980s. In particular, the pluralization of English into English*es* meant that now there were alternatives to the one or two models (British and American) that had hitherto been considered sacrosanct. The norms of grammar, vocabulary, phonology and so on were no longer exclusively those of 'native' Englishes but also those of *nativized* Englishes. At the same time, as 'native' Englishes had lost their exclusivity, 'native' speakers were no longer necessarily the best teachers of English. Also, if English had been acculturated in different contexts, that is, if it had absorbed the cultural specificities of the various settings in which it had relocated, in what way, if at all, should teachers of English include 'culture' in their practice?

7.2   Which English?

Which variety of English should be taught? This is, perhaps, the most obvious question from a World Englishes perspective, according to which 'native-speaker' models aren't relevant outside their won cultural base and should be replaced by the English of the region where teaching and learning take place: Indian English in India, Malaysian English in Malaysia and so on. Two immediate problems, however, arise. One is the fact that many countries in the world don't have an established local variety of English. This is indeed one of the main reasons why research about ELF began: to 'fill a conceptual gap' and provide a model of English alternative to British/American English for teachers and learners in the Expanding Circle (Section 4.5). In this way, a more complete answer to the question addressed here would be a local variety of English, if it exists in the context under scrutiny, otherwise ELF.

Andy Kirkpatrick (2006, 2007, 2008b, 2010a, 2012), who has researched and written about this issue extensively, feels that the two approaches, local English and ELF, can be combined within specific supra-national regions, such as that of ASEAN (Association of South East Asian Nations), where English plays both an intranational role (e.g. in Singapore, Malaysia) and an international role. According to Kirkpatrick (2012), in a region which is richly multilingual like Southeast Asia, the goal of teaching and learning English should be 'radically redefined' so that

> [i]n place of the traditional second language acquisition target of native-like competence and adherence to so-called native speaker norms, the goal of the lingua franca curriculum is for students to be able to use English successfully in regional (and international) settings. Learners no longer need to sound like native speakers when speaking English. . . . Rather,

they need to be able to communicate successfully in multilingual settings. (2012, p. 39)

The second problem is more serious as it concerns the (lack of) recognition of local varieties of English in their respective countries. For example, we've seen (Section 4.4.1) how Singapore English is one of the varieties that have attracted more attention in sociolinguistics, and is also generally considered a well-established variety. However, outside academic circles, the recognition of Singapore English as a valid variety is much less secure. Through the 'Speak Good English Movement' (SGEM) launched in 2000, the government has actively sought to eradicate 'Singlish'. In a letter to the Straits Times, the national newspaper, two representatives of the Ministry of Information and the Ministry of Education explained the government position: 'While Singlish may be a fascinating academic topic for linguists to write papers about, Singapore has no interest in becoming a curious zoo specimen to be dissected and described by scholars' (Liew & Ho, 2008). The English Language Syllabus produced by the Ministry of Education establishes that the model for teaching and learning should be 'internationally acceptable English' and the only type of variation envisaged is with reference to differences between British and American English (Ministry of Education, Singapore, 2010).

In neighbouring Malaysia, the Ministry of Education is even clearer about which model of English it promotes: 'Teachers should use Standard British English as a reference and model for teaching the language. It should be used as a reference for spelling and grammar as well as pronunciation for standardisation' (Ministry of Education, Malaysia, 2012, p. 4). So, the use of Malaysian English for education purposes is simply not contemplated. In public discourse 'there is still an underlying notion that Malaysian English is *wrong* or *incorrect* English as indicated by letters and comments in local newspapers' (Pillai, 2008, pp. 42–43; see also Saraceni, 2010, pp. 100–130).

In this situation, the adoption of local varieties of English is extremely arduous. Indeed, Kirkpatrick and Sussex (2012b) remark how 'Asian Englishes are not an accepted part of syllabuses or curricula, and entity-English retains the prestige of the target model and drives pedagogy and assessment. Textbooks reflect this L1 English focus. L1 models of English, then, are still very much in play' (p. 2). This echoes similar comments about the resistance to change in language pedagogy:

Specific proposals addressing the question as to just what might constitute learning goals instead of the increasingly questioned native-speaker model are scarce indeed. And when we look at curricula, textbooks, and reference materials to draw conclusions as to what constitutes actual course content, we see that native-speaker models remain firmly entrenched. (Seidlhofer, 2011, p. 13)

Based on similarly entrenched notions, as 'native-speaker models' continue to be privileged, 'native speakers' continue to be seen as the ideal teachers of English.

7.3   (Non-)native speakers?

The role and the definition of 'native' and 'non-native' speakers have been discussed at length and for a long time in Applied Linguistics, especially with reference to language education (Rampton, 1990; Davies, 1991, 2003, 2013; Medgyes, 1994; Paikeday, 1998; R. Singh, 1998; Braine, 1999; Doerr, 2009; Bonfiglio, 2010) and continue to be rather contentious issues. The questions over which there is no universal agreement are:

- do 'native speaker' and 'non-native speaker' constitute absolutely separate categories?

- are these terms ideologically loaded and possibly discriminatory?

- do these terms involve extra-linguistic characteristics, such as ethnicity?

- even assuming that such distinct categories do exist, do members of one or the other category necessarily make better teachers of English?

- within a World Englishes frame, can we say that there are 'native speakers' of Outer-Circle Englishes?

7.3.1   *Separate categories?*

As Davies (2013) has pointed out, while research in Second Language Acquisition tends to make an a priori clear-cut distinction between 'native' and 'non-native' speakers, in sociolinguistics the tendency is to see a more nuanced and graded scale between the two notions or, indeed, to reject the terms altogether. He suggests that the following characteristics are normally said to define 'native' speakers:

1   acquisition of L1 in childhood

2   intuitions (in terms of acceptability and productiveness) about idiolectal grammar

3   intuitions about features of the Standard Language grammar which
    are distinct from idiolectal grammar

4   capacity to produce fluent spontaneous discourse, which may exhibit
    pauses mainly at clause boundaries and which is facilitated by a huge
    memory stock of complete lexical items

5   capacity to write creatively

6   capacity to interpret and translate into the first language (L1) of which
    s/he is a native speaker. (Adapted from Davies, 2013, p. 3)

He contends that only the first characteristic is an unchangeable variable,
while 2–6 are 'contingent issues' (p. 4) and thus equally 'accessible' by 'non-
native' speakers. This means that in terms of language proficiency, there
needs to be no substantial difference between people who have acquired a
language from childhood and those who haven't, since all characteristics 2–6
are developed later in life by everybody and don't depend on what language
one is exposed to in the cradle. The reason why it may be relatively easier for
'native' speakers to develop them is simply due to the fact that, after birth,
they are more likely to continue to live in an environment in which their L1 is
the primary language.

   However, this doesn't *automatically* mean that 'native' speakers *do* develop
characteristics 2–6, by osmosis. Being born 'into' a language and continuing
to live in an environment where that language is used does not, in any way,
guarantee that one automatically develops intuitions about that language,
fluency, creativity or the ability to translate into it. These all must be learned,
regardless of the language one was brought up with in childhood. This is
the reason why Davies prefers the term *native user* to designate 'the non-
native speaker (NNS) who lives his/her life professionally and often socially in
English' and argues that 'on international English-language proficiency tests
there is no significant between-group difference between native speakers
and native users' (p. 1). The advantage of the term 'native user' is that it
does without the negativity hard-coded in the *non*-prefix, which defines large
numbers of speakers of English by what they're *not*.

   Being born and raised in a place doesn't give any automatic advantage in
terms of language proficiency. It merely equips someone to operate within
a particular community with more confidence due to the familiarity that one
acquires with the social conventions and cultural references of that community.
Some of these conventions may be linguistic too. In Britain, holding the door
open for the person behind you as you enter a building is just as culturally
conventional as saying *cheers!* in return. Knowing what to say when being
asked about 'school vouchers' or 'membership cards' in supermarkets, or what
it means to 'open a tab' in a pub, or how to pay for a bus fare, or appreciating

and being able to participate in cultural aspects of humour – all these things don't make one a better user of English per se. They merely make one a more confident citizen *in Britain*, perhaps. But for the overwhelming majority of users of English in the world being a confident British citizen is entirely irrelevant. Exactly the same could be said with reference to the United States, Australia and so on.

All of this, of course, is based on rather uniform monolingual situations where children are raised in one language only, according to the country where they are born: somebody born in Italy will be raised with Italian and be a 'native' speaker of Italian, and somebody born in England will be raised with English and be a 'native' speaker of English. In reality, however, sociolinguistic environments are much richer and multilingualism and language diversity are far more common than monolingualism. In many parts of the world – and, increasingly, in Europe too – children aren't necessarily raised with only *one* language and are even less likely to grow up in monolingual environments. What is, in those cases, the value of the distinction between 'native speaker' and 'native user'? It can be argued that we are all *users* of the language(s) we speak in our daily activities. We all use chunks of language(s) according to what it is that we're doing. Nobody uses an 'entire' language, whatever that might be. Everybody uses what Blommaert (2010)'s calls 'truncated repertoires' (and, of course, the notion only really applies if we imagine language as having precise sizes).

7.3.2   *Myths and discrimination*

As it has been said many times, the supposed linguistic superiority of the 'native' speaker is a myth. But, as Barthes (1957/1972) showed, myths can be (very) powerful and 'the native speaker myth . . . persists' (Davies, 2013, p. 157). The conviction that those who 'qualify' as 'native' speakers have an insurmountable linguistic advantage is strong and is a direct consequence of another myth discussed at various points in this book: that languages belong naturally to specific territories and peoples (see Figure 5.2). Thus, somebody who is seen as a member of the people to which a language has a primordial connection is also seen as an ideal speaker of that language. This myth creates very *real* discrimination especially in the employment of teachers of English. For example, it is common for applicants to teaching jobs to be selected exclusively on the basis of their being 'native' speakers and regardless of their qualifications or their ability to use the language effectively outside their own communities. It is equally common for 'native' speakers to receive higher remunerations compared to their 'non-native' colleagues. This is particularly striking when discrimination takes place against local applicants who have studied for years in order to gain a good qualification in the teaching of English as a foreign/second language but are seen as less suitable in comparison to people whose only 'qualification' is a birth-place.

The conviction of the linguistic superiority of the 'native' speaker is common within academic discourse, too. The editors of academic journals, for example, often recommend that manuscripts be proofread by 'native' speakers before submission, in order to guarantee that the language be as accurate as possible if the authors are (thought to be) 'non-native' speakers. Such recommendations completely ignore the fact that writing accurately, especially in academic domains, has nothing to do with '(non-)nativeness' but is something that is acquired through study, practice and explicit metalinguistic awareness, none of which is even remotely related to whichever language(s) someone happens to have been exposed to in childhood. *Expert writer* and *native speaker* are completely unrelated. An yet, if an author is believed to be a 'non-native' speaker, anything that might appear to be 'odd' or 'awkward' or simply 'wrong' in their language is almost instinctively attributed to their being 'non-native'.

Often it's not even just a matter of a birth-place. The myth can acquire racial meanings. That is, the prototypical 'native' speaker is generally represented as a Caucasian, and being 'white' becomes virtually the same as being a 'native' speaker, to the point that it can override birthplace as its main defining trait, thereby adding an extra, even more worrying, layer of 'myth' to the notion. In the ELT job market, 'non-white' people from places that are popularly recognized as 'native English-speaking countries' are clearly in a disadvantaged position compared to their 'white' colleagues.

The advertisement in Figure 7.1 was posted on the job search facility within the UK government website www.gov.uk. The mismatch between the 'teacher-requirements' and the conditions of employment offered couldn't be more conspicuous. Although the advertisement doesn't say this, the requirement to include a photograph with the CV is very likely to be in order to ensure that those appointed are of the 'r/wight' ethnicity.

The correspondence of 'white' with 'native' is almost part of the semantic spaces of certain lexical items. The words *farang*, in Thailand, and *mat salleh*, in Malaysia, for example, refer to 'white' people and this is nearly always synonym to ('native') English speaker. Outside the Inner Circle, people who were brought up with English at home and learned other languages at school will refuse to consider themselves 'native' speakers if they feel they are of the 'wrong' ethnicity. Whereas I have been in semi-surreal situations in which I struggled to find suitable words with which I could explain that despite being 'white' (albeit of a suspiciously darker shade) I was not a 'native' speaker, to the disappointment or approval (depending on their points of view) of my interlocutors.

English teaching positions in China for the September semester

Job Description:
Location: North and South China
Salary: 5,000 – 5,500 RMB per month
Working Hours: 22 hours per week
Teaching age range: 5 – 12 years
Start Date: September 2014
Contract Length: 12 months

Bonuses:
Accommodation: Free fully furnished apartment provided
Utility allowance: All utilities are paid for by the employer (include gas, water and electricity)
Recruitment Fees: N/A
Airfare: 2,000 RMB reimbursed after 12 months
Visa Fee: Condition – reimbursed after 12 months
Airport Pickups: Yes

Teacher Requirements:
Must be from a Native English-speaking country
Age between 22 and 45 years old
No degree required
No experience necessary

To Apply: Please send your up to date CV/resume with photo attached.

FIGURE 7.1 *An English language teaching job advert.*

One of these moments occurred when I participated in a panel discussion during the nineteenth MELTA (Malaysian English Language Teaching Association) International Conference held in Kuching, Sarawak, in June 2010. The discussion was part of a forum on 'The Role Of Native Speaker Teachers and Trainers in Second and Foreign Language Teaching', organized in the wake of the Malaysian Ministry of Education's announcement of its plan to invite 'hundreds of native speakers to act as trainers and consultants to the Malaysian English Language Teaching Community' (MELTA, 2010). Some of the conclusions reached at the forum were:

- Competence and professional training are more important than native-speaker status, as primary criteria for selection of trainers and consultants.

- Trainers need to be fully aware of culture, in terms of not just the social customs but also cultural beliefs about learning and teaching.

- Investing in native speakers from outside the country who will only be in the country on a temporary basis, particularly if they are not prepared for long-term commitment, is not the best way to build a sustainable pool of ESL teachers.

- The measure to bring in a community of sojourners as trainers undermines the expertise and legitimacy of home-grown talent and may have serious implications on Malaysian ESL teacher morale, motivation and self-esteem. (Adapted from MELTA, 2010)

The forum was very engaging and the conference as a whole attracted about 900 teachers both from Malaysia and outside. An event of this type is very useful to bridge the gap between academic community and practitioners. A gap which often remains too wide and keeps the two communities locked in different worlds.

7.4   The paradigm struggles to shift

The necessity to teach and learn English in a way that doesn't depend on models, materials and teachers from the Inner Circle has been argued for a long time (see, e.g. Kirkpatrick, 2012). Yet, just like local varieties of English find little space in teaching materials, 'non-native' speakers continue to be disadvantaged and compared unfavourably to 'native' speakers. Although the push for a paradigm shift has been advocated for 30 years, these ideas have struggled to be accepted outside academia, as seen in the previous sections.

What are the reasons for this situation? In particular, why is there such a conspicuous mismatch between the volume of scholarship that has been produced over the last few decades and actual impact in pedagogical policies and practice that it has (not) had? While it is of course impossible to provide one simple answer, we can probably identify certain major factors that have hindered the transition from theory to practice:

- On a global scale, the teaching of English is a very lucrative industry, driven by the logic of the market. As such, one-English-fits-all and monolingualism are much more efficient and much easier to package, advertise and sell than a multiplicity of different Englishes, let alone the idea that 'English' is a myth and that language is not a thing but part of social practice and not necessarily divided up into discrete entities.

- In fact, the selling and buying of English in this way is made all the easier by the very deeply rooted and commonsensical idea that languages are separate entities, each representing, and belonging to, a country, a 'people', a 'culture', just like national flags or national anthems. This is reflected, for example, in the conviction that learning a language is a richer experience if it involves learning about, and appreciating, cultural aspects of the specific area that the language 'comes from'. The older the connection between that language is thought to have with 'its' area, the more rewardingly 'authentic' it feels to know as much as possible or, better, to be 'immersed' in the culture of that area. So, the allure of British English – or *English* English – can hardly be surpassed, the only serious contender being American English, with the sense of modernity, 'coolness' and sheer power that it exudes.

- In many contexts, in the daily practices of teachers and learners in their classrooms, much of what is discussed within academic domains, that is, in specialized publications and international conferences, is either simply unreachable, or extremely hard to implement. Maley (2010) is unequivocal when he talks about 'the larger delusions which applied linguists and educationists in general suffer from' when they hope that 'the pronouncements they make on the basis of research or policy decisions are valid for classroom practitioners' (p. 37). He refers to a situation where the lived experiences of researchers and classroom teachers are so far apart that they rarely, if ever, meet.

The point made by Maley is certainly true, although there is some evidence that something, at least, is moving in the right direction. For example, some of Maley's former students from Indonesia, who were also my students, have moved on to become teachers of English as well as scholars producing research which they disseminate in international publications, with a strong emphasis on reflective practice (see, e.g. Zacharias, 2013; Zacharias & Manara, 2013; Floris, 2014). This is evidence of what Kumaravadivelu (2012) calls 'proactive research on the part of scholars from the periphery', which 'involves paying attention to the particularities of learning/teaching in periphery countries, identifying researchable questions, investigating them using appropriate research methods, producing original knowledge and applying them in classroom contexts' (pp. 17–18).

In addition, we are reminded of the importance of never losing sight of actual real contexts whenever we generalize about principles and practices. In this regard, there is perhaps a tendency to talk about the teaching and learning of English in relatively uniform and de-contextualized ways. This becomes particularly evident through the use of acronyms that are in regular currency in this field.

7.4.1   Acronyms and the (super-)diversity of language education

The activity of teaching English as a foreign/second language is normally named via a range of acronyms: TEFL (Teaching English as a Foreign Language), TESL (Teaching English as a Second Language), ELT, TESOL. These acronyms also feature in the names of

- professional organizations, such as IATEFL (International Association of Teachers of English as a Foreign Language), Asia TEFL, ThaiTESOL, MELTA and so on;

- academic journals, such as *TESOL Quarterly, ELT Journal, Asian EFL Journal* and so on and

- university courses, such as 'Applied Linguistics and TESOL', and many similar ones.

To some extent, these names objectify the activity of teaching (and learning) English and represent it as fundamentally one *thing* (apart from fairly superficial, and mostly outmoded, differences such as that between 'foreign' language and 'second' language). But if we examine the actual practice 'on the ground', we soon realize that underneath these blanket terms lie a vast range of radically diverse circumstances, motivations, goals, resources, methodologies and so on. Consider the following, real, situations in which the acronyms seen earlier could apply:

- A private, Christian university in Surabaya, Indonesia. Students are wealthy and mainly ethnically Chinese. They learn Business English and their envisaged career paths take them to managerial positions in large companies, often owned and run by their own families. Teachers are both international (mainly from the United States) and local (but generally educated abroad). All subjects are taught in English.

- A state-run secondary school in the same city. The mainly Muslim and ethnically Javanese students learn English as a compulsory component in their curriculum. The content of their English classes has a strong focus on literature. All their teachers are local and most of them have never been abroad. All subjects are taught in Bahasa Indonesia, including, to a very large extent, classes of English language and literature.

- A rural school in the state of Terengganu, in north-east Malaysia. All students are ethnically Malay and Muslim. They learn English as a compulsory subject. Their English teacher is ethnically Indian and has obtained his teacher-training qualification in England, sponsored by the Malaysian Ministry of Education, which explicitly states that 'British English' is the model to be adopted in Malaysian schools.

- A private, very expensive 'international' primary school in Bangkok. Pupils, both Thai and the children of 'expats', learn all subjects in English, and are taught by 'native' speakers only. The curriculum is based on the British system.

- A university in Chiang Mai, Thailand. Students are both local and from other Southeast Asian countries. They learn English as part of a teacher-trainer course. Their teacher is Indonesian.

- A private language school in Edinburgh, specializing in medical English. Students are doctors and nurses wishing to work in the United Kingdom.

- A language school in London. This one specializes in teaching English to immigrants who need to demonstrate an appropriate level of proficiency in English in order to apply for a permit to stay in the country. But the school doesn't teach them English – instead, it sells them certificates for £500.

- A 'pre-sessional' summer course at a British university. The students are mainly wealthy Chinese young people who have not been able to enter good Chinese universities. Their level of proficiency in English is not very good, and their IELTS (International English Language Testing System) scores aren't high enough to meet the entry requirements of the British university they wish to study at. The course, taught by hourly paid part-time teachers, is designed to improve students' proficiency in academic English, in 4 weeks, to a level equivalent to the required IELTS score.

- A language school in the south coast of England, where students from European countries pay for 'all-inclusive' and 'full-immersion' 2-week study-holiday summer courses to improve their English. The students spend most of their out-of-class time socializing in same-nationality groups.

- A centre for refugee support in the same area which offers English language classes to asylum seekers and refugees coming from war-torn regions of the world.

Obviously, the list doesn't even pretend to be exhaustive and could have been infinitely longer. But it nevertheless serves to illustrate how radically different what we rather simplistically call 'language teaching' and/or 'language learning' can be. There is a case for research and academic discourse in general to get closer to this (super-)diverse reality and perhaps avoid, or go beyond, easy 'solutions' for more egalitarianism and equity.

At the same time, the need for egalitarianism and equity extends much further than language pedagogy. Proposals that put forward particular local varieties of English or ELF as appropriate models are well-intentioned, but excessive attention on the *forms* of the language may distract us from the larger issue of the profound inequalities that afflict the world and the forms of neocolonialism that ensure that such inequalities continue to increase. Critically, Kumaravadivelu (2012) remarks:

> In light of the global and local developments both in the society at large and in our professional community, it is only legitimate to ask whether the teaching of EIL [English as an International Language] as a profession has been sensitive to these developments and has come out with a sensible response that is commensurate with the challenges and opportunities. My reading of the prevailing situation leads me to answer the question with a resounding 'no'. What I see is a profession that continues to get entangled in terminological knots and one that easily gets distracted by superficial solutions instead of confronting the underlying causes that call for a radical re-conceptualization. It seems to me that, in order for our profession to meet the challenges of globalism in a deeply meaningful way, what is required is no less than an epistemic break from its dependency on the current West-oriented, Center-based knowledge systems that carry an indelible colonial coloration. (p. 14)

As I discussed in the previous chapter, the extent to which the English language is directly caught in mechanisms that produce inequality is debatable, but English language pedagogy may play a part not so much in informing people that they 'own' English, but in co-constructing awareness of the need to decouple this entity that we call 'English' and all the notions that are too often and too strongly attached to it: 'Britain', 'America', 'white people', 'Christianity', '(neo-)colonialism/', 'the West' and so on.

Kirkpatrick (2012) argues that English language curricula should include 'topics of regional and local cultures' (p. 40) rather than those of 'cultures traditionally associated with English – British or American, for example' (p. 38). Kumaravadivelu (2012) calls this association the 'native speaker episteme', which is not just about a category of teachers, but an entire system of beliefs that depends heavily on principles developed in the Centre (Inner Circle) and exported/imported in the Periphery. He therefore advocates 'a meaningful break from this epistemic dependency if we are serious about sanitizing our discipline from its corrosive effect and sensitizing the field to the demands of globalism and its impact on identity formation' (p. 15). So,

> Breaking the dependency on Western knowledge production will open up avenues for breaking other lateral dependencies pertaining to teaching methods, the teaching of culture, and instructional materials – three of the pedagogic domains where the native-speaker episteme has a direct bearing on what shapes classroom climate and classroom discourse. (p. 18)

7.5   Conclusion: Teaching world Englishes?

How can an episteme shift be implemented within a World Englishes framework? In the introduction to this book, I wrote that the revolutionary drive of World Englishes in the second decade of the twenty-first century was somewhat dampened while its analytical framework found itself struggling to keep up with developments in sociolinguistics. In the early 1980s, the idea of English as equally shared by people around the world who have appropriated the language and moulded it into different varieties expressing the cultural make-up of local contexts represented a very significant step forward from the conception of a monochrome English that was the exclusive property of a handful of nations. This idea, however, gradually began to lose momentum as it seemed to hang tenaciously onto a rather essentialist and nationalistic conception whereby each variety of English was identified with the specific country that gave it its name: Nigerian English in Nigeria, Indian English in India and so on. While the notion of discrete languages separated by fixed borders was being radically questioned in sociolinguistics and recognized as a product of the eighteenth- and nineteenth-century European nation-state ideology, and while, consequently, the concepts of language hybridity, translanguaging, code-meshing and super-diversity began to take centre-stage, the World Englishes framework began to appear less innovative than it had been in the past. The notion of *plurality*, so central in World Englishes, was challenged and re-interpreted as the multiplication of neat singularities. The concept of 'variety' couldn't easily cope with the kind of hybridity which crossed linguistic borders freely and upset 'norms' much more profoundly than did the presence of local 'flavours' in nationally defined Englishes. What used to be the subversive drive of World Englishes began to feel conservative.

The early debates in World Englishes made heavy use of religious metaphors: ideas were labelled as heresies, doctrines, sins, sacred cows and so on. But perhaps institutionalized religion, with its demands of faith and unquestioned adherence to principles, and with its gods, saints and spiritual leaders, isn't a particularly suitable metaphorical domain to represent research and scholarship. Also, the metaphor of a 'field' to represent a broad academic interest shared by a group of scholars should be used with caution and suspicion. Academic 'fields', especially when they are identified by precise names and corresponding acronyms – for example, World Englishes (WE), English as a Lingua Franca (ELF) – can become protective, sectarian and almost *identitarian* and, again, that's not particularly useful.

World Englishes shouldn't be seen as a set of unmovable precepts which, no matter how *new* that may be at one point, are inexorably bound to being superseded by more modern ones. World Englishes should represent a general *attitude*, a *mindset*, of scholars, teachers and students alike, who are *not* happy with blind, a-critical adherence to pre-conceived, never-challenged ideas but are willing to question them and, if necessary, develop them further or replace them with newer ones altogether. The plural in Englishes can continue to be relevant only if it keeps being subversive. The word is always underlined as an 'error' when I type it and I deliberately don't add it to my personal dictionary because I want to be reminded of its fundamental power to upset norms.

So, back to the question with which I opened this section: how can an episteme shift be implemented within a World Englishes framework? It seems to me that in an era where, particularly in the West, the aims of education are being reconfigured so that schools, colleges and universities provide an increasingly expensive 'service' which turns young people into employable clones for whom critical analysis is seen as unnecessary and redundant, it is precisely in education that the seeds of subversion need to be re-planted. It might be a good idea to return, for a moment, to the early days of World Englishes to see whether the pedagogical proposals made then can still be relevant now. Purposefully, this chapter bears the same title as the one which Braj Kachru wrote for the second edition of his classic collection *The Other Tongue*. 'Teaching World Englishes' didn't intend to be the exposition of a set of rules akin to those that might be recommended for the teaching of a religion. On the contrary, it was a call for inspiring a change in mindset. I'd like now to revisit the suggestions that Kachru outlined in the following six points:

1 *Sociolinguistic profile*: an overview of English in its world context with discussion of selected major varieties, their users and uses. A clear distinction to be made between the use of English in a monolingual

society, as opposed to a multilingual society, and its implications (e.g. mixing, switching).

2   *Variety exposure:* an exposition of the repertoire of major varieties of English, native and non-native: their uses and users, specific texts related to various interactional contexts, shared and non-shared features at different linguistic levels.

3   *Attitudinal neutrality:* for teaching purposes, one might focus on one specific variety and at the same time emphasize *awareness* and *functional validity* of other varieties.

4   *Range of uses:* the functional appropriateness of the lectal range of varieties within a specific variety (e.g. from educated varieties to the pidgins and basilects).

5   *Contrastive pragmatics:* the relationships of discoursal and stylistic innovations and their relationsips to the local conventions of culture (e.g. strategies used for persuasion, phatic communion, apologies, condolences and regrets).

6   *Multidimensionality of functions:* the linguistic implications of the functional range, as in, for example, the media, in literary creativity, in administration, in the legal system. (B. B. Kachru, 1992b, pp. 360–361)

It seems to me that Kachru's proposals for innovation in English language education are eminently sensible and can be adapted to the twenty-first century. Significantly, there's far less emphasis on 'models' of English, or the need to codify them, than has been the case in later literature in the field, and more focus on *attitude* and *awareness*. Let's consider the six points.

Sociolinguistic profile

Students need to know *about* English. They need to know the history and geography of English. They need to know about the 'origin of English' myth and its ideological motives. They also need to know about the forces that brought English around the world and why it is important to oppose and eliminate old and new imperialistic discourses that may adhere to it. Ultimately, the connection of the name 'English' to a particular place of 'culture' need not have any more significance than that of an etymological curiosity. There is no need to associate the learning of English to the adoption of any particular cultural value.

Variety exposure and attitudinal neutrality

Students need to experience variability. They need to relate it to their own lives. Not only do they need to be exposed to different accents, words or grammatical conventions, but they also need to see that language boundaries are not at all fixed and that whatever we call 'English' is part of larger linguistic repertoires that people have at their disposal. In other words, students need to be made aware that:

- what we call 'English' is no more than a set of linguistic conventions that are constantly open of (re-)negotiation according to the use we put them to as part of what we do;

- these conventions happen to be shared among a large number of people in the world, and this makes it a practical advantage;

- they don't need to be in competition with, or kept separate from, other conventions that happen to bear different names.

Range of uses, contrastive pragmatics and multidimensionality of functions

These points all relate to the importance of context, register and, therefore, of language-as-practice. Students should know that language isn't something that exists on its own but is an integral part of practice, and the way language manifests itself follows patterns that are determined by the 'multidimensionality of functions'. Students should be made aware that we mould language according to what we do, who we do it with and the role(s) that language plays in it. This shouldn't be taught prescriptively, that is, as sets of rules to follow in different circumstances, but within a broader strategy where contextual negotiation of meanings is more important than adherence to fixed rules.

Within this frame, difference and non-fixity are *organic* to language, not just a consequence of geographical spread. Students should be helped to *challenge*, not reinforce, the idea that each nation has its own variety of English. They should be helped to develop an awareness that they don't belong to a particular class of 'speakers of English' according to their birth-place or ethnic group, both of which involve ideologically constructed boundaries largely outside their own direct control. Learning English need not be seen as a strenuous journey whose ultimate destination is the achievement of 'native-like' status or a linguistic 'visa' into a special 'inner circle'. Learning English means, above all, making it easier to take part, actively and critically, in the practices and discourses that (re-)present, (re-)construct and (re-)shape the global and local worlds we live in.

Key reading

Many publications have been dedicated to pedagogical issues. The following edited volumes cover a wide range of issues from diverse points of view:

- Alsagoff, L., McKay, S. L., Hu, G. & Renandya, W. A. (Eds) (2012). *Principles and Practices for Teaching English as an International Language.* London: Routledge.

- Kirkpatrick, A. & Sussex, R. (Eds) (2012). *English as an International Language in Asia: Implications for Language Education.* Dordrecht: Springer.

- Marlina, R. & Giri, R. (Eds) (2014). *The Pedagogy of English as an International Language.* Dordrecht: Springer.

- Zacharias, N. T. & Manara, C. (Eds) (2013). *Contextualizing the Pedagogy of English as an International Language: Issues and Tensions.* Newcastle upon Tyne: Cambridge Scholars.

References

Académie Française. (n.d.). *Les missions*. http://www.academie-francaise.fr/linstitution/les-missions (Retrieved on 20 March 2014).

Achebe, C. (1965). English and the African Writer. *Transition, 18,* 27–30.

Adams, J. N. (2003). *Bilingualism and the Latin Language*. Cambridge: Cambridge University Press.

Alsagoff, L. (2010a). English in Singapore: culture, capital and identity in linguistic variation. *World Englishes, 29*(3), 336–348.

—. (2010b). Hybridity in ways of speaking: the glocalization of English in Singapore. In L. Lim, A. Pakir & L. Weel (Eds), *English in Singapore: Modernity and Management* (pp. 109–130). Hong Kong: Hong Kong University Press.

—. (December 2012). *Hybridity in Structure: Re-Examining Singapore English Grammar*. Paper presented at the 18th Conference of the International Association for World Englishes, Hong Kong.

Alsagoff, L. & Ho, C. L. (1998). The grammar of Singapore English. In J. A. Foley, T. Kandiah, B. Zhiming, A. F. Gupta, L. Alsagoff, H. C. Lick, L. Wee, I. S. Talib, & W. Bokhorst-Heng (Eds), *English in New Cultural Contexts: Reflections from Singapore* (pp. 127–151). Oxford: Oxford University Press.

Alsagoff, L., McKay, S. L., Hu, G. & Renandya, W. A. (Eds) (2012). *Principles and Practices for Teaching English as an International Language*. London: Routledge.

Anonymous. (27 July 2013). Public Enemy: 'We have always been innovators'. *Gigwise*. Retrieved from http://www.gigwise.com/videos/83184/public-enemy-we-have-always-been-innovators.

Ansre, G. (1979). Four rationalisations for maintaining European languages in education in Africa. *African Languages, 5*(2), 10–17.

Asante, M. K., Jr. (2008). *It's Bigger than Hip Hop: The Rise of the Post-Hip-Hop Generation*. New York: St. Martin's Griffin.

Azodo, A. U. (2008). *Interview with Chimamanda Ngozi Adichie: Creative Writing and Literary Activism*. http://www.iun.edu/~minaua/interviews/interview_chimamanda_ngozi_adichie.pdf.

Bailey, R. W. & Görlach, M. (Eds) (1982). *English as a World Language*. Ann Arbor, MI: University of Michigan Press.

Baker, P. (2010). *Sociolinguistics and Corpus Linguistics*. Edinburgh: Edinburgh University Press.

Barber, C., Beal, J. C. & Shaw, P. A. (2009). *English Language: A Historical Introduction* (Second edn). Cambridge: Cambridge University Press.

Barthes, R. (1972). *Mythologies* (A. Lavers, Trans.). London: Paladin (Original work published 1957).

Baugh, A. C. & Cable, T. (2002). *A History of the English Language* (Fifth edn). London: Routledge.

Beal, J. C. (2010). *An Introduction to Regional Englishes: Dialect Variation in England.* Edinburgh: Edinburgh University Press.

Bergh, A. E. (Ed.) (1903). *The Writings of Thomas Jefferson* (Vol. XIII). Washington, DC: The Thomas Jefferson Memorial Association.

Berns, M. (2009). English as Lingua Franca and English in Europe. *World Englishes, 28*(2), 192–199.

Bex, T. & Watts, R. J. (Eds) (1999). *Standard English: The Widening Debate.* London: Routledge.

Bhatia, A. (2008). Comment 1. *World Englishes, 27*(2), 268–269.

Bisong, J. (1995). Language choice and cultural imperialism: a Nigerian perspective. *ELT Journal, 49*(2), 122–132.

Blommaert, J. (2005). *Discourse: Key Topics in Sociolinguistics.* Cambridge: Cambridge University Press.

—. (2010). *A Sociolinguistics of Globalization.* Cambridge: Cambridge University Press.

—. (2013). Language and the study of diversity. *Tilburg Papers in Culture Studies, Paper 74.* Retrieved from http://www.tilburguniversity.edu/research/institutes-and-research-groups/babylon/tpcs/.

Blommaert, J. & Rampton, B. (2011). Language and superdiversity. *Diversities, 13*(2), 1–21.

Bokhorst-Heng, W. D., Rubdy, R., McKay, S. L. & Alsagoff, L. (2010). Whose English? Language ownership in Singapore's language debates. In L. Lim, A. Pakir & L. Wee (Eds), *English in Singapore: Modernity and Management* (pp. 133–155). Hong Kong: Hong Kong University Press.

Bolton, K. (2003a). *Chinese Englishes: A Sociolinguistic History.* Cambridge: Cambridge University Press.

—. (2–8 September 2003b). English: the Asian way. *Bangkok Post.*

—. (2004). World Englishes. In A. Davies & C. Elder (Eds), *The Handbook of Applied Linguistics* (pp. 367–396). Oxford: Blackwell.

—. (2008). Comment 2. *World Englishes, 27*(2), 270–271.

—. (2012). World Englishes and linguistic landscapes. *World Englishes, 31*(1), 30–33.

—. (2013). World Englishes, globalisation, and language worlds. In N.-L. Johannesson, G. Melchers & B. Björkman (Eds), *Of Butterflies and Birds, of Dialects and Genres: Essays in Honour of Philip Shaw* (Vol. 104, pp. 227–251). Stockholm: Acta Universitatis Stockholmiensis. Retrieved from http://www.english.su.se/publications/books.

Bolton, K. & Graddol, D. (2012). English in China today. *English Today, 28*(3), 3–8.

Bolton, K. & Kachru, B. B. (Eds) (2006). *World Englishes* (Vols. 1–3). London: Routledge.

Bonfiglio, T. P. (2010). *Mother Tongues and Nations: The Invention of the Native Speaker.* Berlin: Mouton de Gruyter.

Bowden, B. (2009). *Empire of Civilization: The Evolution of an Imperial Idea.* Chicago, IL: University of Chicago Press.

Brackmann, R. (2012). *The Elizabethan Invention of Anglo-Saxon England.* Cambridge: D.S. Brewer.

Braine, G. (Ed.) (1999). *Non-native Educators in English Language Teaching.* Mahwah, NJ: Erlbaum.

Braunmüller, K. & Ferraresi, G. (2003). Introduction. In K. Braunmüller & G. Ferraresi (Eds), *Aspects of Multilingualism in European Language History* (pp. 1–13). Philadelphia, PA: John Benjamins.

Brumfit, C. J. (2001). *Individual Freedom in Language Teaching: Helping Learners to Develop a Dialect of Their Own.* Oxford: Oxford University Press.

Bruthiaux, P. (2003). Squaring the circles: issues in modeling English worldwide. *International Journal of Applied Linguistics, 13*(2), 159–178.

Brutt-Griffler, J. (2002). *World English: A Study of its Development.* Clevedon: Multilingual Matters.

Callinicos, A. (2009). *Imperialism and Global Political Economy.* Cambridge: Polity Press.

Cameron, C. H. (1853). *An Address to Parliament on the Duties of Great Britain to India in Respect of the Education of the Natives and their Official Employment.* London: Longman, Brown, Green & Longmans.

Canagarajah, S. (1999). *Resisting Linguistic Imperialism in English Teaching.* Oxford: Oxford University Press.

—. (2006). The place of World Englishes in composition: pluralization continued. *College Composition and Communication, 57*(4), 586–619.

—. (2007). Lingua Franca English, multilingual communities, and language acquisition. *The Modern Language Journal, 91*(1), 923–939.

—. (2013). *Translingual Practice: Global Englishes and Cosmopolitan Relations.* London: Routledge.

Chakrabarty, D. (1992). Postcoloniality and the artifice of history: who speaks for "Indian" pasts? *Representations, 37,* 1–26.

Chomsky, N. (1957). *Syntactic Structures.* The Hague: Mouton.

Chowdhury, R. & Phan Le Ha. (2014). *Desiring TESOL and International Education.* Bristol: Multilingual Matters.

Cogo, A. (2008). English as a Lingua Franca: form follows function. *English Today, 24*(3), 58–61.

Cogo, A. & Dewey, M. (2012). *Analysing English as a Lingua Franca.* London: Continuum.

Considine, J. (2008). *Dictionaries in Early Modern Europe.* Cambridge: Cambridge University Press.

Corthoys, A. & Docker, J. (2010). *Is History Fiction?* (Second edn). Sydney: University of New South Wales Press.

Credit Suisse. (2013). *Global Wealth Report 2013.* Zurich: Research Institute.

Crowley, T. (1996). *Language and History: Theories and Texts.* London: Routledge.

Crystal, D. (2000). On Trying to Be Crystal-Clear: a response to Phillipson. *Applied Linguistics, 21*(3), 415–423.

—. (2003). *English as a Global Language* (Second edn). Cambridge: Cambridge University Press.

—. (2004). *The Stories of English.* London: Penguin.

Davies, A. (1991). *The Native Speaker in Applied Linguistics.* Edinburgh: Edinburgh University Press.

—. (2003). *The Native Speaker: Myth and Reality.* Clevedon: Multilingual Matters.

—. (2013). *Native Speakers and Native Users: Loss and Gain.* Cambridge: Cambridge University Press.

D'Egidio, A. (2014). The tourist gaze in English, Italian and German travel articles about Puglia: a corpus-based study. *ICAME Journal, 38,* 57–72.

Deterding, D. (2007). *Singapore English*. Edinburgh: Edinburgh University Press.

Dewey, M. & Jenkins, J. (2010). English as a Lingua Franca in the global context: interconnectedness, variation and change. In M. Saxena & T. Omoniyi (Eds), *Contending with Globalization in World Englishes* (pp. 72–92). Bristol: Multilingual Matters.

Doerr, N. M. (Ed.) (2009). *The Native Speaker Concept: Ethnographic Investigations of Native Speaker Effects*. Berlin: Mouton de Gruyter.

Dube, S. (2002). Mapping oppositions: enchanted spaces and modern places. *Nepantla: Views from South*, *3*(2), 333–350.

EF. (2013). *EF English Proficiency Index*. http://www.ef.com/epi.

Ellis, G. W. (1915). The psychology of American race prejudice. *The Journal of Race Development*, *5*(3), 297–315.

Esseili, F. (2008). Comment 4. *World Englishes*, *27*(2), 274–275.

Fairclough, N., Mulderrig, J. & Wodak, R. (2011). Critical Discourse Analysis. In T. van Dijk (Ed.), *Discourse Studies: A Multidisciplinary Introduction* (Second edn, pp. 357–378). London: Sage.

Fanon, F. (1967). *Black Skin, White Masks* (C. L. Markmann, Trans.). New York: Grove Press (Original work published 1952).

Ferguson, N. (2003). *Empire: How Britain Made the Modern World*. London: Allen Lane.

—. (11 July 2006). We must understand why racist belief systems persist. *The Guardian*. Retrieved from http://www.theguardian.com/commentisfree/2006/jul/11/comment.race.

Filppula, M. & Klemola, J. (Eds) (2009). Re-evaluating the Celtic hypothesis [special issue]. *English Language and Linguistics*, *13*(2).

Firth, J. R. (1957). *Papers in Linguistics: 1934–1951*. Oxford: Oxford University Press.

Fischer, O. (2013). The role of contact in English syntactic change in the Old and Middle English periods. In D. Schreier & M. Hundt (Eds), *English as a Contact Language* (pp. 18–40). Cambridge: Cambridge University Press.

Fleischman, S. (2000). Methodologies and ideologies in historical linguistics: on working with older languages. In S. C. Herring, P. van Reenen & L. Schøsler (Eds), *Textual Parameters in Older Languages* (pp. 33–58). Amsterdam: John Benjamins.

Floris, F. D. (2014). Learning subject matter through English as the medium of instruction: students' and teachers' perspectives. *Asian Englishes*, *16*(1), 47–59.

Foucault, M. (1972). *The Archaeology of Knowledge*. London: Tavistock.

—. (1977). *Discipline and Punish: The Birth of the Prison* (A. Sheridan, Trans.). New York: Pantheon Books.

Freeborn, D. (2006). *From Old English to Standard English* (Third edn). Basingstoke: Palgrave.

Frost, E. (11 February 2013). New Zealand: Britain but better? *WessexScene.co.uk*. Retrieved from http://www.wessexscene.co.uk/travel/2013/02/11/new-zealand-britain-but-better/.

Gagliardi, C. & Maley, A. (Eds) (2010). *EIL, ELF, Global English: Teaching and Learning Issues* (Vol. 96). Bern: Peter Lang.

Golub, P. S. (2010). *Power, Profit and Prestige: A History of American Imperial Expansion*. London: Pluto Press.

Graddol, D. (1997). *The Future of English?* London: The British Council. Retrieved from www.britishcouncil.org/learning-elt-future.pdf.

—. (2006). *English Next.* London: The British Council. Retrieved from www.britishcouncil.org/learning-research-english-next.pdf.

—. (2010). *English Next India.* London: The British Council. Retrieved from www.britishcouncil.org/learning-english-next-india-2010-book.pdf.

Gramley, S. (2012). *History of English: An Introduction.* London: Routledge.

Gupta, A. F. (1994). *The Step-Tongue: Children's English in Singapore.* Clevedon: Multilingual Matters.

—. (2010). Singapore Standard English revisited. In L. Lim, A. P. Pakir & L. Wee (Eds), *English in Singapore: Modernity and Management* (pp. 57–89). Hong Kong: Hong Kong University Press.

Hadikin, G. (2014). *Korean English: A Corpus-Driven Study of a New English.* Amsterdam: John Benjamins.

Hall, A. J. (2003). *American Empire and the Fourth World.* Montreal: McGill-Queen's University Press.

Halliday, M. A. K. (1978). *Language as Social Semiotic: The Social Interpretation of Language and Meaning.* London: Edward Arnold.

Halliday, M. A. K., McIntosh, A. & Strevens, P. D. (1964). *The Linguistic Sciences and Language Teaching.* London: Longmans.

Hamilton, T. (1833). *Men and Manners in America* (Vol. I). Edinburgh: William Blackwood.

Hardt, M. & Negri, A. (2000). *Empire.* Cambridge, MA: Harvard University Press.

He, D. & Li, D. (2009). Language attitudes and linguistic features in the "China English" debate. *World Englishes, 28*(1), 70–89.

Heath, J. (2001). Borrowing. In R. Mesthrie (Ed.), *Concise Encyclopaedia of Sociolinguistics* (pp. 432–441). Oxford: Elsevier.

Herder, J. G. (2002). Treatise on the origin of language. In M. N. Forster (Ed.), *Herder: Philosophical Writings* (pp. 65–164). Cambridge: Cambridge University Press (Original work published 1772).

Hickey, R. (Ed.) (2012). *Standards of English: Codified Varieties Around the World.* Cambridge: Cambridge University Press.

Higgins, C. (2003). 'Ownership' of English in the outer circle: an alternative to the NS-NSS dichotomy. *TESOL Quarterly, 37*(4), 615–644.

—. (2009). *English as a Local Language: Post-Colonial Identities and Multilingual Practices.* Bristol: Multilingual Matters.

Higham, N. (Ed.) (2007). *Britons in Anglo-Saxon England.* Manchester: Manchester University Press.

Hino, N. (2012). Negotiating indigenous values with Anglo-American cultures in ELT in Japan: a case of EIL philosophy in the Expanding Circle. In A. Kirkpatrick & R. Sussex (Eds), *English as an International Language in Asia: Implications for Language Education* (pp. 157–174). Dordrecht: Springer.

Hoad, T. (2012). Preliminaries: before English. In L. Mugglestone (Ed.), *The Oxford History of English* (Updated edn, pp. 9–38). Oxford: Oxford University Press.

Hobsbawm, E. (1987). *The Age of Empire: 1875–1914.* London: Weidenfeld & Nicolson.

Hobson, J. A. (1902). *Imperialism: A Study.* London: James Nisbet.

Hockett, C. F. (1958). *A Course in Modern Linguistics.* New York: Macmillan.

Hodge, R. & Kress, G. (1988). *Social Semiotics.* Cambridge: Polity Press.

Holborow, M. (1999). *The Politics of English*. London: Sage.

Hu, X. (2005). China English, at home and in the world. *English Today, 21*(3), 27–38.

Hudson, R. A. (1996). *Sociolinguistics* (Second edn). Cambridge: Cambridge University Press.

Huhne, C. (9 February 2014). To do business with India and China, Britain needs to lose its imperial swagger. *The Guardian*. Retrieved from http://www.theguardian.com/commentisfree/2014/feb/09/india-china-britain-empire-soft-power.

Hung, T. T. N. (2012). Hong Kong English. In E. Low & A. Hashim (Eds), *English in Southeast Asia: Features, Policy and Language in Use* (pp. 113–133). Amsterdam: John Benjamins.

Hutnyk, J. (2005). Hybridity. *Ethnic and Racial Studies, 28*(1), 79–102.

Huxham, T. (August 2013). *Tell Me about Eating in Andalucia*. http://ask.metafilter.com/246473/Tell-me-about-eating-in-Andalucia (Retrieved on 9 April 2014).

Hyam, R. (2010). *Understanding the British Empire*. Cambridge: Cambridge University Press.

Irvine, S. (2006). Beginnings and transitions: old English. In L. Mugglestone (Ed.), *Oxford History of English* (pp. 33–60). Oxford: Oxford University Press.

Jenkins, J. (2000). *The Phonology of English as an International Language*. Oxford: Oxford University Press.

—. (2003). *World Englishes: A Resource Book for Students*. London: Routledge.

—. (2006a). Current perspectives on teaching World Englishes and English as a Lingua Franca. *TESOL Quarterly, 40*(1), 157–181.

—. (2006b). Global intelligibility and local diversity: possibility or paradox? In R. Rubdy & M. Saraceni (Eds), *English in the World: Global Rules, Global Roles* (pp. 32–39). London: Continuum.

—. (2007). *English as a Lingua Franca: Attitude and Identity*. Oxford: Oxford University Press.

—. (2009a). English as a Lingua Franca: interpretations and attitudes. *World Englishes, 28*(2), 200–207.

—. (2009b). *World Englishes: A Resource Book for Students* (Second edn). London: Routledge.

—. (2013). *English as a Lingua Franca in the International University: The Politics of Academic English Language Policy*. London: Routledge.

Jenkins, J., Cogo, A. & Dewey, M. (2011). Review of developments in research into English as a Lingua Franca. *Language Teaching, 44*(3), 281–315.

Joseph, J. E. (2004). *Language and Identity: National, Ethnic, Religious*. Basingstoke: Palgrave.

—. (2006). *Language and Politics*. Edinburgh: Edinburgh University Press.

Kachru, B. B. (1965). The Indianness in Indian English. *Word, 21*, 391–400.

—. (1966). Indian English: a study in contextualization. In C. E. Bazell, J. C. Catford, M. A. K. Halliday & R. H. Robins (Eds), *In Memory of J.R. Firth* (pp. 224–287). London: Longman.

—. (1971). English in India: a Pan-Indian and international link. *English around the World, 4*, 1–7.

—. (1975). Lexical innovations in South Asian English. *International Journal of the Sociology of Language, 4*, 55–74.

—. (1976). Models of English for the third world: white man's linguistic burden or language pragmatics? *TESOL Quarterly, 10*(2), 221–239.

—. (Ed.) (1982). *The Other Tongue: English Across Cultures*. Urbana, IL: University of Illinois Press.

—. (1983). Models of New Englishes. In J. Cobarrubias & J. A. Fishman (Eds), *Progress in Language Planning: International Perspectives* (pp. 145–170). Berlin: Mouton.

—. (1985). Standards, codification and sociolinguistic realism: the English language in the outer circle. In R. Quirk & H. Widdowson (Eds), *English in the World: Teaching and Learning the Language and Literatures* (pp. 11–30). Cambridge: Cambridge University Press.

—. (1987). The spread of English and sacred linguistic cows. In P. H. Lowenberg (Ed.), *Georgetown University Round Table on Languages and Linguistics 1987* (pp. 207–228). Washington, DC: Georgetown University Press.

—. (1991). Liberation linguistics and the Quirk Concern. *English Today, 7*(1), 3–13.

—. (1992a). The second diaspora of English. In T. Machan & C. Scott (Eds), *English in Its Social Contexts: Essays in Historical Sociolinguistics* (pp. 230–252). Oxford: Oxford University Press.

—. (1992b). Teaching World Englishes. In B. B. Kachru (Ed.), *The Other Tongue: English across Cultures* (Second edn, pp. 355–365). Champaign, IL: University of Illinois Press.

—. (1992c). World Englishes: approaches, issues and resources. *Language Teaching, 25*(1), 1–14.

—. (2009). Asian Englishes in the Asian Age: contexts and challenges. In K. Murata & J. Jenkins (Eds), *Global Englishes in Asian Contexts: Current and Future Debates* (pp. 175–193). Basingstoke: Palgrave.

Kachru, B. B., Kachru, Y. & Nelson, C. L. (Eds) (2006). *The Handbook of World Englishes*. Oxford: Blackwell.

Kachru, B. B. & Nelson, C. (1996). World Englishes. In S. L. McKay & N. H. Hornberger (Eds), *Sociolinguistics and Language Teaching* (pp. 71–102). Cambridge: Cambridge University Press.

Kachru, B. B. & Smith, L. E. (1985). Editorial. *World Englishes, 4*(2), 209–212.

Kachru, Y. & Nelson, C. L. (2006). *World Englishes in Asian Contexts*. Hong Kong: Hong Kong University Press.

Kachru, Y. & Smith, L. E. (2008). *Cultures, Contexts, and World Englishes*. London: Routledge.

Kirkpatrick, A. (2006). Which model of English: native-speaker, nativized or Lingua Franca? In R. Rubdy & M. Saraceni (Eds), *English in the World: Global Rules, Global Roles* (pp. 71–83). London: Continuum.

—. (2007). *World Englishes: Implications for International Communication and English Language Teaching*. Cambridge: Cambridge University Press.

—. (2008a). English as the official language of ASEAN: features and strategies. *English Today, 24*(2), 27–34.

—. (2008b). Learning English and other languages in multilingual settings: principles of multilingual performance and proficiency. *Australian Review of Applied Linguistics, 31*(3), 1–11.

—. (2010a). *English as a Lingua Franca in ASEAN: A Multilingual Model*. Hong Kong: Hong Kong University Press.

—. (Ed.) (2010b). *The Routledge Handbook of World Englishes*. London: Routledge.

—. (2012). English as an International Language in Asia: implications for language education. In A. Kirkpatrick & R. Sussex (Eds), *English as an International Language in Asia: Implications for Language Education* (pp. 29–44). Dordrecht: Springer.

Kirkpatrick, A. & Sussex, R. (Eds) (2012a). *English as an International Language in Asia: Implications for Language Education*. Dordrecht: Springer.

—. (2012b). Introduction. In A. Kirkpatrick & R. Sussex (Eds), *English as an International Language in Asia: Implications for Language Education* (pp. 1–12). Dordrecht: Springer.

Kirkpatrick, A. & Xu, Z. (2002). Chinese pragmatic norms and 'China English'. *World Englishes*, *21*(2), 269–279.

Klemola, J. (2013). English as a contact language in the British Isles. In D. Schreier & M. Hundt (Eds), *English as a Contact Language* (pp. 75–87). Cambridge: Cambridge University Press.

Koh, M. (1 October 2012). Why parents push kids so hard for PSLE. *The Straits Times*.

Kövecses, Z. (2010). *Metaphor: A Practical Introduction*. Oxford: Oxford University Press.

Kumaravadivelu, B. (2012). Individual identity, cultural globalization, as teaching English as an international language. In L. Alsagoff, S. L. McKay, G. Hu & W. A. Renandya (Eds), *Principles and Practices for Teaching English as an International Language* (pp. 9–27). London: Routledge.

Lakoff, G. & Johnson, M. (1980). *Metaphors We Live by*. Chicago: University of Chicago Press.

Lamb, S. M. (2004). What is a language? In J. Webster (Ed.), *Language and Reality: Selected Writings of Sydney Lamb* (pp. 394–414). London: Continuum.

Lawrence, C. B. (2012). The Korean English linguistic landscape. *World Englishes*, *31*(1), 70–92.

Lee, J. S. (2004). Linguistic hybridization in K-Pop: discourse of self-assertion and resistance. *World Englishes*, *23*(3), 429–450.

Leimgruber, J. R. E. (2013). *Singapore English: Structure, Variation and Usage*. Cambridge: Cambridge University Press.

Levine, P. (2013). *The British Empire: Sunrise to Sunset* (Second edn). London: Routledge.

Liew, C. B. & Ho, P. (12 December 2008). Good English the way to go. *The Straits Times*. Retrieved from http://www.moe.gov.sg/media/forum/2008/12/good-english-the-way-to-go.php.

Lim, L. (2012). Standards of English in South-East Asia. In R. Hickey (Ed.), *Standards of English: Codified Varieties around the World* (pp. 274–293). Cambridge: Cambridge University Press.

Locher, M. A. & Strässler, J. (Eds) (2008). *Standards and Norms in the English Language*. Berlin: Mouton de Gruyter.

Low, E. L. (2010). English in Singapore and Malaysia: differences and similarities. In A. Kirkpatrick (Ed.), *The Routledge Handbook of World Englishes* (pp. 229–246). London: Routledge.

—. (2012). Singapore English. In E. Low & A. Hashim (Eds), *English in Southeast Asia: Features, Policy and Language in Use* (pp. 35–53). Amsterdam: John Benjamins.

Lowenthal, D. (1998). *The Heritage Crusade and the Spoils of History.* Cambridge: Cambridge University Press.

Macaulay, T. B. (1967). Minute on Indian Education. In G. Young (Ed.), *Prose and Poetry* (pp. 719–730). Cambridge, MA: Harvard University Press (Original work published 1835).

Mahboob, A. & Barratt, L. (Eds) (2014). *Englishes in Multilingual Contexts.* Dordrecht: Springer.

Makoni, S. B. (2011). Sociolinguistics, colonial and postcolonial: an integrationist perspective. *Language Sciences, 33*(4), 680–688.

Maley, A. (2010). The reality of EIL and the Myth of ELF. In C. Gagliardi & A. Maley (Eds), *EIL, ELF, Global English: Teaching and Learning Issues* (Vol. 96, pp. 25–44). Bern: Peter Lang.

Malinowski, B. (1923). The problem of meaning in primitive languages. In C. K. Ogde & I. A. Richards (Eds), *The Meaning of Meaning* (pp. 296–336). London: Routledge & Kegan Paul.

—. (1935). *Coral Gardens and Their Magic* (Vol. II). London: George Allen & Unwin.

Marlina, R. & Giri, R. (Eds) (2014). *The Pedagogy of English as an International Language.* Dordrecht: Springer.

Marshall, H. (1908). *Our Empire Story.* London: Thomas Nelson & Sons.

Matsuda, A. (Ed.) (2012). *Principles and Practices of Teaching English as an International Language.* Bristol: Multilingual Matters.

Mauranen, A. (2012). *Exploring ELF: Academic English Shaped by Non-native Speakers.* Cambridge: Cambridge University Press.

Mauranen, A. & Ranta, E. (Eds) (2009). *English as a Lingua Franca: Studies and Findings.* Newcastle upon Tyne: Cambridge Scholars.

Maurer, F. (1953). *Nordgermanen und Alemannen* (Third edn). Bern: Francke.

Mayhew, A. (1926). *The Education of India: A Study of British Educational Policy in India, 1835–1920, and of Its Bearing on National Life and Problems in India Today.* London: Faber & Gwyer.

McArthur, T. (1993). The English language or the English languages? In W. F. Bolton & D. Crystal (Eds), *The English Language* (pp. 323–341). London: Penguin Books.

McKenzie, R. M. (2010). *The Social Psychology of English as a Global Language: Attitudes, Awareness and Identity in the Japanese Context.* Dordrecht: Springer.

McLellan, J. (2010). Mixed codes or varieties of English? In A. Kirkpatrick (Ed.), *The Routledge Handbook of World Englishes* (pp. 425–441). London: Routledge.

Medgyes, P. (1994). *The Non-Native Teacher.* London: Macmillan.

Meinig, D. W. (1986). *The Shaping of America: A Geographical Perspective on 500 Years of History* (Vol. I, pp. 1492–1800). New Haven, CT: Yale University Press.

Melchers, G. & Shaw, P. (2003). *World Englishes: An Introduction.* London: Arnold.

—. (2011). *World Englishes: An Introduction* (Second edn). London: Hodder Education.

MELTA. (June 2010). *A Report on the Forum "To Go Or Not To Go Native: The Role of Native Speaker Teachers and Trainers in Second and Foreign Language Teaching" held at the 19th MELTA International Conference.* Retrieved from http://www.melta.org.my/images/MELTA_Native_Speaker_Forum_Report_2010.pdf.

Mencken, H. L. (1921). *The American Language: An Inquiry into the Development of English in the United States* (Second edn). New York: A.A. Knopf.

Mesthrie, R. (2006). Anti-deletions in an L2 grammar: a study of Black South African English mesolect. *English World-Wide, 27*(2), 111–145.

Mesthrie, R. & Bhatt, R. M. (2008). *World Englishes: The Study of New Linguistic Varieties*. Cambridge: Cambridge University Press.

Millar, R. M. (2007). *Trask's Historical Linguistics*. London: Hodder Education.

Milroy, J. (2002). The legitimate language. In R. Watts & P. Trudgill (Eds), *Alternative Histories of English* (pp. 7–25). London: Routledge.

Milroy, J. & Milroy, L. (2012). *Authority in Language: Investigating Standard English* (Fourth edn). London: Routledge.

Ministry of Education, Malaysia. (2012). *Kurikulum Standard Sekolah Rendah*. Putrajaya: Curriculum Development Centre.

Ministry of Education, Singapore. (2010). *English Language Syllabus 2010*. Singapore: Curriculum Planning and Development.

Modiano, M. (2001). Ideology and the ELT practitioner. *International Journal of Applied Linguistics, 11*(2), 159–173.

Mufwene, S. S. (2010). The role of mother-tongue schooling in eradicating poverty: a response to *Language and Poverty*. *Language, 86*(4), 901–932.

Mugglestone, L. (2003). *Talking Proper: The Rise of Accent as Social Symbol* (Second edn). Oxford: Oxford University Press.

—. (2012). Introduction: a history of English. In L. Mugglestone (Ed.), *The Oxford History of English* (Updated edn, pp. 1–8). Oxford: Oxford University Press.

Munslow, A. (2006). *Deconstructing History* (Second edn). London: Routledge.

Muysken, P. (2011). Code-switching. In R. Mesthrie (Ed.), *The Cambridge Handbook of Sociolinguistics* (pp. 301–314). Cambridge: Cambridge University Press.

Nelson, C. L. (2011). *Intelligibility in world Englishes: Theory and Application*. London: Routledge.

Ngũgĩ wa Thiong'o. (1986). *Decolonising the Mind: The Politics of Language in African Literature*. Portsmouth, NH: Heinemann.

—. (24 July 2013). *HARDtalk with Ngũgĩ wa Thiong'o*. http://www.bbc.co.uk/programmes/b037bt3l. British Broadcasting Corporation.

Norton, B. (1997). Language, identity, and the ownership of English. *TESOL Quarterly, 31*(3), 409–429.

Nunan, D. (2012). *What Is This Thing Called Language?* (Second edn). Basingstoke: Palgrave Macmillan.

Okara, G. (1963). African Speech . . . English words. *Transition, 3*(10), 15–16.

O'Leary, J. (1995). Prince says Americans are ruining the language. *The Times*, 24 March 1995.

Oppenheimer, S. (2006). *The Origins of the British: A Genetic Detective Story*. London: Constable & Robinson.

Otsuji, E. & Pennycook, A. (2010). Metrolingualism: fixity, fluidity and language in flux. *International Journal of Multilingualism, 7*(3), 240–254.

—. (2013). Unremarkable hybridities and metrolingual practices. In R. Rubdy & L. Alsagoff (Eds), *The Global–Local Interface and Hybridity* (pp. 83–99). Bristol: Multilingual Matters.

Page, R. I. (1995). *Runes and Runic Inscriptions*. Woodbridge: The Boydell Press.

Paikeday, T. M. (1998). *The Native Speaker is Dead!* Toronto: Paikeday.

Panitch, L. & Gindin, S. (2004). *Global Capitalism and American Empire*. London: Merlin.

Parakrama, A. (2012). The *Malchemy* of English in Sri Lanka: reinforcing inequality through imposing extra-linguistic value. In V. Rapatahana & P. Bunce (Eds), *English Language as Hydra: Its Impacts on Non-English Language Cultures* (pp. 107–132). Bristol: Multilingual Matters.

Park, J. S.-Y. & Wee, L. (2012). *Markets of English: Linguistic Capital and Language Policy in a Globalizing World*. London: Routledge.

Pattison, J. E. (2008). Is it necessary to assume an apartheid-like social structure in Early Anglo-Saxon England? *Proceeding of the Royal Society, 275*(1650), 2423–2429.

Pennycook, A. (1998). *English and the Discourses of Colonialism*. London: Routledge.

—. (2003). Global Englishes, Rip Slyme, and performativity. *Journal of Sociolinguistics, 7*(4), 513–533.

—. (2007a). *Global Englishes and Transcultural Flows*. London: Routledge.

—. (2007b). The myth of English as an international language. In S. Makoni & A. Pennycook (Eds), *Disinventing and Reconstituting Languages* (pp. 90–115). Clevedon: Multilingual Matters.

—. (2010a). *Laguage as a Local Practice*. London: Routledge.

—. (2010b). Rethinking Origins and Localizations in Global Englishes. In M. Saxena & T. Omoniyi (Eds), *Contending with Globalization in World Englishes* (pp. 196–210). Bristol: Multilingual Matters.

—. (2012). Afterword: could Heracles have gone about things differently? In V. Rapatahana & P. Bunce (Eds), *English Language as Hydra: Its Impacts on Non-English Language Cultures* (pp. 255–262). Bristol: Multilingual Matters.

Phillipson, R. (1992). *Linguistic Imperialism*. Oxford: Oxford University Press.

—. (1996). Linguistic imperialism: African perspectives. *ELT Journal, 50*(2), 160–167.

—. (1999). Voice in Global English: Unheard Chords in Crystal Loud and Clear. *Applied Linguistics, 20*(2), 265–276.

—. (2008a). Lingua Franca or Lingua Frankensteinia? English in European integration and globalisation. *World Englishes, 27*(2), 250–267.

—. (2008b). The linguistic imperialism of neoliberal empire. *Critical Inquiry in Language Studies, 5*(1), 1–43.

—. (2009). *Linguistic Imperialism Continued*. Hyderabad: Orient Blackswan.

—. (2012a). English: from British empire to corporate empire. *Sociolinguistic Studies, 5*(3), 441–464.

—. (13 March 2012b). Linguistic imperialism alive and kicking. *The Guardian*. Retrieved from http://www.theguardian.com/education/2012/mar/13/linguistic-imperialism-english-language-teaching.

Pillai, S. (2008). Speaking English the Malaysian way – correct or not? *English Today, 24*(4), 42–45.

Platt, J. T., Weber, H. & Ho, M. L. (1983). *Singapore and Malaysia*. Amsterdam: John Benjamins.

—. (1984). *The New Englishes*. London: Routledge & Kegan Paul.

Prator, C. H. (1968). The British heresy in TESL. In J. Fishman, C. Ferguson & J. Das Gupta (Eds), *Language Problems of Developing Nations* (pp. 459–476). London: Wiley.

Pride, J. B. (Ed.) (1982). *New Englishes*. Rowley, MA: Newbury House.
—. (1985). [Review of *English as a World Language*, by R. W. Bailey and M. Görlach]. *Language in Society, 14*(3), 379–387.
Prodromou, L. (2010). *English as a Lingua Franca: A Corpus-Based Analysis*. London: Continuum.
Quirk, R. (1985). The English language in a global context. In R. Quirk & H. G. Widdowson (Eds), *English in the World: Teaching and Learning the Language and Literatures* (pp. 1–6). Cambridge: Cambridge University Press.
—. (1990). Language varieties and standard language. *English Today, 6*(1), 3–10.
Rampton, M. B. H. (1990). Displacing the 'native speaker': expertise, affiliation, and inheritance. *ELT Journal, 44*(2), 97–101.
Rao, R. (1938). *Kanthapura*. London: George Allen & Unwin.
Rapatahana, V. & Bunce, P. (Eds) (2012). *English Language as Hydra: Its Impacts on Non-English Language Cultures*. Bristol: Multilingual Matters.
Reuters. (12 March 2014). *Gambia to Stop Using "Colonial Relic" English – President*. Retrieved from http://uk.reuters.com/article/2014/03/12/uk-gambia-language-idUKBREA2B23N20140312
Reynolds, S. (1985). What do we mean by 'Anglo-Saxon' and 'Anglo-Saxons'? *Journal of British Studies, 24*(4), 395–414.
Roberts, A. (2006). *A History of the English-Speaking Peoples since 1900*. London: Weidenfeld & Nicolson.
Rothkopf, D. (1997). In praise of cultural imperialism? *Foreign Policy, Summer 97*(107), 38–53.
Rubdy, R. (2013). Hybridity in the linguistic landscape: democratizing English in India. In R. Rubdy & L. Alsagoff (Eds), *The Global–Local Interface and Hybridity: Exploring Language and Identity* (pp. 43–65). Bristol: Multilingual Matters.
Rubdy, R. & Alsagoff, L. (2013). The cultural dynamics of globalization: problematizing hybridity. In R. Rubdy & L. Alsagoff (Eds), *The Global–Local Interface and Hybridity* (pp. 1–14). Bristol: Multilingual Matters.
Rubdy, R., McKay, S. L., Alsagoff, L. & Bokhorst-Heng, W. D. (2008). Enacting English language ownership in the Outer Circle: a study of Singaporean Indians' orientations to English norms. *World Englishes, 27*(1), 49–67.
Rubdy, R. & Saraceni, M. (Eds) (2006). *English in the World: Global Rules, Global Roles*. London: Continuum.
Rushdie, S. (3 July 1982). The Empire writes back with a vengeance. *The Times*.
Said, E. (1978). *Orientalism: Western Conceptions of the Orient*. London: Routledge & Kegan Paul.
Sapir, E. (1929). The status of linguistics as a science. *Language, 5*(4), 207–214.
Saraceni, M. (2008a). Comment 7. *World Englishes, 27*(2), 280–281.
—. (2008b). English as a Lingua Franca: between form and function. *English Today, 24*(2), 20–26.
—. (2010). *The Relocation of English: Shifting Paradigms in a Global Era*. Basingstoke: Palgrave.
—. (2013). The language of Malaysian and Indonesian users of social networks. In R. Rubdy & L. Alsagoff (Eds), *The Global–Local Interface and Hybridity* (pp. 191–204). Bristol: Multilingual Matters.
Saussure, F. (1983). *Cours de Linguistique Générale*. London: Duckworth (Original work published 1916).

Saxena, M. & Omoniyi, T. (Eds) (2010). *Contending with Globalization in World Englishes*. Bristol: Multilingual Matters.

Schendl, H. (2011). Beyond boundaries: code-switching in the leases of Oswald of Worcester. In H. Schendl & L. Wright (Eds), *Code-Switching in Early English* (pp. 47–94). Berlin: Mouton de Gruyter.

Schendl, H. & Wright, L. (2011). Code-switching in early English: historical background and methodological and theoretical issues. In H. Schendl & L. Wright (Eds), *Code-Switching in Early English* (pp. 15–45). Berlin: Mouton de Gruyter.

Schneider, E. (2007). *Postcolonial English: Varieties Around the World*. Cambridge: Cambridge University Press.

—. (2011). *English Around the World: An Introduction*. Cambridge: Cambridge University Press.

Schreier, D. & Hundt, M. (2013). Introduction: nothing but a contact language .. . . In D. Schreier & M. Hundt (Eds), *English as a Contact Language* (pp. 1–17). Cambridge: Cambridge University Press.

Seargeant, P. (2009). *The Idea of English in Japan: Ideology and the Evolution of a Global Language*. Bristol: Multilingual Matters.

—. (Ed.) (2011). *English in Japan in the Era of Globalization*. Basingstoke: Palgrave.

—. (2012a). English in the world today. In P. Seargeant & J. Swann (Eds), *English in the World: History, Diversity, Change* (pp. 5–35). London: Routledge.

—. (2012b). *Exploring World Englishes: Language in a Global Context*. London: Routledge.

Seargeant, P. & Swan, J. (Eds) (2012). *English in the World: History, Diversity, Change*. London: Routledge.

Seargeant, P., Tagg, C. & Ngampramuan, W. (2012). Language choice and addressivity strategies in Thai–English social network interactions. *Journal of Sociolinguistics*, *16*(4), 510–531.

Sedlatschek, A. (2009). *Contemporary Indian English: Variation and Change*. Amsterdam: John Benjamins.

Seidlhofer, B. (2001). Closing a conceptual gap: the case for a description of English as a Lingua Franca. *Journal of Applied Linguistics*, *11*(2), 133–158.

—. (2004). Research perspectives on teaching English as a Lingua Franca. *Annual Review of Applied Linguistics*, *24*, 209–239.

—. (2006). English as a Lingua Franca in the Expanding Circle: what it isn't. In R. Rubdy & M. Saraceni (Eds), *English in the World: Global Rules, Global Roles* (pp. 40–50). London: Continuum.

—. (2009a). Accommodation and the idiom principle in English as a Lingua Franca. *Intercultural Pragmatics*, *6*(2), 195–215.

—. (2009b). Common ground and different realities: World Englishes and English as a Lingua Franca. *World Englishes*, *28*(2), 236–245.

—. (2011). *Understanding English as a Lingua Franca*. Oxford: Oxford University Press.

Shi, X. (2013). The glocalization of English: a Chinese case study. *Journal of Developing Societies*, *29*(2), 89–122.

Shrank, C. (2000). Rhetorical constructions of a national community: the role of the King's English in mid-Tudor writing. In A. Shepard & P. Withington (Eds), *Communities in Early Modern England: Networks, Place, Rhetoric* (pp. 180–198). Manchester: Manchester University Press.

Singh, I. (2005). *The History of English: A Student's Guide*. London: Hodder Education.

Singh, R. (Ed.) (1998). *The Native Speaker: Multilingual Perspectives*. New Delhi: Sage.

Smith, J. (2012). English and Englishes. In P. Seargeant & J. Swan (Eds), *English in the World: History, Diversity, Change* (pp. 197–230). London: Routledge.

Smith, L. E. (1976). English as an international auxiliary language. *RELC Journal*, *7*(2), 38–42.

—. (2009). Dimensions of understanding in cross-cultural communication. In K. Murata & J. Jenkins (Eds), *Global Englishes in Asian Contexts: Current and Future Debates* (pp. 17–25). Basingstoke: Palgrave.

Smith, N. (2003). *American Empire: Roosevelt's Geographer and the Prelude to Globalization*. Berkeley, CA: University of California Press.

Sonntag, S. K. (2003). *The Local Politics of Global English: Case Studies in Linguistic Globalization*. Lanham, MD: Lexington Books.

Stockwell, R. P. & Minkova, D. (2009). *English Words: History and Structure* (Second edn). Cambridge: Cambridge University Press.

Svartvik, J. & Leech, G. (2006). *English: One Tongue, Many Voices*. Basingstoke: Palgrave.

Tan, L. (2011). Divergences in the English-language news media in Singapore. *Asian Englishes*, *14*(2), 4–20.

Tan, P. K. W. & Rubdy, R. (Eds) (2008). *Language as Commodity: Global Structures, Local Marketplaces*. London: Continuum.

Taylor, C. (2013). Searching for similarity using corpus-assisted discourse studies. *Corpora*, *8*(1), 81–113.

Tongue, R. K. (1974). *The English of Singapore and Malaysia*. Singapore: Eastern Universities Press.

Trakulkasemsuk, W. (2012). Thai English. In E.-L. Low & A. Hashim (Eds), *English in Southeast Asia* (pp. 101–111). Amsterdam: John Benjamins.

Tristram, H. L. (Ed.) (2006). *The Celtic Englishes IV: The Interface between English and the Celtic Languages*. Potsdam: Potsdam University Press.

Urry, J. & Larsen, J. (2011). *The Tourist Gaze 3.0* (Third edn). London: Sage.

Van Coetsem, F. (1988). *Loan Phonology and the Two Transfer Types in Language Contact*. Dordrecht: Foris.

van Gelderen, E. (2006). *A History of the English Language*. Amsterdam: John Benjamins.

Vertovec, S. (2007). Super-diversity and its implications. *Ethnic and Racial Studies*, *30*(6), 1024–1054.

—. (2010). Towards post-multiculturalism? Changing communities, conditions and contexts of diversity. *International Social Science Journal*, *61*(199), 83–95.

von Humboldt, W. (1999). *On Language: The Diversity of Human Language Structure and Its Influence on the Mental Development of Mankind* (Second edn) (M. Losonsky, Ed. and P. Heath, Trans.). Cambridge: Cambridge University Press (Original work published 1836).

Warner, G. (June 2010). *We Need an Academy of English to Save Our Beautiful Language*. http://blogs.telegraph.co.uk/news/geraldwarner/100042575/we-need-an-academy-of-english-to-save-our-beautiful-language/ (Retrieved on 10 February 2014).

Watts, R. J. (2011). *Language Myths and the History of English*. Oxford: Oxford University Press.

Webster, N. (1783). *A Grammatical Institute of the English Language. Part I*. Hartford: Hudson & Goodwin.

—. (1789). *Dissertations on the English Language*. Boston, MA: Isaiah Thomas.

Whorf, B. L. (1956). Languages and Logic. In J. B. Carroll (Ed.), *Language, Thought, and Reality: Selected Writings of Benjamin Lee Whorf* (pp. 233–245). Boston, MA: The MIT Press (Original work published 1941).

Widdowson, H. (1994). The ownership of English. *TESOL Quarterly, 28*(2), 377–389.

Wierzbicka, A. (2006). *English: Meaning and Culture*. Oxford: Oxford University Press.

—. (2010). *Experience, Evidence, and Sense: The Hidden Cultural Legacy of English*. Oxford: Oxford University Press.

Winford, D. (2010). Contact and borrowing. In R. Hickey (Ed.), *The Handbook of Language Contact* (pp. 170–187). Oxford: Blackwell.

Wolf, H.-G. (2009). *World Englishes: A Cognitive Sociolinguistic Approach*. Berlin: Mouton de Gruyter.

Wright, L. (2011). On variation in medieval mixed-language business writing. In H. Schendl & L. Wright (Eds), *Code-Switching in Early English* (pp. 191–218). Berlin: Mouton de Gruyter.

Wright, S. (2011). Language and nation building in Europe. In B. Kortmann & J. van der Auwera (Eds), *The Languages and Linguistics of Europe: A Comprehensive Guide* (pp. 775–790). Berlin: Mouton de Gruyter.

Wu, A. (July 2009). *NNEST of the Month: Robert Phillipson*. http://nnesintesol. blogspot.co.uk/2009/07/robert-phillipson.html.

Yano, Y. (2009). The future of English: beyond the Kachruvian Three Circle Model? In K. Murata & J. Jenkins (Eds), *Global Englishes in Asian Contexts: Current and Future Debates* (pp. 208–225). Basingstoke: Palgrave.

Young, V. A., Barrett, R., Young-Rivera, Y. & Lovejoy, K. B. (2014). *Other People's English: Code-Meshing, Code-Switching, and African American Literacy*. New York: Teachers College Press.

Zacharias, N. T. (2013). Navigating through the English-medium-of-instruction policy: voices from the field. *Current Issues in Language Planning, 14*(1), 93–108.

Zacharias, N. T. & Manara, C. (Eds) (2013). *Contextualizing the Pedagogy of English as an International Language: Issues and Tensions*. Newcastle upon Tyne: Cambridge Scholars.

Index